2024 AHRMA

AHRMA REGION SERIES & CLASS PARTNERS

AHRMA NATIONAL SUPPORTING PARTNERS

HOT SHOT WELDING

Toad Town Racing

BILL DOKIANOS

LAW TIGERS

FRANK SCHOENBECK

**EVENT AMBASSADOR
NEW JERSEY MOTORSPORTS PARK
BOB BLAKELY**

DOUGLAS LAFEVRE AND COMPANY

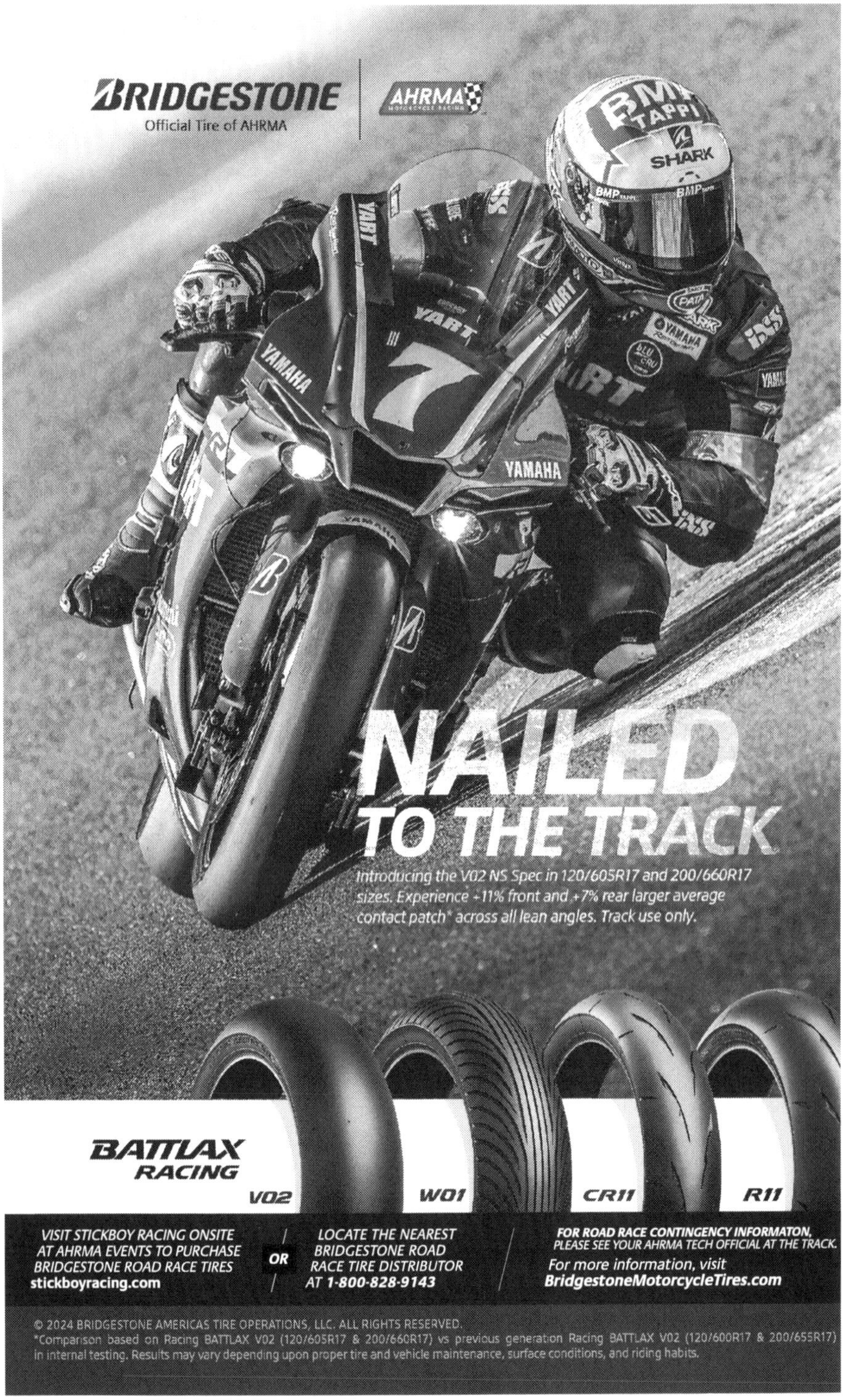

BRIDGESTONE
Official Tire of AHRMA
AHRMA
NAILED
TO THE TRACK
Introducing the V02 NS Spec in 120/605R17 and 200/660R17 sizes. Experience +11% front and +7% rear larger average contact patch* across all lean angles. Track use only.
BATTLAX RACING
V02
W01
CR11
R11
VISIT STICKBOY RACING ONSITE AT AHRMA EVENTS TO PURCHASE BRIDGESTONE ROAD RACE TIRES
stickboyracing.com
OR
LOCATE THE NEAREST BRIDGESTONE ROAD RACE TIRE DISTRIBUTOR AT 1-800-828-9143
FOR ROAD RACE CONTINGENCY INFORMATON, PLEASE SEE YOUR AHRMA TECH OFFICIAL AT THE TRACK.
For more information, visit
BridgestoneMotorcycleTires.com
© 2024 BRIDGESTONE AMERICAS TIRE OPERATIONS, LLC. ALL RIGHTS RESERVED.
*Comparison based on Racing BATTLAX V02 (120/605R17 & 200/660R17) vs previous generation Racing BATTLAX V02 (120/600R17 & 200/655R17) in internal testing. Results may vary depending upon proper tire and vehicle maintenance, surface conditions, and riding habits.

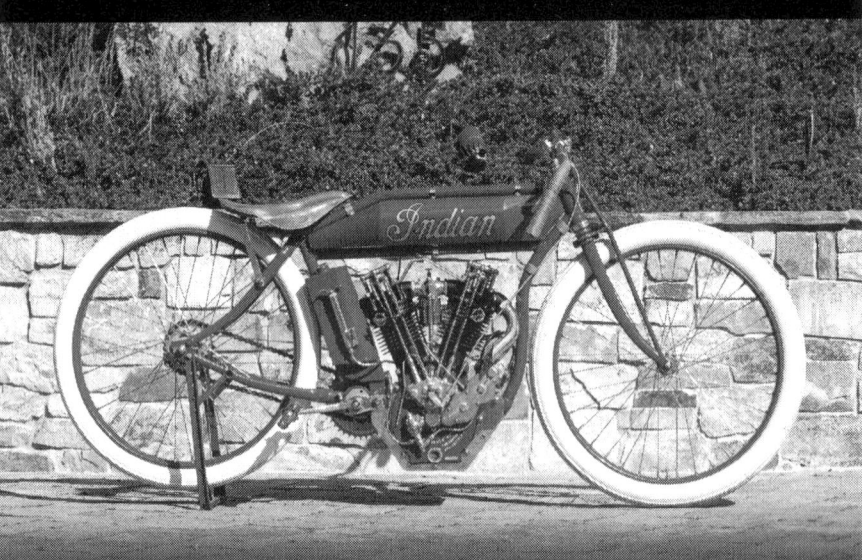

TABLE of CONTENTS

Section 1 – Introduction 1
Section 2 – Definitions..................... 1
Section 3 – Events and Race
   Procedures....................................... 3
   Organization of AHRMA Events 3
   Machine Eligibility........................... 3
   Tech Inspection................................ 4
   Rider Eligibility................................ 6
   Rule Interpretation, Application....... 8
   Road Race Procedures....................... 8
   Road Race Flags 10
   Pit Bikes 11
   Race Number Policies 11
Section 4 – Entry Procedure 12
   Entry Fees....................................... 13
   Pre-Entries...................................... 13
   Refunds 13
   One Event/Weekend Membership.... 13
Section 5 – Officials and Duties 14
   Race Director.................................. 14
   Referee 14
   Safety Director (Control) 14
   Starter 14
   Chief Registrar and Scorer 14
   Technical Inspector......................... 15
   Corner Workers 15
Section 6 – Offenses, Penalties,
   Protests and Appeals 16
   Offenses 16
   Penalties 17
   Protests 18
   Appeals 19
Section 7 – Duties of AHRMA-Affiliated
   Clubs and Promoters 19
Section 8 – Classes for AHRMA
   Race Meets 21
   Vintage Road Race 21
   Vintage Superbike 22
   Next Gen Superbike 22
   Sound of Thunder........................... 22
   Battle of Twins ® 23
   Thruxton Cup Challenge 23
   Sound of Singles ®......................... 23
   Open Two-Stroke 23
   Formula Thunder 23
   Formula Lightning........................... 23
   Phillip Island Challenge 23
   Two-Stroke Classic.......................... 23
   Vintage Motocross........................... 23
   Post Vintage Motocross.................... 24
   Observed Trials 25
   Dirt Track and TT............................ 25
   Vintage Cross Country 26
   Post Vintage Cross Country 26
   Next Gen Motocross........................ 26
Section 9 – General Road Racing Rules.. 27
   Rider Eligibility............................... 27
   Machine Eligibility.......................... 28
   Tech Inspection............................... 28
   Lockwire Requirements 29
   Numbers, Number Plates................. 31
   Scoring, Series Points, Awards........ 32
   Mechanical Requirements,
      Vintage Classes 33
      Battle of Twins® 38
      Sound of Singles® 38
      Sound of Thunder.................... 38
Section 10 – Requirements for
   Road Racing Classes....... 42
   Performance Index 42
   Grand Prix: 500 Premier, 350 GP,
      250 GP, 200 GP Plus 43
   Formula: Formula 750, Formula 500,
      Formula 250, Formula 125,
      Formula Vintage...................... 48
   Classic: Class C, Class C Handshift,
      Pre-1940 GP, Classic Sixties......... 51
   Sportsman....................................... 55
   Novice Historic Production.............. 57
   British European American
      Racing Series (BEARS®) 59
   Vintage Superbike 59
   Next Gen Superbike 63
   Sidecar 73
   Exhibition 79
   Sound of Thunder........................... 80
   Battle of Twins® 80
   Thruxton Cup Challenge 81
   Sound of Singles®.......................... 82
   Open Two-Stroke 82
   Formula Thunder 82
   Formula Lightning........................... 82
   Phillip Island Challenge 83
   Two-Stroke Classic.......................... 84
Section 11 – Vintage Motocross........ 86
   Classes, Eligibility........................... 86
   Tech Inspection, Modifications 94
   Motocross Rider Grading System 98

Equipment Required of all
  Motocross Riders 99
Scoring at MX Events 99
Series Points, Awards 99
Race Procedures 100
Section 12 – Post Vintage Motocross 101
Historic: Classes, Eligibility 102
Grand Prix: Classes, Eligibility 105
Ultima: Classes, Eligibility 106
Additional Classes 107
Tech Inspection, Modifications 108
General Motocross Rules 110
Section 13 – Observed Trials 111
Classes 111
Tech Inspection, Modifications 113
Class, Ability Levels 114
Event Procedures 116
Definitions for Trials Rules 117
Series Points, Awards 119
Section 14 – Dirt Track 120
Rider Eligibility, Equipment 121
Dirt Track and TT Classes 122
Race Procedures 125
Dirt Track Technical Inspection,
  Modifications 125
TT Technical Inspection,
  Modifications 127
Series Points, Awards 127
Section 15 – Cross Country 128
Classes 129
Equipment Required of all
  Cross Country Riders 130
Race Procedures 130
Series Points, Awards 131
Numbers and Number Plates 131
Section 16 – Next Gen Motocross 131
General Rules 131
Numbers and Number Plates 131
Technical Inspection 132
Courses 132
Pre-Modern Classes 132
Next Gen Classes 134
Two-Stroke Classes 135
Additional Classes 136
General Motocross Rules 137

**Section 17 – AHRMA,
  The Organization 137**
The Origins of AHRMA 137
AHRMA Organization 138
Getting More Involved 138
Competition Opportunities 138
AHRMA Membership 139
Benevolent Fund 139
Agreement Not to Sue and to
  Indemnify 140
Communications 140
Special Awards 141
**Section 18 – AHRMA Member Code
  of Conduct 143**
Offenses 143
Submission of a Complaint 144
Enforcement and Penalties 145
Appeals 145
Section 19 – For More Information 146
Rules & Eligibility Committees 146
Awards Committee 146
Risk Management Committee 147
Benevolent Fund Advisory
  Committee 147
Editorial Review Committee 147
AHRMA Racing Officials 147
Off-Road Regions 147
AHRMA National Offices 148
Rule Change Proposal Form 148
Eligibility Request Form 149
AHRMA Membership Application 149
Refund/Credit Request Form 149
Minor Release and Waiver of
  Liability and Indemnity
  Agreement 149
NOTES 150

cover artwork: Chris Siarkiewicz

■ SECTION 1 - INTRODUCTION

The American Historic Racing Motorcycle Association is a member-owned 501(c)(4) not-for-profit organization dedicated to enhancing the sport of historic motorcycle racing. Since 1989, AHRMA has provided an appropriate environment to showcase vintage and alternative modern racing motorcycles in the disciplines of road racing, motocross, dirt track, trials, and cross country. With more than 3,400 members, AHRMA is the largest vintage racing group in North America and is one of the world's leading vintage motorcycle organizations.

AHRMA

8913 Town and Country Circle #1093
Knoxville, TN 37923
Website: www.ahrma.org

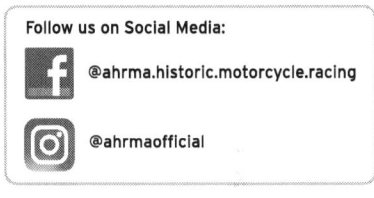

IMPORTANT NOTE: Rules and wording that are new for this year are underlined for your convenience.

■ SECTION 2 - DEFINITIONS

The following definitions and abbreviations are provided to clarify the meaning and intent of this handbook.

AHRMA "Regional Championship" or AHRMA "State Championship": A single meet per year as authorized in writing by AHRMA; the terms "area," "regional," "national" and "national championship" or "series championship" shall not be used in relation to AHRMA events without written permission of AHRMA.

Amateur riders: Participants in an AHRMA amateur event.

Amateur meet: An event in which prizes, trophies, certificates, or merchandise are awarded to the participant.

cc: Cubic centimeters.

Complete lap: A lap in which all participating riders have passed the finish line under the green flag.

cu. in.: Cubic inches.

DNF: "Did not finish." Points may be awarded; consult the rules for each form of competition.

Entrant: Every person who participates in an AHRMA competition event as a rider, official, sponsor, mechanic, or crew member.

Event: Organized competition consisting of one, two or three days of competition.

GP-kitted: Low handlebars (two-inch maximum rise above the top of the fork crown), rearset footrests (at or aft of the swingarm pivot), no lights, no street equipment, or related brackets of any type (factory-welded brackets may be retained). Fairings are encouraged (required in Formula 750).

Historic Cup Series: Events or meets that comprise the annual AHRMA-approved National-championship road racing series.

License: The one-year All Form Competition License purchased in conjunction with AHRMA membership. This license is subject to all rules and specifications outlined herein and falls into one of four categories:
1. **Active** - Unrestricted competition race license
2. **Student** - Restricted competition race license allowing full race privileges subject to wearing a safety vest at events
3. **Probation** - Restricted competition race license subject to race director and referee discretion
4. **Suspended** - Competition race privileges have been denied; member is not currently permitted to participate in race events

Like design: Any motorcycle or part produced or reproduced after a cutoff date that is essentially unchanged from that produced prior to the cutoff (e.g., 1974 Norton Commando is essentially the same as the '72 model).

Machine: One frame, its frame number, one engine in that frame and that engine's serial number.

Major components: Unless otherwise specified, includes frames, forks, hub assemblies, crankcases, cylinders, heads, and gearboxes.

Management system: A series of sensors or monitoring devices attached to different points on the engine, exhaust system or intake system to signal ECM for dynamic programmed correction or adjustments for optimum engine performance.

Manufacturer: The original equipment manufacturer for the machine; not a distributor for the machine; not a dealer for the machine; not the constructor of a "special."

Meet: A competitive activity including but not limited to roadrace, motocross, observed trials, sidecar, or dirt track; also, may refer to road riding or concours d'elegance.

Member: As used herein, a person who by virtue of paying AHRMA the appropriate fee, and by agreeing to abide by AHRMA's rules, regulations and requirements, is entitled to participate in AHRMA activities and events for a specified period of time, and as otherwise set forth in AHRMA's Bylaws. Members may either be full members, who are entitled to participate in all AHRMA events or competitions with voting rights, or associate members, who are generally persons interested in supporting historic motorcycle competition and do not have voting rights.

Moto: Timed or set number of laps in event.

Motorcycle: A two-wheeled motorized vehicle of street or competition variety; single-engined; not a sidecar.

MSR: AHRMA's event registration, provided by MotorsportReg; can be accessed by visiting ahrma.motorsportreg.com

OEM: Original Equipment Manufacturer.

OHV and OHC: Overhead-valve and overhead-cam engines; for example, a Triumph Bonneville and Norton Manx, respectively.

Performance index: When a motorcycle is demonstrably faster or slower than others in its displacement group, it may, at the discretion of the review committee, be assigned to another class.

Period: The period in history encompassed by a class.

Piston displacement (or displacement): The volume swept by the piston or pistons at each stroke; may be measured in cubic inches or cubic centimeters.

Pit crew: Any mechanics or assistants to the rider entered in a meet.

Promoter: Any official AHRMA-approved organization holding, proposing to hold, or otherwise organizing an AHRMA event. Promoters shall be approved in writing by AHRMA. "Promoter" may be substituted for "organizer."

Race day: Part of an "Event." (All AHRMA disciplines with the exception of Cross Country ISDT events.)

Rider: Any person (or in the case of Sidecar events, the sidecar driver and passenger) who has signed the required entry forms and who competes in a meet.

Sidecar: A motorcycle permanently attached to a single-wheeled sitting or kneeling platform; single-engined; not a motorcycle.

Sidevalve (SV) or flathead: An engine with valves that are not operated in an OHV or OHC manner; e.g., a Harley-Davidson KR.

Valves: All references to the number of intake/exhaust valves are the number of valves per cylinder.

■ SECTION 3 - EVENTS AND RACE PROCEDURES

3.1 ORGANIZATION OF AHRMA EVENTS

An AHRMA event may be organized by AHRMA or other clubs, organizations, or promoters approved in writing in advance by AHRMA. Some event fees may be deemed non-refundable by AHRMA.

3.1.1 The name or emblem of AHRMA or use of AHRMA rules shall be associated only with events approved by AHRMA. Organizers shall not distribute or use AHRMA entry forms prior to obtaining AHRMA approval.

3.1.2 AHRMA reserves the right to postpone, reschedule or cancel any scheduled event.

3.1.3 Every attempt will be made to run all events, rain or shine. No refund of entry fees will be made in the event of any form of inclement weather. In the event of a forced cancellation, AHRMA has the discretion to determine refund policy for that event.

3.1.4 No entrants, pit crew, photographers or media shall have consumed or be under the influence of any intoxicant or drugs of any nature which could affect their normal mental or physical ability.

3.1.5 Valid passes must be in the possession of all entrants, photographers, or media during the entire time of their participation. Fraudulent use of any pass will be penalized as deemed appropriate.

3.1.6 When AHRMA competition events are held in conjunction with a non AHRMA event and it is necessary to combine classes, AHRMA classes should only be combined with AHRMA classes.

3.2 MACHINE ELIGIBILITY

3.2.1 All motorcycles competing in an AHRMA event must meet these rules of eligibility. For any motorcycle that requires eligibility approval, the entrant must use the Eligibility Request Form (see section 19.10). The completed form must be accompanied by three photos (one of each side and one of the engine) and returned to the AHRMA Executive Director before the race date.

3.2.2 Eligibility will be determined by the AHRMA Rules and Eligibility Committee, subject to the right of appeal. See Section 17 for contact information for committee members.

3.2.3 Questions of eligibility at the racetrack will be determined by the AHRMA Race Director. (See Section 5 regarding AHRMA race officials and their powers and duties.)

3.2.4 With the realization that vintage motorcycle racing takes place throughout the world, and that these events are governed by different rule-making organizations with differing sets of rules, AHRMA, the primary sanctioning body of vintage motorcycle racing in the United States, will give consideration to non-North American entries that do not conform to AHRMA rules. In certain cases, foreign entrants may be permitted to compete in a separate Exhibition Class only, provided there is sufficient proof of eligibility with their own vintage racing organization. Such entrants must apply at least 60 days before any AHRMA event in which they wish to participate.

3.2.5 There will be a compliance period of 90 days from the date of issue for rule changes affecting mechanical requirements. Safety-related or class changes are effective immediately upon publication unless otherwise specified.

3.2.6 Two AHRMA decals must be conspicuously displayed on each motorcycle.

3.3 TECHNICAL INSPECTION

3.3.1 All motorcycles must be scrutinized and approved by the Technical Inspector before participating in any practice sessions or race meets and must bear an official AHRMA sticker affirming the inspection. All prior stickers must be removed before the Technical Inspector will issue a new seal. Final approval rests with the Technical Inspector, and such approval may be revoked at any time. Motorcycles may be subjected to additional inspection at any time. A recommendation to the Race Director or Chief Technical Inspector that a machine be inspected may be made by any race meet official or by any participant in the meet. The decision to inspect shall be by the Chief Technical Inspector. After a crash, the machine must be submitted to the chief Technical Inspector prior to returning to the track. Failure to do so can result in the levying of penalties described under rule 6.2.

3.3.2 All riders' protective clothing and equipment must be scrutinized and passed by Tech before a rider's motorcycle is approved. The selection of the clothing is the rider's prerogative. AHRMA only inspects the clothing for obvious damage and unsuitability. If this determination is made, then the user will be refused entrance to the track. It is the responsibility of the rider to select a helmet and apparel which will provide appropriate protection. Although AHRMA approves materials, the association does not endorse or guarantee specific products or manufacturers. Riders must rely on their own judgment in the selection of helmets and apparel for safety and durability.

3.3.3 If a Technical Inspector suspects a motorcycle of being ineligible for the class in which it is entered, the inspector may recommend to the Race Director that the machine be inspected for conformation with class rules.

3.3.4 All machines must meet certain minimum safety requirements. The primary emphasis of this inspection is race-worthiness of the equipment used. The burden of complying with the rules regarding eligibility of a motorcycle for a specific category of competition rests with the entrant. The Inspector retains the right to reject or ask for problem correction on any machine that does not meet the established standards, either during the formal inspection process, or at any time thereafter upon re-inspection of the machine.

3.3.5 Modifications to the motorcycle must be consistent with the spirit of the class (i.e., "period modification") and must be approved by the Race Director or Eligibility Inspector. Appearance and workmanship of reasonable standards shall be enforced.

3.3.6 Motorcycles must be neat and clean. Specifically, motorcycles that are dirty, or show bodywork damage, or that are partially or totally in primer, or that do not bear the prescribed identification marks, shall not be approved for competition.

3.3.7 Tires must be in good condition (as determined by the Technical Inspector) and may not be recaps or retreads. Tires will be inspected and must be of modern racing compound only. No slicks or hand-cut slicks are allowed, except in Next Gen Superbike, Sound of Singles, Battle of Twins, Sound of Thunder, Open Two-Stroke and Formula Lightning

3.3.8 All motorcycles, except for certain dirt-track machines, must be equipped with front and rear brakes that operate and are in good working order.

3.3.9 All motorcycles must have a self-closing throttle.

3.3.10 Headlight and taillight must be taped if glass or plastic lenses are left in place.

3.3.11 All hoses or lines that carry fluid must be secured at all connecting points by means of screw- or clamp-type hose clamps and safety wire, or a spring-type hose clamp and safety wire.

3.3.12 No fluid leaks are permitted.

3.3.13 Oily motorcycles shall be prohibited from practice and racing.

3.3.14 Helmets must be used in all AHRMA competitions and practices. Helmets worn in road racing and dirt track must be full-face type and certified by the manufacturer by having a sticker affixed to the helmet stating the helmet meets or exceeds the Snell M2015, FIM BSI 6658 Type A ("Blue Label"), FIM ECER22.05 or FIM JIST 8133:2000 standard. **All helmets used in road racing and dirt track must have been manufactured within the prior 60 months of the date of competition and meet Snell (or equivalent) standard at the time of manufacture.** Only OEM chin-strap fasteners may be used (no aftermarket quick-release fasteners are allowed). This change is provisional for the 2022 season only. All helmets must be intact, and no modification may be made to their construction that alters the helmet from the condition it was tested and approved. The helmet is made to provide protection and is not a platform to attach foreign objects. Cameras or other accessories are NOT permitted to be attached to the rider's helmet.

Helmets worn in vintage and post vintage motocross and cross county may be open- or full-face type and certified by the manufacturer by having a sticker affixed to the helmet stating the helmet meets or exceeds at least one of the following standards: U.S. Department of Transportation (DOT) FMVSS 218; Snell M2010; Europe's ECE 22-05 'P', 'NP' or 'J'; or Japan's JIS T 8133:2007. It is recommended that motocross and cross country helmets be removed from service after five years from date of manufacture; helmets greater than five years old – but no more than 10 years old – may be used at the discretion of the Tech Inspector. Only OEM chin-strap fasteners may be used.

Helmets worn in vintage trials may be half, open or full-face type and must meet or exceed U.S. Department of Transportation (DOT) motorcycle standards or equivalent international standards.

All helmets are subject to inspection by AHRMA competition officials to ensure compliance. This inspection does not warrant the condition of a participant's helmet. It is the responsibility of the participant to ensure his/her helmet is in good and safe condition. Riders are prohibited from using damaged helmets. If there is any question regarding the condition of a helmet, an appropriate helmet expert should be contacted for inspection and advice.

3.4 RIDER ELIGIBILITY
3.4.1 GENERAL
- a) All riders in AHRMA events, including roadrace (including Sidecar passengers), motocross, dirt tracks, cross country, and trials, must be full members of AHRMA. Additionally, all AHRMA Road Racers must hold an AHRMA Digital Roadrace or Active, Student or Probationary License.
- b) Four classes of Digital Roadrace Licensing
    1. ACTIVE - Unrestricted competition license
    2. STUDENT- Restricted competition race license allowing full race privileges subject to wearing a safety vest at events and monitoring of performance by race control
    3. PROBATION - Restricted competition race license subject to Race Director and Referee discretion
    4. REVOKED - Competition race privileges have been denied; member is not currently permitted to participate in race events
- c) **Control and Administration of Race Licenses.** For **Active** and **Suspended**, no further administration is required. MSR features a rider "type" whereby members with a full license are permitted to register at future events, and riders with a suspended license are prohibited from registering for any future events. For **Student**, it will be the responsibility of the student to inform the Race School Director or other AHRMA official that they have complied with the requirement to participate in three race weekends covering six separate days so their license can be changed from Student to Regular status. MSR will support this by allowing the Race School Director to run reports before each race event listing all registered racers who are in this class. Educational materials can be prepared during school instruction to inform students of the race license structure and their responsibility to monitor their status and report when they have met the requirements to be full ACTIVE members. The Referee, Race Director, or their designee with MSR administration privileges will be authorized to change the status of student racers as it can be verified in MSR that they have complied with the three-race requirement. For **Probation**, it will be the responsibility of the Race Director and Referee to monitor and update the subject race license in accordance with the documented terms of the probation.
- d) Riders must present proof of medical insurance coverage before being permitted to compete in an AHRMA National-championship event.
- e) AHRMA non-racing members are not eligible to compete in AHRMA events.
- f) No rider under the age of majority may compete without the written consent of all legal guardians. AHRMA's minimum rider age is 18 for road race, and 16 for motocross, cross country and select classes for dirt track. See section 19.13 for Minor Release and Waiver of Liability and Indemnity Agreement information. If under 21, proof of age is required.
- g) Each rider is responsible for the behavior and actions of any personnel, either family or crew, affiliated with him/her. Any punitive action required as a result of actions by family or crew will be levied against the rider.
- h) It is the responsibility of every rider to inform race officials of any rider's medical condition which may be worsened by participation at that particular event.
- i) Competitors for ALL disciplines are required to carry a medical card that provides an emergency contact and pertinent medical information for first responders in case of an incident while participating in any AHRMA sanctioned event. The card is to be placed in an AHRMA-supplied break-away lanyard worn around the neck. An alternative to the lanyard worn around the neck is the AHRMA approved Medical Data card holder placed on the helmet.

j) All entries must be signed by the individual rider who plans to compete, and no rider may practice or compete without properly registering.
k) There is no limit to the number of classes a rider may compete in on a given day. However, the referee may remove a rider from the track who appears to be fatigued and no longer riding safely.
l) Children are allowed in the paddock area but must be controlled at all times by a responsible adult. Proper compliance is the sole judgment of the race officials. Pets may be kept in the paddock area only if they are constrained by leash or locked in a vehicle. Pets and children are banned from pit road (exception would be an individual who was a properly licensed mechanic, meeting the age requirement). See Section 6 for Offenses & Penalties.
m) All riders must have a fire extinguisher with a minimum recharge rating of 5BC available at all times in their pit area. All extinguishers must carry current recharge tags. Note: A "5BC" extinguisher extinguishes B- and C-class fires. B-class fires involve flammable liquids such as gasoline or grease. C-class fires involve electrical equipment. The "5" indicates, roughly, how many square feet of fire the extinguisher can extinguish.
n) Each rider shall be responsible for leaving his or her pit area in a clean and acceptable condition at the end of the race meet.
o) Each rider shall be responsible for arranging the removal of his or her motorcycles, motor vehicles and trailers at the end of the race meet.
p) All riders in an AHRMA event must attend the rider's meeting. Roll call may be held, and absentees may be penalized.
q) An AHRMA region may not discriminate against AHRMA members from outside its region. Any AHRMA member willing to travel and compete in the required number of events to qualify for an AHRMA regional series shall be eligible for that series' awards.
r) Proof of membership should be on all entry forms. This includes membership number and expiration date.

3.4.2 EQUIPMENT REQUIRED OF ALL ROADRACE RIDERS

The following must be worn at all times when riding on the active course, hot lanes, or warm-up areas:

a) A riding suit of leather, leather and Kevlar, or Kevlar, with appropriate padding, as approved by tech inspection. It must be one-piece construction or, if a two-piece suit is worn, the upper and lower pieces must be securely fastened together. Tech inspection by AHRMA does not warrant the condition of a participant's riding suit. It is the responsibility of participants to ensure that their riding suit is in good and safe condition. Participants are encouraged to have their riding suit examined by appropriate experts if they have questions regarding its condition.
b) Leather gloves with no holes or other openings, except breathing holes.
c) Leather or plastic boots of sufficient height to overlap the bottom of the trouser leg at all times, and in no case less than eight-inches tall (except Sidecar passengers).
d) Road racing helmets must be of full-face construction. (See 3.3.14)
e) Face shields must be shatter resistant. Face shield tear-offs may be used under the following conditions: 1) Tear-off pull-tabs must be cut off; 2) Both sides of the tear-off must be taped or otherwise firmly affixed to the shield; 3) Tear-offs may not be removed and deposited anywhere on the racetrack or hot pit.
f) The use of back protection is mandatory.
g) Sparking knee pucks and toe pucks are prohibited.

- h) The use for competition of any of the above items shall be subject to the reasonable judgment of the Tech Committee. All of the above gear must be presented and approved by the Technical Inspector.
- i) **NEW ROADRACE RIDERS:** A person with no previous road racing experience, first-time AHRMA competitors, or riders designated by a race official (or any rider wishing to do so), must wear an orange vest (supplied by AHRMA) until he/she competes in six events, or until he/she is released by AHRMA officials. New, novice AHRMA roadracers may not be permitted to ride at certain venues.
- j) Helmet-mounted video cameras are not allowed. Video camera mounting brackets must be bolted to the motorcycle, and cameras must be tethered to the motorcycle.

3.5 RULE INTERPRETATION AND APPLICATION

- a) Principle Rule of Interpretation and Application: AHRMA rules are intended to ensure AHRMA events are conducted in a manner which is as fair as possible for all competitors consistent with the interests of safety, the sport and prompt and final competition results. On occasion, circumstances will arise that are either unforeseen or otherwise extraordinary, in which strict application of AHRMA rules may not achieve this goal. In such unusual circumstances, AHRMA officials, as a practical matter, may make a determination regarding the conduct of the race, the eligibility of a competitor, or similar matters that is not contemplated by or is inconsistent with AHRMA rules, in order to achieve this goal. Such determinations are reviewable by the AHRMA Board of Trustees.
- b) Finality of Interpretation and Application. The interpretation and application of AHRMA rules by AHRMA officials at the track is subject to the Protest and Appeal process. However, no event will be re-run.

3.6 ROAD RACE PROCEDURES

- a) In pre-entry events, a deadline will be established before the event, normally 14 days. Grid positions will be based on points earned by a rider in that class. The class champion will be awarded the pole position for the entire season he or she carries the No. 1 plate. (This gridding and number privilege does not carry over into other classes.) Riders who are post-entered will be gridded at the rear of the grid, or at the Race Director's discretion.

    If heat races are run, heat race results will determine grid positions for the final or main event. Where the total number of entrants exceeds safe track density, riders will be required to run heat races prior to the main. Riders will be gridded for the main event, starting with the winner of each heat, and then alternating succeeding riders from each heat until the field is complete. Riders who fail to qualify for the final may, at the Race Director's discretion, be allowed to practice with qualifiers at all subsequent practice sessions for that event.

- b) A first, second, and third call will be made prior to each race. Motorcycles will gather at the entrance to the track (or designated pre-grid area) at this time.
- c) A five-minute sign will be displayed at the start/finish line. Motorcycles will then be allowed to take one hot lap. Those competitors who do not wish to take a warm-up lap will report to the pit steward for instructions. The procedure for placing them on the grid will be outlined at the rider's meeting.
- d) At a time designated by the Referee, the track will be closed to competitors. Those riders who have not begun their hot lap nor reported for direct gridding will be barred from competition in that particular event.

e) When the two-minute board is displayed, motorcycles should be in their respective grid positions and all persons other than grid marshals and the starter must be clear of the track. Riders entering the track after the two-minute board is displayed must start from the hot pit after the main grid is clear.
f) When the one-minute board is displayed, all riders on the starting grid must be in their respective positions. Riders arriving late to the grid must start at the rear of the grid. Riders with stalled motorcycles must raise their arm to get the attention of the starter and grid marshals. At that time, the starter and grid marshals will address the problem.
g) When the one-minute board is displayed in the horizontal position, no motorcycles will be permitted to enter the racetrack/hot pit. At this time, all competing motorcycles should be in gear. All competing riders should have their leathers zipped and face shields down. The green flag will be shown within 10 seconds of the display of the horizontal one-minute board. Riders may start at the first sign of the green flag waving.
h) Multiple waves may be used in road racing. Riders in the second or third wave of a race (identified on the posted grid sheets) will see a grid marshal on the grid with a wave board identifying the wave number. The grid marshal will make eye contact with all riders, show a waving clutch hand, and expect each rider to return the signal, indicating that his/her machine is not in gear and that he/she is waiting for the appropriate wave. The grid marshal will remain in that position, holding the wave board until the preceding wave has left the grid and the starter has gone back to the one-minute board. Once the grid marshal moves off the grid and takes the wave board down, the starter will wave the green flag, signaling the start for that wave.
i) No movement of wheels is allowed until after the green flag is displayed. If movement is detected, the rider may be penalized one lap (see rule 3.7h).
j) In races if the red flag is displayed before the leader has completed less than half the scheduled laps, the race will be restarted with original grids. The race lap count will be lessened by 1 (one) lap to allow for additional warm up lap. If the leader has completed more than half the scheduled laps before the red flag is displayed, the race will be deemed complete and scored by the last completed lap by the field. If a rider causes a red flag after the leader has completed more than half of scheduled laps, the offending rider will receive a DQ. Race Control, Referee and Director will determine if rider, track conditions or other circumstances caused the red flag.
k) Any rider leaving the course shall re-enter the course safely without an attempt to shorten the course from the point where he/she left. Exiting the track via the designated track exit is the only approved location. Exiting the track by any other route is grounds for disqualification.
l) The responsibility for the decision to pass another motorcycle rests with the overtaking rider. Any rider appearing to be deliberately blocking another motorcycle seeking to pass may be black-flagged.
m) Hand/leg signals:
    1. Before entering the pits from the course, riders should signal by raising an arm or extending a leg.
    2. If a rider's speed slows significantly, for any reason, the rider should signal by raising an arm or extending a leg.
n) In the case of a heat race, the entry is considered a permanent rider/motorcycle combination and any change in the combination will result in that entrant motorcycle being placed at the rear of the grid for the feature event.
o) A motorcycle that has crashed may not continue in the race and must be re-teched before the next race in which it is entered or before the same race is restarted.

- p) Weaving is cause for disqualification, and the rider may be subject to a fine.
- q) If, for any reason, a rider is forced to stop the motorcycle on the course during an event, it should be the rider's first duty to place the motorcycle in such a manner as to cause no danger or obstruction to other competitors.
- r) Riders may obtain no assistance during the race other than from their pit crews and in the pits. This does not preclude assistance by race officials for safety reasons.
- s) Motorcycles may not be pushed while on the course, except to remove them from a hazardous position to one of greater safety.
- t) During an event it is expressly forbidden to ride any vehicle in the direction opposite to that in which the event is being run without specific approval of a race official.
- u) At no time shall anyone but authorized attendants be on pit road. At no time shall anyone under 16 years of age be on pit road, pre-grid, or track area.
- v) The Race Director, at his/her discretion, may limit the number of attendants on the pit road for any given event.
- w) The only person allowed at the track wall on pit road is the crew member signaling the rider.
- x) Should a pit-bound rider overshoot his pit, the motorcycle must either be pushed back by hand, or else continue for another lap. No motorcycle may be ridden back to the pit under conditions which would constitute a hazard.
- y) Refueling in the pits must be done with the engine off and the rider off of the bike. A crew member must stand by with a ready fire extinguisher.
- z) Speeds in the paddock area are limited to 20 mph or less, or as dictated by the policy of the track where the event is being held. Although the hot pit is considered part of the track surface, riders are limited to "reasonable and proper" speeds in the hot pit due to the presence of staff and race personnel. A rider may be penalized for excessive speed, by either himself or his crew, in the paddock or pits.
- aa) Once a rider has left the hot grid or racetrack to return to the paddock, he cannot return to the race, including a restart, unless ordered by the Race Director.

3.7 ROAD RACE FLAGS

The following flag signals shall be obeyed *without question*:

- a) **GREEN:** A race is under way at the instant the green flag is displayed. When displayed, the green flag indicates the course is clear.
- b) **STATIONARY YELLOW:** A stationary yellow flag indicates a *potentially dangerous situation on or near the track*. Passing is allowed.
- c) **WAVING YELLOW:** A waving yellow flag indicates a hazard or obstacle on the track. **No passing** is allowed, from the flag station showing the waving yellow flag until beyond the incident.
- d) **RED:** A red flag means the race has been suspended. Competition must cease immediately, with all riders slowing to a safe speed (approximately 25 mph) and proceeding in a safe manner to the hot pit area, where the grid marshal/starter will give further instructions. The red flag will be displayed at start/finish as well as other locations where necessary and proper. The racer causing the red flag may be disqualified, at the discretion of the Race Director.
- e) **WHITE:** A white flag, displayed only at the start/finish line, indicates one lap to go. This flag is a courtesy and may not always be displayed.
- f) **WHITE & GREEN CROSSED:** White and green flags crossed indicates the race is halfway through. This flag is a courtesy and may not always be displayed.

g) **BLACK:** A black flag indicates a safety or mechanical problem. The black flag will be displayed, along with the rider's competition number, at start/finish. The rider must leave the track surface as early as safely possible, preferably in the area of corner workers, where they can inform the rider of the problem. Failure to comply with a black flag may result in disqualification. The rider must not proceed without approval of a race official.

h) **BLACK FLAG WITH SOLID-ORANGE CIRCLE:** The "Meatball" indicates a rules violation. The rider must report to the pit steward on the **next** lap. Failure to comply will result in penalties.

i) **YELLOW WITH VERTICAL RED STRIPES:** A yellow flag with vertical red stripes indicates oil or a foreign substance has been spilled or a slippery or dangerous condition exists somewhere on the track. *Take care* and *be prepared*! The debris flag may be used at the corners to indicate a mechanical wave-off.

j) **WHITE WITH RED CROSS:** A white flag with a red cross indicates an ambulance is on the course. This flag is displayed from the corner immediately preceding the location of the ambulance, the corner where the ambulance has stopped and at start/finish.

k) **CHECKERED:** A checkered flag indicates the end of the race (or practice session). Riders should proceed to the designated track exit. (See rule 9.6.1.)

3.8 PIT BIKES

a) Pit bikes are permitted as transportation in the pit and paddock areas, subject to track policy. All pit bikes must be identified with the rider's competition number and must meet the number plate requirements of rule 9.5 (front plate only). Improper use or identification of a pit bike may result in impoundment of that pit bike for the remainder of the meet.

3.9 RACE NUMBER POLICIES

3.9.1 **NUMBERS AND NUMBER PLATES:** All road racing, motocross and dirt track competition numbers will be assigned by AHRMA's race directors. All competitors must display their AHRMA-assigned number unless granted prior permission to run a different number and number plate color at that event only.

3.9.2* **RACE NUMBER CONFIGURATION:** Race number configuration is as follows. Race numbers that are in existence prior to July 1st, 2022 that do not comply with these requirements must be changed by December 31st, 2023.

a) Allowed in race numbers:
- 1-3 (one to three) positions
- Numbers (i.e. 0-9) (see disallowed - single-digit "0" and single-digit "1" are not allowed as race numbers)
- "1" following alpha letter
- If following letter used, the letter must be upper case
- If following letter used, the letter must be at least 3" (3 inches) tall

b) Disallowed in race numbers:
- More than 1 (one) letter
- More than 3 (three) positions (i.e. no four-digit numbers or combinations of numbers and letters in any form)
- The following letters: B, D, I (capital "i"), O, S, and Z
- Punctuation marks or special symbols (i.e. quotation marks, periods, commas, etc)
- Leading letters
- Leading zeros
- Single-digit 0 (zero) or single-digit 1 (one)

* No. 1 Championship race numbers are assigned, and are therefore exempt from this policy.

3.9.3 **RELEASING ASSIGNED NUMBERS:** Numbers will be released back into available race number inventory as follows:
- Full member has not raced within the past 24 months (2 years); does not apply to off-road disciplines (motocross and cross country - trials does not have permanent number assignments) - exceptions may be made by race directors
- Lifetime member has not raced within the past 24 months (2 years); does not apply to off-road disciplines (motocross and cross country - trials does not have permanent number assignments) - exceptions may be made by race directors
- Associate member is not eligible to hold a race number
- Membership lapses, or has been expired, for more than 6 (six) months
- Numbers assigned to weekend members expire when the membership expires

■ SECTION 4 - ENTRY PROCEDURE

4.1 In order to compete in any AHRMA-permitted event, riders must sign appropriate forms and waivers. By signing the form, every entrant agrees to be subject to the rules of this book and any supplements.

4.2 Registration may be completed online or submitted by fax or mail. Appropriate forms and waivers must be signed in ink by riders, and by parents or legal guardians, as required. Entrants and photographers/media physically entering sanctioned events are required to sign a liability release and waiver prior to their participation and to have such liability release and waivers signed by a parent or legal guardian, as necessary. When signing the required liability release and waivers, entrants, photographers/media, and parents agree not to sue AHRMA for any injury occurring to themselves or their property at AHRMA events and further agree to reimburse AHRMA for all losses or costs it suffers as a result of their participation at AHRMA-approved events.

4.3 Only United States currency, personal checks, money orders or MasterCard, Visa, Discover and American Express credit cards will be accepted for payment of entry fees for AHRMA events. PayPal is accepted for online registration only.

4.4 **Bad checks:** A $25 fee will be added to the face value of every returned check. Failure to redeem a dishonored check within 10 days of notification will result in the rider being dropped from the license rolls. Reinstatement will only be possible following the redemption of the check and a new license application, accompanied by full fees.

4.5 ENTRY FEES
a) Entry fees vary, depending on the event and location.
b) All AHRMA events allow riders 70 years of age or older discounted race fees for each AHRMA sanctioned round in any discipline. Online pre-entry or in-person post-entry race fees will be discounted to $35 for the first class entry of each discipline. The fee for additional classes will be at normal additional-class rates.
c) Discounts do not apply to road race practice fees.

4.6 PRE-ENTRIES
a) All AHRMA dirt track, motocross, cross country and roadrace National events will be pre-entry unless instructed otherwise. Trials will be post-entry, except for certain events, which will be advertised as pre-entry.
b) Some events may be pre-entry only. Conditions of pre-entry will be contained in all advertisements and published in *AHRMA MAG*.
c) When a pre-entry is received, the rider will be entered in the event and placed on the grid or start list of the appropriate class entered.
d) All entries received after the pre-entry deadline will be returned and refunded.
e) Unless entries are limited, post-entries will be accepted for all AHRMA Nationals. Riders may post-enter classes based upon available grid space, at the designated higher post-entry fee for the first class entered.
f) Registration officials may determine at any time that an entry list is full and refuse further entries.
g) Participants may be required to purchase additional insurance, gate pass, pit or paddock passes, as determined by the individual track or promoter. At National events, AHRMA membership is required for any pass other than general admission.

4.7 EVENT REFUNDS*
a) Event refunds will be issued only to riders who have completed an Event Refund/Credit Request Form. The form may be obtained from and returned to registration or tech at an event or submitted online. See section 19.12 for Refund/Credit Request Form. Requests for refunds will not be accepted via telephone or email.
b) A rider contacting the AHRMA event registrar up through the day of the event will be refunded the full amount, less a per-entry administrative fee ($10 for Road Race, $5 for Off-road and Dirt Track). A rider filing for refund not more than 14 days after the event will be settled at 50-percent of the total entry. After that time, there will be no refund. This policy applies to National events, unless noted otherwise on the entry form.
c) If a rider's machine goes on track the day the request is dated, there shall be no refund for that day. Any following days if applicable are due a refund.
d) Some events may be deemed no refund by AHRMA.

*Off-road may also offer credits at their discretion.

4.8 ONE EVENT/WEEKEND MEMBERSHIP:
A One Event/Weekend Membership may be available to all disciplines at a reduced price and may be converted to a Full Membership within 30 days.* A One Event/Weekend Membership does not include any series points, the *AHRMA MAG* subscription, the AHRMA Handbook, or voting privileges. Weekend members are not eligible to have permanent race numbers assigned.

* This could vary at the race director's discretion.

■ SECTION 5 - OFFICIALS AND DUTIES

It is the duty of every AHRMA official, promoter or club official to make every effort to ensure the events are run in accordance with the procedures and standards set forth in this Handbook. Further, all operations and decisions must be made without respect to individual competitors, but rather to the fair and honest representation of all participants.

5.1 **RACE DIRECTOR:** Responsible for the overall activities of an event, including performance of the staff. In some cases, this job description will be filled by two individuals, in others, by one. This position includes handling rules interpretation, administrative errors, and conduct of all participants. Race director may also function as the referee.

5.2 **REFEREE:** Holds Riders Safety meetings, settles disputes, protests, oversees tech inspection operations, addresses eligibility and specific class requirement issues, and assists Race Director as needed.

5.3 **SAFETY DIRECTOR (Control):** Responsible to the Race Director for the coordination and placement of all safety-related personnel, including medical. Will work in close harmony with the Race Director, Starter, Medical, and Corner Marshals in an effort to achieve maximum safety in procedures and an understanding by all of emergency protocol. The Safety Director is also responsible for physical impediments regarding the safe operation of the course. Safety orientations will be delivered by the Safety Director to all new
novice riders.

5.4 **STARTER:** The Starter is responsible for the safe operation of the grid and track areas during practice or race events.

5.5 **CHIEF REGISTRAR AND SCORER:** The Chief Registrar and Scorer shall operate directly under the supervision of the Race Director and shall be responsible for accepting, certifying, and processing all entries and credentials for racers, crews, officials, and other non-racers and be responsible for all scoring activities of the event. Duties are:
   a) Accept, certify, and process all entries and credentials for racers, crews, officials, and other non-racers.
   b) Maintain records and lap charts for all competing motorcycles.
   c) Compile and post the grid sheets for endurance races, heat races, and feature races as well as compile the official race results.
   d) Work closely with the announcer and press officials to provide results or race information as quickly as possible.
   e) Coordinate assistants for registration and scoring activities.
   f) Answer all inquiries from racers or crew regarding registration, scoring or related issues.
   g) Train new workers for assignment as assistants for registration or scoring.
   h) Inform Starter of halfway point in the race, one lap to go in the race, and the leader's progress.

5.6 TECHNICAL INSPECTOR: The Technical Inspector shall work directly under the supervision of the Race Director to ensure all competing motorcycles and racers are in compliance with the rules. A machine that passes Tech Inspection is not automatically certified as eligible for the class in which it's entered. However, the Tech Inspector is authorized to make eligibility determinations.

Duties are:
- Inspect and approve every machine and rider before they are allowed on the track.
- Conduct inspection of motorcycles (including discretionary teardowns) at the request of the Race Director (Referee).
- Accept and administer protests received from a rider.
- Train Technical Inspection Assistants and supervise all assistants.
- Assemble the fields of motorcycles into the order specified by registration prior to the race.
- Supervise the entry of motorcycles into the pit lane and direct traffic in the pit lane.

5.7 CORNER WORKERS:

5.7.1 CORNER CAPTAIN: The Corner Captain has the sole authority of the proper operation of the corner. On matters of race control on his corner, his decision will supersede the advice or decision of any race official except the Race Director of the event.

Duties include:
- Direct all activities on his corner.
- Ensure the proper display of all flags on his corner.
- Sole authority for calling a waving yellow flag or ambulance.
- Direct the return to the course of any motorcycle stopped on or off the course.
- Submit a written report of any accident at his corner, plus any reports requested by the Race Director.
- Instruct novice personnel.
- The Corner Captain shall wear a distinguishable article of clothing (such as an International Orange poncho) and carry a whistle.

5.7.2 FLAGMAN
- Shall face traffic at all times.
- Shall inform riders of track conditions ahead with the appropriate flags under the direction of the Corner Captain.

5.7.3 BACK-UP MAN
- Shall face downstream from traffic.
- Shall transmit commands from the Corner Captain to the Flagman.
- Shall inform riders of track conditions ahead with the appropriate flags under the direction of the Corner Captain.

5.7.4 RADIO/PHONE OPERATOR
- Is the communication link between the corner and Central Control.
- Relays information between corner personnel and Central Control at all times the corner is in operation.
- Records all incidents occurring on the corner.

5.7.5 **SAFETY CREW**
- Shall operate under the direction of the Corner Captain.
- Must be familiar with all emergency equipment on the corner and their use.
- Render any assistance to the rider that will increase his safety.

■ SECTION 6 - OFFENSES, PENALTIES, PROTESTS & APPEALS

6.1 OFFENSES

In order to provide for fair competition and control, penalties may be assessed against any entrant deemed to be in breach of the AHRMA competition rules. Such breaches may include, but are not limited to, the following offenses:

6.1.1 Failure to obey the instruction of a recognizable race official.

6.1.2 Any action with the goal or effect to deprive or defraud the organization, promoter, racetrack, or sponsor of their proper and just financial considerations.

6.1.3 Attempted bribery, or acceptance of a bribe by anyone connected to the operation or participation in a race event. An entrant shall be responsible for all acts of his or her crew.

6.1.4 Reckless or dangerous riding, or an act exhibiting a disregard for the safety of any participant or any other person, including the offender. An entrant shall be responsible for all acts of his or her crew.

6.1.5 Any action with the goal or effect of participation of an ineligible rider or motorcycle in competition.

6.1.6 Failure to follow any announced or posted rules specific to a certain racetrack or facility.

6.1.7 Any action that causes upset or disturbance within the area where the event is being held, including behavior problems in local businesses as well as private property.

6.1.8 Any action with the goal or effect to deceive, defraud or cheat competitors, AHRMA, including but not limited to an engine displacement too large for the class, etc.

6.1.9 No rider shall knowingly operate a motorcycle on any paved surface while it is leaking oil. Once a rider becomes aware the motorcycle is leaking oil on a paved surface, he must promptly pull off, shut down and either push back to the paddock or wait to be picked up by the track crew. Under no circumstances shall the rider attempt to ride the motorcycle to the paddock under power. Any motorcycle which leaks oil on the track surface (including entrance, exit or staging areas) is deemed to have been immediately impounded by the Race Director. The motorcycle must be brought immediately and without detours to tech inspection for evaluation by the Chief Technical Inspector, who will determine the cause of the leak and instruct the rider on the corrective action to be taken. The bike remains in impound status until released by the Race Director. Once repairs have been made, the motorcycle must be re-teched before it may be operated. The Race Director, with the assistance of the Executive Director, will issue a written report of each such incident. This report will be distributed to the rider, to all AHRMA officials, and will be published in *AHRMA MAG*. Any rider who fails to comply will be subject to severe sanction.

6.1.10 Loan of a license to any other competitor will result in a one-year suspension and $500 fine. Participation of any in the act of allowing an unlicensed or unregistered party to ride on the track will result in the same penalty. This includes loan of equipment or other forms of deception.

6.1.11 Physical violence, acts of hate or discrimination, sexual harassment, or any unlawful abuse of any other participant or official will result in suspension that will continue for a term deemed appropriate by the Executive Director and Executive Committee and payment of a $500 minimum fine. Additionally, illegal acts may result in prosecution by local authorities.

6.1.12 **"Burnouts"** are not allowed anywhere on the track premises at any event.

6.1.13 **Wheelies** are not permitted in the pit or paddock area of any event.

6.1.14 Failure or refusal to tear down an engine for examination or measurement at the request of a race official will be penalized with loss of racing privileges for up to 13 months by the rider.

6.1.15 The use of alcohol or other intoxicating/debilitating substances by a competitor, participant, crew or official is forbidden, until competition is complete.

6.2 PENALTIES

6.2.1 **Specific penalties range from reprimand to banishment. The hierarchy of penalties follows:**

a) **Fines:** Fines from $25 to $150 may be levied by race officials. Fines from $25 to $500 may be levied in lieu of or in addition to other penalties, based upon the severity of the infraction and the recommendations of the race officials.

b) **Assessments:** The Executive Director or the Board of Trustees may assess an AHRMA member costs incurred by the association, including, but not limited to, phone, travel, AHRMA staff time and Board members' time (at a rate of $25 per hour), incurred as a result of actions of a member that are not in the normal and usual course of the association's business. Such assessment shall be due and payable within 10 days of mailing to the member's last known address. Failure to pay such assessment shall be subject to possible suspension. **Reprimands:** Entrants will be given written reprimands for minor infractions committed by themselves or crew where a written record of the situation seems desirable. All written reprimands will be sent from the AHRMA office.

c) **Loss of Points:** Offenses more serious than satisfied by reprimand may result in partial or total loss of points earned year-to-date.

d) **Removal from Events:** Entrants may be removed from an individual meet for breach of rules or conduct.

e) **Probation:** In cases of offenses that are repeats of previous reprimands, or of a significantly more blatant nature, an entrant may be placed on probation for a fixed period. Probation may only be levied after review of the case by the AHRMA Executive Director. Probations may be published in *AHRMA MAG* at the discretion of the Executive Director.

f) **Suspension:** Competition licenses may be suspended for violation of probation, as well as flagrant breach of AHRMA rules. Suspension shall begin with notification by registered letter from the National Office. Suspension may be imposed only by the AHRMA Executive Director <u>when confirmed by a majority vote of the Board of Trustees.</u> Membership may be retained and *AHRMA MAG* received while the member is suspended from competition. Suspended members are not in good standing and may not vote for trustees. Suspensions will be published in *AHRMA MAG*.

g) **Banishment:** In cases of the most flagrant breaches, or with entrants who are habitual and deemed incorrigible, banishment will be applied. This punishment will include lifetime loss of AHRMA license and membership rights. Banishment will only be levied by a majority vote of the AHRMA Board of Trustees and will always result in being published in *AHRMA MAG*.

6.2.2 Where a competitor has been found to have used an ineligible performance-related component, the penalty shall be loss of accumulated season points and results for any class in which that machine was ineligible. A second infraction in any 12-month period shall result in the rider's suspension for up to 13 months.

6.2.3 Any rider refusing to allow an inspection of his machine by race officials will be disqualified from that event and may lose all accumulated season points for that class. In addition, that rider will be suspended for up to 13 months at the discretion of the Executive Director.

6.2.4 When a competitor is found to be out of compliance with a rule that does not affect performance (a non-performance rule), the competitor shall be warned by the Race Director or Referee, without loss of race standing. A second failure to comply with a non-performance rule can result in loss of points and results for any class in which that machine was ridden at that event.

6.3 PROTESTS

6.3.1 Protests are generally based on entrant conduct, claimed motorcycle illegality or ineligibility; however, they may be for other reasons.

6.3.2 **Protest Procedures:** All protests must be initiated in writing. Visual and scoring protests or protests regarding unsportsmanlike and/or dangerous riding may be initiated by a person in the same race or moto as the machine and/or rider being protested. An internal protest may be initiated only by a person in the same category and displacement class as the machine and/or rider being protested. A protest fee (cash only; see fee schedule below) is required to initiate a protest. A protest must be presented to a race referee within 30 minutes after the posting of the provisional results. If the protest is upheld, the entire fee will be returned. If the protest is disallowed, the protest fee will be disbursed at the discretion of the Executive Director of AHRMA. Protests must be specific. The race director may order the teardown of any machine, whether or not a protest has been filed.

Once a protest is filed, the protested motorcycle shall be immediately impounded by race officials, pending determination of the protest. The inspection will be conducted under the supervision of the Technical Inspector. The inspection will generally be at the race event; however, the inspection may be at such place(s) as the Technical Inspector deems necessary. The Technical Inspector will have up to 10 days to determine the validity of the protest and may impound the protested equipment for that period. Race officials are not limited in their determination of illegality or ineligibility to the matter protested (i.e., if in the course of their inspection other illegalities or basis for ineligibility are found, penalties may be imposed). Once a protest is lodged regarding machine illegality or ineligibility, the responsibility of proving a legality or eligibility rests with the protested entrant. Failure to provide the necessary proof of legality or eligibility will
uphold the protest.

6.3.3 **Types of Protests/Fees:** There are three types of equipment protests regarding machine illegality: visual, internal and fuel. The equipment protest fee is $10 for all protests except for an internal equipment protest, which follows the fee schedule shown below:

    Flathead and two-stroke $100
    Single-cylinder pushrod four-stroke $125
    Single-cylinder overhead cam four-stroke $150
    Pushrod twin, triple or four $200
    Pre-1974 and like-design OHC twin, triple or four $250
    Modern twin, triple, OHC and/or water-cooled, top end $500
    Modern twin, triple, OHC and/or water-cooled, bottom end.........$1000

• All other protest fees are $10; there is no fee for a scoring protest.

6.3.4 **Results of Protests:** Trophies, placing and points affected by a protest will be withheld until the protest has been settled. When a protest is upheld, race officials must make a decision regarding the penalty.

6.3.5 The decision regarding the protest will be made by the Race Director.

6.3.6 **Records of Protest:** A copy of every protest will be kept on file by AHRMA for a period of five years.

6.4 APPEALS

6.4.1 Entrants have the right to appeal decisions of the Rules and Eligibility Committee and decisions on protests.

6.4.2 The appeal shall be in writing, postmarked within 30 days of the decision appealed and mailed to the Executive Director of AHRMA. If an appeal is filed, the initial decision is stayed pending the decision of the Appeals Committee (except for matters of safety, as solely determined by the Executive Director of AHRMA).

6.4.3 The appeal shall be accompanied by an appeal fee of $250. Disposition of the appeal fee shall be made by the Appeals Committee, which may decide to return or retain all or a portion of the fee.

6.4.4 Appeals will be heard by an Appeals Committee established by the Board of Trustees. The Committee shall consist of three members, as appointed from time to time by the Board of Trustees. The Board of Trustees may appoint such Appeals Committee on a case-by-case basis or establish a standing committee. The number of committees, the length of committee service and the persons serving on the committee(s) shall be at the sole discretion of the Board of Trustees.

6.4.5 The appeal will include a hearing, either in person or by phone, as the committee determines. The committee will consider all information presented, both oral and written, within 30 days of the hearing. No attorneys are permitted to represent any party. The decision of the committee is final. The decision will be published in *AHRMA MAG* and will identify the parties, the dispute, the decision, and the penalty (if any).

■ SECTION 7 - DUTIES OF AHRMA-AFFILIATED CLUBS AND PROMOTERS

The purpose of this section is to describe duties and responsibilities of clubs and promoters who run AHRMA-approved events and who use this AHRMA Handbook. In order to provide uniformity and consistency for historic motorcycle competitive events, AHRMA encourages the use of its Handbook, which includes these general duties. (**Note:** As used here, promoter may also mean "promoting club.").

7.1   All events require an AHRMA permit.
7.2   All conditions of entry should be contained in the advertisement and entry application.
7.3   At all public AHRMA activities the promoter should display, in a conspicuous place, a notice, warning spectators witnessing events that they assume all risks for any injuries or damages resulting from that competition or its related activity.
7.4   The promoter is responsible for adequate fencing and other means of crowd control to protect the spectators from injury during the meet.
7.5   At closed-course race meets (roadrace, motocross, etc.) dangerous obstacles should be removed from the course and the surrounding area. Posts or trees along the course should be padded. Outside fencing and guardrails which do not completely reach the ground, or any interruptions in fencing should be padded with hay bales or equivalent padding.
7.6   Promoters must take adequate measures for the control of dust on the track.
7.7   Promoters of meets where speed is a determining factor must have an ambulance with operating oxygen supply and attending physician or qualified first-aid personnel at all times. There shall be an operative fire extinguisher with a minimum of a 5BC rating at the starting line at all events. No meet or practice session shall be started until this equipment is at the track.
7.8   If a rider or spectator is injured or dies during the sanctioned period, the promoter **must forward a detailed report, including photographs, to AHRMA** concerning the circumstances of the incident. This should include names of witnesses, persons involved, details on track and weather conditions, and any other pertinent or helpful information. The report should include the promoter club name, any permit number and date of the meet.
7.9   A promoter must not make false announcements, advertise, or otherwise disseminate information to the press or public which is incorrect or misleading.
7.10 All advertisements should carry the words "AHRMA Permitted" and display the official AHRMA logo, publication-quality copies of which are available on written request to the AHRMA National Office or download it from the Member Resources section at www.ahrma.org. The words "area," "regional," "national" or "state championship" shall not be used without the appropriate sanction or written permission.
7.11 The promoter shall provide a location, which is properly enclosed, for engine inspection and measurements; and to have winning engines ready for measurement on completion of the meet when required, at the discretion of the Referee or race officials.
7.12 The promoter shall have the responsibility to see that all AHRMA rules are enforced at permitted events. Failure to adhere to these rules at AHRMA-sanctioned meets shall nullify the sanction and approval for that meet.
7.13 It is the sole responsibility of the promoter to ensure compliance with all rules relating to or directed to safety, and to otherwise act to promote safety of the meet.
7.14 It is the sole responsibility of the promoter to determine that the facility meets the underwriting criteria of the insurance carrier and to purchase the required spectator and participant liability insurance in amounts and with coverage criteria as set by AHRMA. Proof of insurance by a carrier admitted in the state of the event must be provided to AHRMA at least 30 days before the event. If the required liability insurance is not purchased, the permit and approval for that day's meet will be declared null and void.

7.15 All clubs and promoters seeking an AHRMA permit must agree to conduct the event pursuant to such terms and conditions as AHRMA will establish from time to time.

■ SECTION 8 - CLASSES FOR AHRMA RACE MEETS

8.1 VINTAGE ROAD RACE

a) **500 PREMIER:** 1968 and earlier 500cc four-stroke OHV/OHC, or 750cc sidevalve machines. See Section 10.2.1.

b) **350 GRAND PRIX:** 1968 and earlier 350cc four-stroke machines; 350cc air-cooled, single-cylinder, two-strokes with a maximum of five speeds; 250cc liquid-cooled, single-cylinder two-strokes; and 250cc air-cooled, twin-cylinder two-strokes with a maximum of six speeds. See Section 10.2.3.

c) **250 GRAND PRIX:** 1968 and earlier 250cc four-stroke machines; 250cc air-cooled, single-cylinder two-strokes with a maximum of five speeds; 175cc liquid-cooled two-stroke singles; 175cc air-cooled, twin-cylinder, two-strokes with a maximum of six speeds. See Section 10.2.4.

d) **200 GRAND PRIX PLUS:** This class combines a variety of engine designs and displacements, based on an index of performance. See Section 10.2.5.

e) **FORMULA 750:** Fully GP-kitted four-stroke machines up to four cylinders, manufactured as 600-750cc and built prior to December 31, 1972. See Section 10.3.1.

f) **FORMULA 500:** Fully GP-kitted two-stroke and certain four-stroke machines up to 500cc, based on an index of performance. See Section 10.3.2.

g) **FORMULA 250:** Fully GP-kitted two-stroke air-cooled machines, including singles up to 360cc and twins up to 250cc, and certain four-strokes. See Section 10.3.3.

h) **FORMULA 125:** Air-cooled, twin-shock, steel-framed Grand Prix bikes up to 125cc, plus certain GP-kitted street and enduro machines. See Section 10.3.4.

i) **FORMULA VINTAGE:** Open to machines eligible for 500 Premier, Formula 750, Formula 500, and Sportsman 750. Additional models are eligible; for the complete listing, see Section 10.3.5.

j) **CLASS C:** Intended for AMA "Class C" machines manufactured prior to December 31, 1951, as '51 models. Also, **CLASS C HANDSHIFT,** a championship class run together with, but scored separately from, Class C. See Section 10.4.1.

k) **PRE-1940 GRAND PRIX:** 1940 and earlier Grand Prix or modified street machines, including 500cc OHV and OHC, and 750cc sidevalve machines. See Section 10.4.2.

l) **CLASSIC SIXTIES:** 1960s-era and earlier Grand Prix/Clubman 350-500cc four-stroke OHV and OHC, and 750cc sidevalve machines.

CLASSIC SIXTIES 650: 1960s-era 650cc OHV and 883cc sidevalve machines, run with but scored separately from Classic Sixties. See Section 10.4.3.

m) **SPORTSMAN:** 1972 and earlier four-stroke, street bike-based machines, divided into 350, 500 and 750cc classes. See Section 10.5.

n) **NOVICE HISTORIC PRODUCTION:** 1978 and earlier production street machines with the standard OEM frame, swingarm, fork and handlebar mounts. Engines use the original OEM bore and stroke. Classes are **Lightweight** (four-strokes up to 500cc, 250cc two-strokes and certain 350cc two-strokes) and **Heavyweight** (four-strokes up to 750cc and 350-500cc two-strokes). This class is intended for novice riders. See Section 10.6.
o) **BEARS® (BRITISH EUROPEAN AMERICAN RACING SERIES):** Two-cylinder pushrod machines built up through 1968, competing under Formula 750 specifications. See Section 10.7.
p) **SIDECAR:** Vintage and modern three-wheeled machines. See Section 10.10.
q) **EXHIBITION:** Non-competitive exhibition or "rolling display" rides. See Section 10.11. Guidelines available from the AHRMA National office.

8.2 VINTAGE SUPERBIKE
a) **HEAVYWEIGHT:** Unlimited displacement twins and pushrod triples, and displacement-limited fours and sixes built up through the 1982 model year. See Section 10.8.3.
b) **MIDDLEWEIGHT:** Unlimited displacement singles, limited pushrod twins, OHC twins, pushrod triples and OHC fours built up through the 1982 model year. See Section 10.8.3.
c) **LIGHTWEIGHT:** Singles, twins and multis using performance indexes for smaller bikes. See Section 10.8.3.

8.3 NEXT GEN SUPERBIKE
a) **NEXT GEN SUPERBIKE:** Based on the mid-1980s to early-'90s U.S. Superbikes which were production machines available from the showroom floor. See Section 10.9.1.
b) **NEXT GEN SUPERBIKE 2:** 1990s to early-2000s U.S. Superbikes. See Section 10.9.2.
c) **NEXT GEN SUPERBIKE 3:** Late 1980s to mid 2000s U.S. Superbikes. See Section 10.9.5
d) **NEXT GEN SUPERBIKE LIGHTWEIGHT:** A lightweight class to showcase what was raced in the '80s through the early '90s. See Section 10.9.3.
e) **NEXT GEN SUPERBIKE MIDDLEWEIGHT:** A middleweight class to showcase what was raced in the '80s through the early '90s. See Section 10.9.4.

8.4 SOUND OF THUNDER
a) **SOUND OF THUNDER 1 (SoT1):** Unlimited displacement four-stroke single-, twin- and three-cylinder machines; rotary engines; Open Two-Strokes. See Section 10.12.1.a.
b) **SOUND OF THUNDER 2 (SoT2):** Any Sound of Singles machine or Motard, liquid-cooled twins to 850cc, unlimited air-cooled twins, triples to 675cc, and two-strokes to 250cc. See Section 10.12.1.b.
c) **SOUND OF THUNDER 3 (SoT3):** Harley-Davidson XR1200, pushrod OHV twin-cylinder machines to 1000cc, OHC two- or three-valve twins to 805cc, SOHC liquid-cooled V-twins to 750cc, OHC liquid-cooled four-valve twins to 650cc. Pushrod OHV machines over 900cc must run under Supersport specifications See Section 10.12.1.c.
d) **SOUND OF THUNDER 4 (SoT4):** Any single or twin cylinder four-stroke production motorcycle up to 400cc sold in the U.S. with a street-legal VIN. The Ninja 400 is limited to Supersport specifications (see 9.8.1) otherwise it must compete in SOT3.

8.5 BATTLE OF TWINS®
a) **0-904cc**: Open to air-cooled twins 0 - 904cc. See Section 10.13.
b) **905cc-OPEN**: Open to air-cooled twins 905cc - Open. See Section 10.13.

8.6 THRUXTON CUP CHALLENGE
Open to lightly modified 865cc air-cooled Triumph Thruxtons and Harley-Davidson Sportsters. See Section 10.14.

8.7 SOUND OF SINGLES®
a) **SOUND OF SINGLES 1 (SoS1):** Unlimited displacement single-cylinder four-strokes. See Section 10.15.1.a.
b) **SOUND OF SINGLES 2 (SoS2):** Liquid-cooled, single-cylinder four-stroke motorcycles up to 450cc and air-cooled four-strokes to 610cc. See Section 10.15.1.b.
c) **SOUND OF SINGLES 3 (SoS3):** Certain 250-350cc single-cylinder machines with GP-style chassis and 300-400cc machines with Production chassis. See Section 10.15.1.c.
d) **MOTARD:** Motocross, off-road, dual-sport and motard-specific single-cylinder machines of unlimited displacement. See Section 10.15.1.d.

8.8 OPEN TWO-STROKE
Open to any two-stroke motorcycle, regardless of displacement, number of cylinders, frame type, cooling type or date of manufacture. See Section 10.16.

8.9 FORMULA THUNDER
Open to all Next Gen Superbike, Sound of Thunder, Sound of Singles and Battle of Twins motorcycles. See Section 10.17.

8.10 FORMULA LIGHTNING
Open to any zero-emission motorcycle. See Section 10.18.

8.11 PHILLIP ISLAND CHALLENGE
Open to machinery of large displacement vintage era engines to have an organization to race with that currently does not exist anywhere else. See Section 10.19.

8.12 TWO-STROKE CLASSIC
For Grand Prix or Factory road racing two-stroke 250/350cc motorcycles built from January 1974 through December 1984. Only genuine race bikes are allowed; modified street bikes are not eligible. See Section 10.21.

8.13 VINTAGE MOTOCROSS
a) **PREMIER LIGHTWEIGHT:** Certain pre-modern-era machines up to 250cc. See Section 11.1.1.
b) **PREMIER 350:** Certain 1960s-era four-stroke machines 300-350cc. See Section 11.1.2.
c) **PREMIER 500:** Pre-1965-era machines up to 500cc. See Section 11.1.3.
d) **PREMIER OPEN TWINS:** Non-unit-construction twin-cylinder machines manufactured as 600cc and larger. See Section 11.1.4.
e) **100cc MOTOCROSS:** 88-100cc two-stroke and 88-120cc four-stroke production machines up to 1974. See Section 11.1.5.
f) **CLASSIC 125:** 125cc two-strokes and four-strokes up to 150cc, manufactured through December 1971 and any like machines. See Section 11.1.6.

g) **CLASSIC 250:** Specific 250cc and smaller two-stroke machines introduced just after the Premier Lightweight era, and 350cc non-unit motorcycles. See Section 11.1.7.
h) **CLASSIC 500:** Specific motorcycles introduced just after the Premier 500 era. See Section 11.1.8.
i) **EARLY SPORTSMAN STOCK:** 250 and 500cc classes for lightly modified machines from the early portion of the Sportsman era. See Section 11.1.9-10
j) **SPORTSMAN:** 125, 250 and 500cc classes for machines up to model year 1974. See Section 11.1.11-13.
k) **SPORTSMAN OPEN TWINS:** Twin-cylinder machines up to model year 1974. See Section 11.1.14.
l) **OPEN AGE:** Any rider on any eligible vintage machine. See Section 11.1.15.
m) **40+:** Riders aged 40 and older on any eligible vintage machine. See Section 11.1.16.
n) **50+:** Riders aged 50 and older on any eligible vintage machine. See Section 11.1.17.
o) **60+:** Riders aged 60 and older on any eligible vintage machine. See Section 11.1.18.
p) **70+:** Riders aged 70 and older on any eligible vintage machine. See Section 11.1.19.
q) **WOMEN:** Female riders on any eligible vintage machine. See Section 11.1.20.

8.14 POST VINTAGE MOTOCROSS
a) **HISTORIC 125:** Certain 125cc and smaller motorcycles built up to and including the 1977 model year as the first-generation of long-travel machines. See Section 12.1.2.
b) **HISTORIC 250:** Certain 126-250cc motorcycles built up to and including the 1977 model year as the first-generation of long-travel machines. See Section 12.1.3.
c) **HISTORIC 500:** Certain 325-460cc two-strokes and four-strokes up to 636cc built up to and including the 1977 model year as the first-generation of long-travel machines. See Section 12.1.4.
d) **HISTORIC FOUR-STROKE:** Certain four-stroke machines built up to and including the 1978 model year with up to 636cc. Overhead-cam machines are limited to 500cc See Section 12.1.5.
e) **GRAND PRIX 125:** Certain post-1977 motorcycles, 88-125cc. See Section 12.2.2.
f) **GRAND PRIX 250:** Certain post-1977 motorcycles, 126-250cc. See Section 12.2.3.
g) **GRAND PRIX 500:** Certain post-1977 motorcycles, 325-500cc two-stroke and up to 580cc four-stroke. See Section 12.2.4.
h) **ULTIMA 125:** Certain motorcycles up to 125cc that do not have disc brakes or power-valve type mechanism built directly into the engine. See Section 12.3.2.
i) **ULTIMA 250:** Certain 126-250cc motorcycles that do not have disc brakes or power-valve type mechanism built directly into the engine. See Section 12.3.3.
j) **ULTIMA 500:** Certain 325-580cc motorcycles that do not have disc brakes or power-valve type mechanism built directly into the engine. See Section 12.3.4.
k) **ULTIMA FOUR-STROKE:** Certain 200cc-580cc four-stroke motorcycles produced after the Historic period, including those with single-shock rear suspension or newer engine technology. See Section 12.3.5.
l) **OPEN AGE:** Any rider on any eligible machine. See Section 12.4.1.

- m) **40+:** Riders aged 40 and older on any eligible machine. See Section 12.4.2.
- n) **50+:** Riders aged 50 and older on any eligible machine. See Section 12.4.3.
- o) **60+:** Riders aged 60 and older on any eligible machine. See Section 12.4.4.
- p) **70+:** Riders aged 70 and older on any eligible machine. See Section 12.4.5.
- q) **WOMEN:** Female riders on any eligible machine. See Section 12.4.6.

8.15 OBSERVED TRIALS
- a) **PREMIER HEAVYWEIGHT:** Pre-1965-era machines 350cc and larger. See Section 13.1.1.
- b) **PREMIER LIGHTWEIGHT:** Pre-1965-era machines up to 250cc. See Section 13.1.2.
- c) **RIGID LIGHTWEIGHT:** Any non-swingarm machine up to 300cc. See Section 13.1.3.
- d) **RIGID HEAVYWEIGHT:** Any non-swingarm machine 301cc or larger. See Section 13.1.4
- e) **GIRDER FORK:** Any rigid-frame, girder-fork machine. See Section 13.1.5.
- f) **MODERN CLASSIC:** Any unit-construction machine up to model year 1979. See Section 13.1.6.
- g) **CLASSIC:** Kit-framed two-strokes up to model year 1974 with 175cc or smaller OEM engine, and Spanish four-speeds to 250cc in original OEM frame. See Section 13.1.7.
- h) **MODERN TWIN SHOCK:** Post 1979 factory-designed twin shock motorcycles with drum brakes and air-cooled engines. See Section 13.1.8.
- i) **BEGINNER:** A non-championship class for beginning trials riders on any motorcycle eligible for AHRMA trials. See Section 13.1.9.
- j) **VINTAGE YOUTH CLASSES:** AHRMA Vintage Youth Classes are open to any rider through 14 years old. See section 13.1.10
- k) **AIR COOLED MONO (ACM):** with drum brakes only. Trials machines manufactured just after the twin shock era, but before significant performance advances were introduced to trials bike technology. See section 13.1.11.

8.16 DIRT TRACK and TT
- a) **DINOSAUR:** 1951 and earlier 500cc OHV and 750cc sidevalve. See Section 14.2.1.
- b) **LIGHT BRAKELESS:** Open to all machines 1968 and older up to and including 300cc. See Section 14.2.2.
- c) **HEAVY BRAKELESS:** Open to all machines 1968 and older 301cc and above. See Section 14.2.3.
- d) **SPORTSMAN:** 1974 and earlier dirt trackers, divided into classes for 125s, 0-250cc, 251-600cc and 601-750cc machines. See Section 14.2.4-7.
- e) **LIGHT VINTAGE:** Open to all machines 1990 and older up to and including 300cc. See Section 14.2.11.
- f) **HEAVY VINTAGE:** Open to all machines 1990 and older 301cc and above. See Section 14.2.12.
- g) **50+:** Riders aged 50 and older on any AHRMA class-eligible machine. See Section 14.2.10.
- h) **SPANISH CUP:** All air-cooled Spanish motorcycles (Bultaco, Montesa, and Ossa) to 360cc. See Section 14.2.9.
- i) **SEVENTIES SINGLES:** Post-vintage era four-stroke machines up to 600cc, such as those that competed in the late 1970's. See section 14.2.8.

- j) **NOVICE:** A non-championship class run at selected events for entry-level riders on Sportsman-eligible machines. See Section 14.2.13.
- k) **SUPPORT CLASSES:** Veteran (30+) may be run as support classes at the promoter's discretion. Also includes Modern Support classes. See Section 14.2.14.
- l) **EXHIBITION CLASSES:** AHRMA dirt track exhibition classes include:
  1. Board Track and like-design dirt track machines
  2. Two-valve speedway machines (on soft tracks where conditions allow. See Section 14.2.15.)

8.17 VINTAGE CROSS COUNTRY
- a) **100cc:** 88-100cc two-stroke and 88-120cc four-stroke machines. See Section 15.1.1.a.
- b) **SPORTSMAN 200:** Motorcycles manufactured as 88-200cc. See Section 15.1.1.b.
- c) **SPORTSMAN OPEN:** Motorcycles manufactured as 201cc and larger. See Section 15.1.1.c.
- d) **CLASSIC:** Includes all machines eligible for Classic classes in vintage MX. See Section 15.1.1.d.
- e) **PREMIER:** Includes all machines eligible for Premier classes in vintage MX. See Section 15.1.1.e.
- f) **50+:** Riders aged 50 and older on any eligible machine. See Section 15.1.1.f.
- g) **60+:** Riders aged 60 and older on any eligible machine. See Section 15.1.1.g.
- h) **70+:** Riders aged 70 and older on any eligible machine. See Section 15.1.1.h.
- i) **WOMEN:** Females riders on any eligible machine. See Section 15.1.1.i.

8.18 POST VINTAGE CROSS COUNTRY
- a) **HISTORIC 200:** Historic-class machines manufactured as 88-200cc. See Section 15.1.2.a.
- b) **HISTORIC OPEN:** Historic-class machines manufactured as 201cc and larger. See Section 15.1.2.b.
- c) **POST VINTAGE 200:** Grand Prix and Ultima-class machines manufactured as 88-200cc. See Section 15.1.2.c.
- d) **POST VINTAGE OPEN:** Grand Prix and Ultima-class machines manufactured as 201cc and larger. See Section 15.1.2.d.
- e) **50+:** Riders aged 50 and older on any eligible machine. See Section 15.1.2.e.
- f) **60+:** Riders aged 60 and older on any eligible machine. See Section 15.1.2.f.
- g) **70+:** Riders aged 70 and older on any eligible machine. See Section 15.1.2.g.
- h) **WOMEN:** Female riders on any eligible machine. See Section 15.1.2.h.
- i) **PRE-MODERN:** Certain machines equipped with front disc/rear drum brakes. See Sections 16.5.1-16.5.5

8.19 NEXT GEN MOTOCROSS
Novice classes shall not be combined in any Intermediate or Expert class race. All Novice classes shall run in Novice-only motos. There are no displacement divisions in any Novice class. See section 16.5.1.
- a) **PRE-MODERN 125:** Certain two-stroke motorcycles 100-125cc that were produced within the guidelines of the Pre-Modern class specifications. See Section 16.5.2.
- b) **PRE-MODERN 250:** Certain two-stroke motorcycles 126-250cc that were produced within the guidelines of the Pre-Modern class specifications. See Section 16.5.3.

c) **PRE-MODERN 500:** Certain two-stroke motorcycles 280-500cc that were produced within the guidelines of the Pre-Modern class specifications. See Section 16.5.4.
d) **PRE-MODERN FOUR-Stroke:** Certain four-stroke motorcycles 250-600cc that were produced within the guidelines of the Pre-Modern class specifications. See Section 16.5.5.
e) **NEXT GEN 1 - 125:** Certain two-stroke motorcycles 100-125cc that were produced within the guidelines of the Next Gen 1 class specifications. See Section 16.2.1.
f) **NEXT GEN 1 - 250:** Certain two-stroke motorcycles 126-250cc that were produced within the guidelines of the Next Gen 1 class specifications. See Section 16.2.2.
g) **NEXT GEN 1 - 500:** Certain two-stroke motorcycles 256-500cc that were produced within the guidelines of the Next Gen 1 class specifications. See Section 16.2.3.
h) **MILLENIUM TWO-STROKE- 125:** Certain two-stroke motorcycles 100-125cc that were produced within the guidelines of the Millennium class specifications. See Section 16.7.2.
i) **MILLENIUM TWO-STROKE - 250:** Certain two-stroke motorcycles 126-250cc that were produced within the guidelines of the Millennium class specifications. See Section 16.7.3.
j) **CURRENT TWO-STROKE - 125AM:** two-stroke motorcycles 100-125cc that were produced within the guidelines of the Current 2-Stroke class specifications. See Section 16.7.4.
k) **CURRENT TWO-STROKE - 250AM:** two-stroke motorcycles 126-250cc that were produced within the guidelines of the Current 2-Stroke class specifications. See Section 16.7.5.
l) **TWO-STROKE UNLIMITED:** This class shall not have OEM production machine restrictions, unlimited modifications are allowed, two-stroke engines ONLY. No displacement limits. See Section 16.7.7.
m) **40+:** Expert & Intermediate: Any Bike of this Generation is eligible for this class. See Section 16.8.1.
n) **50+:** Expert & Intermediate: Any Bike of this Generation is eligible for this class. See Section 16.8.1.
o) **60+:** Expert & Intermediate: Any Bike of this Generation is eligible for this class. See Section 16.8.1.

■ SECTION 9 - GENERAL ROAD RACING RULES

Every effort should be made to comply thoroughly with the following competition rules.

9.1 RIDER ELIGIBILITY

9.1.1 New AHRMA roadracers are required to provide evidence that in the past two years they have either successfully completed an accredited roadrace school or competed with another roadrace organization acceptable to AHRMA, including but not limited to AMA, CCS, WERA, AFM, etc. The minimum age for riders is 18. New, novice AHRMA roadracers may not be permitted to ride at certain venues.

9.2 MACHINE ELIGIBILITY

9.2.1 A motorcycle can bump-up one class but may be ridden in any class for which it is eligible under class guidelines, including that listed in the bump-up schedule below. With safety and fair competition in mind, the following schedule applies:

- a) 200 GP into 250 GP
- b) 250 GP into 350 GP
- c) 350 GP into 500 Premier
- d) 350 GP two-strokes into Formula 250
- e) 350 Sportsman into 500 Sportsman
- f) 500 Sportsman into 750 Sportsman
- g) Pre-1940 into Class C
- h) Class C into Classic Sixties
- i) Classic Sixties (500cc)
- j) Classic Sixties 650 to BEARS
- k) Formula 125 into Formula 250
- l) Formula 250 into Formula 500
- m) Formula 500 into Formula 750
- n) BEARS into Formula 750
- o) 500 Premier, Formula 500 & 750 and 750 Sportsman into Formula Vintage
- p) Novice Historic Production may not bump into any other class
- q) Vintage Superbike Lightweight into Vintage Superbike Middleweight
- r) Vintage Superbike Middleweight into Vintage Superbike Heavyweight
- s) Vintage Superbike Heavyweight into Formula Vintage
- t) Next Gen Superbike Lightweight into Next Gen Superbike Middleweight
- u) Next Gen Superbike Middleweight four-stroke into Next Gen Superbike
- v) Next Gen Superbike Middleweight two-stroke into Open Two-Stroke
- w) Next Gen Superbike into Next Gen Superbike 2
- x) Next Gen Superbike 2 into Next Gen Superbike 3
- y) Next Gen Superbike 3 into Formula Thunder

9.2.2 Sound of Singles (SoS), Sound of Thunder (SoT) and Battle of Twins (BoT) machines may enter any class in which the machine is eligible under the class guidelines.

9.2.3 Depending upon size of grids, entries may be run together and scored separately at the Race Director's option.

9.2.4 No roadrace class will be eliminated or consolidated without first being officially placed on a one-year probation. The probationary period is intended to give competitors an opportunity to support the class and show that it is viable.

9.3 TECHNICAL INSPECTION

- a) All turn signals, luggage racks and mirrors must be removed. Non-essential brackets, braces, grab rails, and chain guards may be removed. Centerstands and sidestands must be removed.
- b) Parts of the motorcycle that have sharp edges or corners and that present a cutting hazard must be smoothed or covered with at least 1/8-inch of rubber or other approved padding. These parts include, but are not limited to, foot controls and sidestand lugs.
- c) The motorcycle seat or fender must extend rearward beyond the line drawn vertically through the rear axle.
- d) If used, oil coolers must be securely mounted in a protected area. Manufacturer-approved oil lines or properly installed aftermarket lines and fittings must be used. Oil coolers, if used, must be frame-mounted (no fork-mounted oil coolers).

e) An unbreakable catch tank or reservoir of at least six-ounce capacity must be provided for **any** breather hoses venting the following: cambox or top end, crankcase, primary, gearbox, oil tank, and radiator or coolant tanks. Catch tanks must be situated so they will not normally overflow unless more than two-thirds full. Liquid-cooled machines **must use only water** or "WaterWetter" as a coolant, and a separate six-ounce catch tank must be provided.

f) **Oil containment.** Oil containment systems are required on all road racing machines. Oil containment pans on wet-sump engines must be designed to hold the capacity of the engine sump with nominal reserve. Material used must be durable, fastened safely, and removable for inspection, if required. All machines fitted with split or two-piece fairings must be fitted with an internal oil containment system. The pan must have a retaining dam at the rear. Two-stroke and dry-sump machines must use a pan with a minimum capacity of one quart, or approved oil-absorbing material covered with an impermeable layer of material and a screen backing and fastened securely. Oil-absorbing material, securely retained in the bottom of the pan, is **strongly recommended.** All oil containment systems are subject to approval by technical inspection.

g) Kickstarters may not be retained on roadracers, except in Class C and Pre-1940 on Handshift machines only. The kickstarter may be retained on supermoto-type machines, provided the lever is equipped with a secondary restraint, such as an elastic band.

h) All machines must be equipped with effective silencers, and exhaust systems must include sound-attenuation material or devices. Open pipes and reverse cone megaphones are not effective silencers. Exceptions may be granted for exhibition purposes only. All exhaust systems must exit toward the rear of the motorcycle.

Sound testing will take place at AHRMA National events. The AHRMA sound limit is 105 dB(a). The sound level will be measured while the machine is on the track during practice sessions and racing events. A static test may be used off-track with the sound meter held 45° off the centerline of the silencer and 48" from the tip, and the throttle held at ½ redline. If the machine is found to be not in compliance with the AHRMA limit of 105 dB(a) or a track-imposed lower limit in either test, the machine will not be allowed to continue until it is brought into compliance. No refunds of entry fees will be issued. The limit of 105dB(a) will be imposed for all machines on the track and in the pits, including generators.

9.4 LOCKWIRE REQUIREMENTS

Because historic racing motorcycles have unique characteristics of construction, AHRMA has developed specific lockwiring requirements for roadracers. As a general rule-of-thumb, "If in doubt, lockwire it." **Note:** Only stainless steel lockwire may be used. The following regulations apply in addition to those outlined earlier in this Handbook.

a) Primary case filler, drain and level-check plugs must be lockwired.
b) Crankcase filler, drain and level-check plugs must be lockwired.
c) Transmission filler, drain and level-check plugs must be lockwired.
d) Any primary case, crankcase or transmission inspection plug must be lockwired.
e) Any primary case, crankcase or transmission overflow or vent hoses must be lockwired.
f) Oil filter nuts and oil filter plugs must be lockwired.
g) Fuel tank overflow lines must be secured and have a catch bottle or one-way valve provided.

h) Lockwiring of carburetor drain plugs, or securing with a fuel-proof sealant, is encouraged.
i) All flexible oil lines must be a reinforced oil- and gas-resistant hose, and must be secured by lockwire as a secondary security, in addition to a swaged fitting or hose clamp. Total-loss oiling is not permitted. Any machine with a non-recirculating oiling system must be equipped with unbreakable catch bottles and/or a "select pad" diaper system of sufficient capacity. **Oil must not be deposited on the track.**
j) All fuel and oil lines must be securely clamped or secured by other acceptable means and will be pull-tested during tech inspection.
k) All fork drains must be lockwired or securely taped.
l) Exhaust systems must be securely mounted and bolts lockwired. A secondary security system is encouraged and may be required at the Tech Inspector's discretion.
m) Brake torque arm bolt lockwiring is required.
n) If not lockwired, axle nuts must be secured with a cotter pin or other acceptable means.
o) Foot brake pedal pivot bolts and nuts must be lockwired.
p) All brake rods and cables with threaded adjusters must be wired or cotter-pinned to prevent the loss of the adjuster nut.
q) Throttle cable(s) must be lockwired to the carburetor linkage or body. If throttle cables are not crimped into the twistgrip or inline adjusters, they must also be wired to retain cable(s) in ferrules.
r) All disc brake caliper attaching bolts must be lockwired.

9.5 NUMBERS AND NUMBER PLATES

9.5.1 For race number policies, please see SECTION 3.9

9.5.2 Roadrace class champions from the previous year may display the No. 1 plate on their machine (see rule 3.6a). In combined-class racing, No. 1 plates must also display an upper-case letter (such as 1E). When used, letters must be four inches tall. Case designation below is for registration software purposes only. Upper case letters only should be used on number plates. For Next Gen, please use the same number assignments.

Number/letter combinations for each class are:

Class	Code	Class	Code
500 Premier	1	Next Gen Superbike	1Y
2 Stroke Classic 250GP	1W	Next Gen Superbike 2	1v
2 Stroke Classic 350GP	1X	Next Gen Superbike 3	1r
350 Grand Prix	1A	Next Gen Superbike Lightweight	1s
250 Grand Prix	1B	Next Gen Superbike Middleweight	1z
200 Grand Prix Plus	1C	Formula Thunder	1n
Formula 750	1D	Battle of Twins 900cc	1a
Formula 500	1E	Battle of Twins 900cc-Open	1m
Formula 250	1F	Sound of Thunder 1	1b
Formula 125	1G	Sound of Thunder 2	1c
Pre-1940 GP	1H	Sound of Thunder 3	1d
Class C Handshift	1I	Sound of Thunder 4	1u
Class C Footshift	1K	Open Two-Stroke	1e
Classic Sixties	1L	Sound of Singles 1	1f
Classic Sixties 650	1M	Sound of Singles 2	1g
Sportsman 750	1N	Sound of Singles 3	1h
Sportsman 500	1P	Motard	1j
Sportsman 350	1Q	Formula Lightning	1k
Formula Vintage	1R	Thruxton	1t
BEARS	1S	Phillip Island Challenge	1p
Vintage Superbike Heavyweight	1T		
Vintage Superbike Middleweight	1V		
Vintage Superbike Lightweight	1Z		

9.5.3 All vintage roadrace numbers must be black on a white background, except: Sportsman, black numbers on "school bus yellow" background, and Novice Historic Production, red numbers on white background, Sports-man and Novice Historic Production machines use 10x12-inch rectangular number plates; all others use rectangular plates 10x12-inches or oval plates no smaller than 9x11-inches.

9.5.4 All Vintage Superbike numbers must be white numerals on a green background

9.5.5 BoT, SoS and SoT machines may use any number plate background color; numbers can either be black or white, whichever provides the best visibility.

9.5.6 Numbers must be at least seven-inches high, block style, with a stroke width of one-inch and legible. There must be no less than 1/2-inch of space between numbers, and between the numbers and the outside edge of the number plate. If a rider's assigned number will not fit into a 9x11-inch oval, a larger background may be used, up to a 10x12-inch rectangle.

9.5.7 All machines must display three number plates -- one mounted on the front and one on each side, mounted in such a manner that it will not be blocked by the rider in the normal racing (seated) position.

9.5.8 Any violations constitute grounds for disqualification.

9.6 SCORING AND SERIES POINTS, AWARDS

9.6.1 **RACE FINISHES:** The race is officially ended for all contestants at the completion of the lap the winner is given the checkered flag.

    a) Should the checkered flag be displayed later than the official distance, the finishing order will be decided on the basis of the official distance. Under any other circumstance, the winner is the leader at the time the checkered flag is displayed.

    b) Should a rider be given the checkered flag with or ahead of the actual winner, the rider will be scored as having completed the race in the race position the rider was running at that time.

    c) Riders not yet receiving the checkered flag will be scored in order of finish and laps completed.

9.6.2 A "did not finish" (DNF) scores points in order of stoppage, but a "did not start" (DNS) will not receive points. A rider will score points if he is the sole class competitor. A rider must complete one full lap to be scored.

9.6.3 Results will be posted as soon as possible after the finish of a race. Once posted, there will be a 30-minute review time. If a rider believes there is an error in scoring, he or she must draft a written protest and deliver it to an AHRMA official or Referee within 30 minutes of the provisional results being posted. Unprotested results will stand. Any discrepancies will be resolved at the track. All results posted on the AHRMA website are considered final and can only be modified under direction of the Roadrace Director. This process is subject to appeal.

9.6.4 If two classes are run together in one race, a rider may ride one motorcycle in one class and also be scored in the other class, provided the machine is eligible and entered in that other class. The rider shall start from the least favorable wave or grid position.

9.6.5 Points will be awarded at all roadraces according to the following schedule. National-championship events also award regional-championship points for the region in which the event takes place.

National Series awards are based on a rider's best finishes in one-half of the total number of races up to 20, in the series, rounded up to the next whole number if necessary (e.g., in a 19-race series, a rider's 10 best finishes count). A rider must score points in at least two events to be eligible for National series awards. Criteria for Regional Series Awards will be defined and published prior to the first event of the year. Yearly schedule changes to events and locations may change the regional series criteria. Year-end scoring ties will be broken by the greatest number of first-place finishes, then second-place finishes, third place, etc. <u>within the best finishes.</u> If still tied, the position will be awarded to the rider with the better results in any head-to-head, on-track meetings. In the event of an absolute tie, the oldest rider wins.

    a) All machines must have a functioning AMB transponder mounted on either fork leg not more than 42 inches from the ground with the mounting pin up, during all races. It is the responsibility of the rider to have the AMB transponder charged and mounted properly, or the rider will not be scored in the respective race.

    b) The racer must use their registered transponder on any bike they race.

    c) If a racer wants to be manually scored, a fee of $50 per day will be charged. The racer must notify the Race Director prior to the race to be manually scored

d) Scoring of a racer with a malfunctioning transponder will be at the discretion of the Race Director.
e) AMB timing and scoring results are to be used to determine the final finishing positions. Results on www.mylaps.com are not official AHRMA results. Official AHRMA results will be posted on www.ahrma.org.

Finish Position	Points	Finish Position	Points	Finish Position	Points
1	1000	21	64	41	20
2	835	22	58	42	19
3	700	23	53	43	18
4	590	24	49	44	17
5	499	25	45	45	16
6	424	26	42	46	15
7	362	27	39	47	14
8	311	28	36	48	13
9	268	29	34	49	12
10	232	30	32	50	11
11	202	31	30	51	10
12	176	32	29	52	9
13	154	33	28	53	8
14	136	34	27	54	7
15	120	35	26	55	6
16	107	36	25	56	5
17	95	37	24	57	4
18	85	38	23	58	3
19	77	39	22	59	2
20	70	40	21	60	1

9.7 MECHANICAL REQUIREMENTS FOR VINTAGE CLASSES

9.7.1 All major components must be OEM parts or accurate, detailed replicas of the same parts using the same type materials and technologies. Major components may not be newer than the cutoff date specified for a class (i.e., no post-period inverted forks in the vintage or Vintage Superbike classes). Composite materials not of the period cannot be used in any form in a vintage machine without prior approval of the Vintage Roadrace Rules & Eligibility Committee. The burden of authenticating is on the rider. Press clippings and photos with identifiable dates may be helpful.

9.7.2 **ENGINES**
a) Engines of any type, falling into the classes listed, may compete.
b) Engines must be naturally aspirated (no turbos). Superchargers are allowed only on Pre-1940 GP machines, if original equipment
c) Allowable overbore is a class's maximum displacement plus the following limits, or the specific machine displacement, as in the performance-indexed classes (such as 200 Grand Prix Plus and Classic Sixties 650): Four stroke cylinders may be overbored by a maximum of .080", singles; .060", twins; .040", triples; and .040", fours. Two stroke cylinders may be overbored by a maximum of .080". To determine displacement limits, .080", .060", <u>and</u> .040", as appropriate, shall be subtracted from the actual bore prior to calculation. **Note:** These limits do not apply to Class C and Pre-'40 classes, which have a maximum overbore of .080".
d) The formula for calculating engine displacement in any class is: Bore x bore x .7854 x stroke x number of cylinders.

- e) A six-ounce-minimum catch tank or reservoir must be provided for any breather hoses venting the following: Cambox or top end, crankcase, primary, transmission, oil tanks, and radiator or coolant tanks. Such catch tanks must be situated so that they will not normally overflow.
- f) Total-loss primary chain oilers must be equipped with a system to prevent spillage onto the track.
- g) All fluid plugs and fittings with oil or coolant behind them must be securely fastened or lockwired.
- h) Liquid-cooled motorcycle engines must use only water or "WaterWetter" as a coolant, and a separate, six-ounce catch tank must be fitted.
- i) Machines with chain-driven primary must have a chain guard.
- j) Conversion to toothed-belt primary drive is encouraged as a safety measure.
- k) Hydraulically-assisted clutches are prohibited.

9.7.3 FRAMES
- a) Frames shall be free of cracks and kinks.
- b) All welds shall be structurally sound.
- c) Road racing motorcycles must have both front and rear suspension (except Pre-'40, Class C and Sidecar).
- d) No part of the seat or other parts to the rear may stand more than 37 inches above the ground when the motorcycle is unladen.
- e) Unladen motorcycles must be capable of leaning at least 50 degrees to either side before contacting the ground (tires excepted).
- f) Frames and swingarms must be made in the same type (tubing style) and manner as original or period. An eligibility request must be submitted for any frame or swingarm redesign or modification. A diagram of an approved tubular reinforced swingarm eligible for Formula and Sportsman machines is shown below. This swingarm was documented as having been constructed by Big D Cycle in 1971. Round-tube swingarms are encouraged on all vintage-class machines. Box-section swingarms may be fitted, but must be of stamped-steel construction, or maximum 2" x 1.25" cross-section steel. Aluminum-alloy swingarms are allowed but must have been manufactured before the class cut-off date, or a replica thereof.

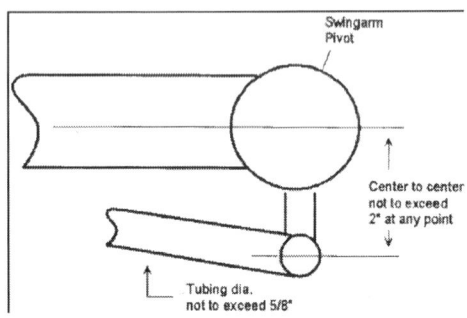

- g) The motorcycle seat or fender must extend rearward beyond the line drawn vertically through the rear axle.
- h) Gas-filled shocks are permitted, but remote or external reservoirs are not, unless fitted as original equipment.

i) Monoshock or cantilever rear suspension is prohibited except Vincent original equipment. Machines that were factory equipped with them are eligible. Example: Yamaha TZ750 in Formula Vintage. Two rear shock/spring units are required and must not be inclined forward more than 45-degrees from vertical, one shock on each side of the machine.

9.7.4 TANKS
a) All tanks, whether for fuel, oil, or coolant, **must be leak-free and securely mounted.**
b) Fuel tanks **must be fitted** with readily accessible shut-off valves in working order. Machines fitted with electric fuel pumps are exempt from the inline shut-off valve requirement.
c) Positive clamping is **mandatory** on all oil, fuel, and coolant line connections. Slip fits are not permitted.

9.7.5 TIRES & RIMS
a) Road racing tires must be of modern racing compound (only DOT-type permitted). No slicks, soft rain tires or hand-cut slicks are permitted in vintage classes. Tires must be treaded and not excessively worn.
b) Wheels must be wire-spoke-type in Classic, Grand Prix, and Sportsman categories. Spokes must be in good condition. Formula classes may use period cast wheels. Astralite (stamped) type wheels are prohibited, except in Vintage Superbike.
c) Tire warmers are allowed on vintage motorcycles with treaded tires.

9.7.6 RIM SIZES
a) **Grand Prix (200 GP+, 250 GP, 350 GP and 500 Premier):** Rim diameter must be at least 18 inches and not exceed WM3 (2.15 inches), except where fitted as original equipment (e.g., Ariel Arrow), minimum diameter 16 inches.
b) **Formula 750:** Rim diameter must be at least 18 inches and not exceed WM4 (2.5 inches) front and WM5 (3.0 inches) rear. Harley-Davidson XR750s may use WM6 (3.5 inches) when fitted with original Morris magnesium wheels. No Astralite wheels.
c) **Formula 500:** Rim diameter must be at least 18 inches not exceed WM4 (2.5 inches) front and WM5 (3.0 inches) rear.
d) **Formula 250:** Rim diameter must be at least 18 inches and not exceed WM4 (2.5 inches) front and WM4.5 (2.75 inches) rear.
e) **Formula 125:** Rim width may not exceed WM3 (2.15 inches) front or rear.
f) **Classic (Pre-'40, Class C, Classic Sixties):** Rim diameter must be at least 18 inches and not exceed WM3 (2.15 inches), except in Class C and Pre-'40 when fitted as OEM (H-D and Indian), minimum diameter 16 inches.
g) **Sportsman:** Rim diameter must be at least 18 inches and not exceed WM3 (2.15 inches) front and WM4 (2.5 inches) rear. WM4 (2.5 inches) front rims and WM5 (3.0 inches) rear rims are permitted on 750s only.
h) **Novice Historic Production:** Maximum rim width WM3 (2.15 inches) front and WM4 (2.5 inches) rear.
i) **Vintage Superbike:** Maximum rim width is 3.5 inches front and 4.5 inches rear.

RIM WIDTH MEASURMENTS	
SIZE	WIDTH (inches)
WM 2	1.85
WM 3	2.15
WM 4	2.5
WM 4.5	2.75
WM 5	3.0
WM 6	3.5
As measured inside the rim, from inside shoulder to inside shoulder	

9.7.7 **BRAKES**
   a) Efficient front and rear brakes are required.
   b) Front disc brakes, where allowed, must be of the period; steel, rigid-mounted type; maximum diameter 12 inches. Caliper must be the two-piston period type. Discs permitted only in Sportsman and Formula categories—single front disc or drum in Sportsman 750, Historic Production Heavyweight and Formula 250; dual front discs or drum in Formula 500 and Formula 750. All GP and Classic classes must use drum front brakes.
   c) Rear discs are permitted, provided they are period equipment. Rear discs are not permitted in Classic Sixties, Class C and Pre-1940 classes.
   d) Any type of period drum brake is acceptable. Hydraulically-operated drum brakes are prohibited. Refer to Class C, Pre-1940 and Classic Sixties rules for restrictions.
   e) Air scoops, if fitted, must have screens and be clear of all working parts.

9.7.8 **HANDLEBARS & CONTROLS**
   a) Handlebars must have a minimum width of 18 inches and a maximum width of 32 inches (except Class C and Pre-1940).
   b) Handlebars, levers, and the rider's hands must have at least one-inch clearance between the fuel tank or enclosed-type fairings, and at least two inches with cut-out-type fairings.
   c) Handlebars shall permit the front wheel to be turned at least 20 degrees to each side from a straight-ahead position.
   d) Hand-control levers must have ball ends at least 1/2-inch in diameter. Front brake lever protectors are strongly encouraged.
   e) All controls must operate effectively and reliably.
   f) All foot controls must be free from sharp or ragged edges.
   g) Steering dampers may be added or changed.
   h) All motorcycles must be equipped with a functional, handlebar-mounted kill switch. If the motorcycle is equipped with a magneto where an operational kill switch cannot be fitted, the carburetor settings must be such that a running engine shuts off when the throttle is fully closed.
   i) Throttles must be self-closing, or the machine must be equipped with a deadman switch mounted on the handlebar and attached to the rider.

9.7.9 FOOTRESTS
a) Footrests must be positioned for ready access to applicable controls.
b) Footrests may be solid or folding. If folding, they must fold up and to the rear at a 45-degree angle and must be spring-loaded to prevent folding accidently.
c) Only one pair of footrests may be fitted per machine.
d) Footrests must be free of sharp or cutting edges.

9.7.10 FAIRINGS
a) Fairings, if used, must be mounted at no fewer than three points.
b) Fairings must not extend forward of a vertical line drawn through the forward-most part of the front tire. The front wheel must be visible from the side, and it must be possible to see the rider completely, in the normal riding position, from either side and from above with the exception of the forearms and hands.
c) No streamlining may be attached to the rider or the helmet. Leathers with "aero humps" are permitted.
d) Dustbin fairings are permitted only on pre-1957 GP-class roadracers.
e) Period fairings only. No fairings in Sportsman classes.

9.7.11 FUEL
a) Gasoline only; maximum 115 octane [using formula (R+M)/2].
b) Race gas available to all competitors at each event will be used as a standard for testing. Street gas with boosters or additives will be illegal if it exceeds the standard.
c) No fuel may be carried on a motorcycle except in tanks securely mounted for that purpose.

9.7.12 EXHAUST NOISE
a) Sound testing will take place at all AHRMA National events. See rule 9.3h.
b) All two-stroke machines must compete with effective silencers.
c) Exceptions may be granted for exhibition purposes only.

9.7.13 EXHAUST SYSTEMS
a) Period-style exhaust systems are encouraged.
b) All exhaust systems must exit toward the rear of the motorcycle.

9.7.14 CARBURETORS
a) Flat-slide or Lectron-type and injection-type carburetors are not permitted. "Power jet" and "pumper" type carburetors are not permitted unless such mechanisms are disconnected or removed. Fuel injection is not permitted. Period carburetors are encouraged. Smoothbore carburetors with concentric float bowls are not permitted, except where they were fitted as original equipment or supplied as factory kits on that model motorcycle. Modern replacement smoothbore carburetors are not permitted.
b) A restrictor plate may be used where a minimum carburetor size is specified. A restrictor plate must be at 1/8-inch thick with a constant diameter bore no larger than the required maximum diameter.

9.7.15 IGNITION:
Conversion to electronic (pointless) ignition is permitted in all classes. Ignitions may be relocated on/in the engine, and programmable and/or digital systems are allowed. Electronic engine-management systems are not permitted. Any system that provides dynamic (vehicle in motion) electronic adjustments via rider selection or any other means is illegal.

9.7.16 REED VALVES:
Reed petals may be metal, fiber or carbon fiber. No cage restriction.

9.7.17 **GENERAL:** Two AHRMA decals of an approved design must be displayed in a conspicuous or readily-visible position on the motorcycle. Decals are available at technical inspection at no cost to the competitor.

9.8 MECHANICAL REQUIREMENTS FOR BATTLE OF TWINS®, SOUND OF SINGLES® AND SOUND OF THUNDER

a) **ENGINE MODIFICATIONS:** Unless specified, there are no restrictions on engine modifications. A competitor may modify the engine to any degree, as long as the class displacement limits are not exceeded. Engines may not have their bore and/or stroke reduced to meet class limits. Engines must be naturally aspirated (no turbos or superchargers), except four-stroke singles in Sound of Thunder.

b) **FRAMES**
1. Any frame manufactured by an OEM or any reputable aftermarket frame manufacturer is allowed. Custom frames are eligible, but only the highest standard of workmanship will be permitted. Frame modifications are allowed; however, they must be declared and brought to the attention of the Tech Inspector for inspection of quality and eligibility. Any frame considered inadequate by the Tech Inspector will not be allowed to race. This decision may be appealed to the Race Director only at that event. Contact the AHRMA office for clarification of confirmation of eligibility.
2. Frame modifications: Gusseting and strengthening is allowed, as long as it is done in a professional, safe, workmanlike manner.
3. Swingarms may be strengthened or changed to a different style or type, provided they are safe and tight in the frame.
4. Frames shall be free of cracks and kinks.
5. All welds shall be structurally sound.

c) **WHEELS:** Rim diameter must be no smaller than 16 inches. Rim width should comply with the tire manufacturer's recommendations.

d) **TIRES:** Slicks, DOT or rain tires may be used in all SoS/BoT/SoT classes except Thruxton Transatlantic Challenge. Tires must be of a modern racing compound and must not show excessive wear. Tire warmers are permitted in all SoS/BoT/SoT classes.

e) **BRAKES:** Efficient front and rear brakes are required.

f) **SUSPENSION:** Motorcycles must have both front and rear suspension.

g) **EXHAUST:** All machines must be equipped with effective silencers, and exhaust systems must include sound-attenuation material or devices. Open pipes and reverse-cone megaphones are **not** effective silencers. Exceptions may be granted for exhibition purposes. All exhaust systems must exit toward the rear of the motorcycle. See Sec 9.3 h) for description of testing.
Sound testing will take place at AHRMA National events. The AHRMA sound limit is 105 dB(a).

h) **FLUIDS AND FLUID CONTROL**
1. All liquid-cooled machines must use only water or "WaterWetter" for cooling. Antifreeze, ethylene glycol or other additives are prohibited. A separate catch tank of at least six ounces must be fitted to catch any overflow.
2. All fluid plugs and fittings with oil or coolant behind them must be securely fastened or lockwired.

3. A six-ounce-minimum catch tank or reservoir must be provided for any breather hoses venting the following: cambox or top end, crankcase, primary, transmission and oil tanks. Such catch tanks must be situated so that they will not normally overflow.
4. All tanks, whether for fuel, oil, or coolant, must be leak-free and securely mounted.
5. On machines not fitted with an electric fuel pump, fuel tanks must be fitted with readily accessible shut-off valve(s)/petcock(s) in working order.
6. Positive clamping is mandatory on all oil, fuel, and coolant line connections. Slip fits are not permitted.

i) **CONTROLS AND FOOTRESTS**
1. Handlebars must have a minimum width of 18 inches and a maximum width of 32 inches.
2. Handlebars, levers, and the rider's hands must have at least one-inch clearance between the fuel tank or enclosed-type fairings, and at least two inches with cut-out-type fairings.
3. Handlebars shall permit the front wheel to be turned at least 20 degrees to each side from a straight-ahead position.
4. Hand-control levers must have ball ends at least 1/2-inch in diameter. Front brake lever protectors are required, and must be of safe, workmanlike construction.
5. All controls must operate effectively and reliably.
6. Steering dampers may be added or changed.
7. Motorcycles must be equipped with a functional, handlebar-mounted kill-switch.
8. Throttles must be self-closing.
9. Footrests must be positioned for ready access to applicable controls.
10. Footrests may be solid or folding. If folding, they must fold up and to the rear at a 45-degree angle and must be spring-loaded to prevent folding accidently. Only one pair of footrests may be fitted per machine.
11. Footrests and foot controls must be free of sharp or cutting edges.

j) Unladen motorcycles must be capable of leaning at least 50 degrees to either side before contacting the ground (tires excepted).

k) **BODYWORK**
1. Fairings, if used, must be mounted at no fewer than three points.
2. Fairings must not extend forward of a vertical line drawn through the forward-most part of the front tire. The front wheel must be visible from the side, and it must be possible to see the rider completely, in the normal riding position, from either side and from above with the exception of the forearms and hands.
3. The motorcycle seat or fender must extend rearward beyond a line drawn vertically through the rear axle.
4. No streamlining may be attached to the rider or the helmet. Leathers with "aero humps" are permitted.

l) **FUEL**
1. Gasoline only; maximum 115 octane [using formula (R+M)/2]. Race gas available to all competitors at each event will be used as a standard for testing. Street gas with boosters or additives will be illegal if it exceeds the standard.
2. No fuel may be carried on a motorcycle except in tanks securely mounted for that purpose.

m) Two AHRMA decals of an approved design must be displayed in a conspicuous or readily-visible position on the motorcycle. Decals are available at technical inspection at no cost to the competitor.

9.8.1 SUPERSPORT

The following are the allowable modifications for Supersport spec, where required by certain classes. Only the modifications listed in this section are permitted. No other changes are allowed. If it doesn't say you **may** do it, then you **may not**.

a) **ELIGIBILITY:** Eligible Supersport machines must be sold by the manufacturer in the U.S. to the general public with full EPA and DOT approval (EPA/DOT approval not required for supermoto-type machines in Motard). A list of eligible motorcycles is available from the AHRMA office. No updating or backdating of parts is allowed. The frame will determine the year and model of the motorcycle. All other parts must be from that year and model of motorcycle. Motorcycles must display a valid U.S. VIN number on the main frame.

b) **GENERAL:** The following items must be removed: Turn signals, mirrors, headlight. Taillight/brakelight must be removed or disabled. Taillight lens may be retained but must be taped over. Horn must be removed or disabled. Sidestand must be removed. The following items may be removed: Grab rails, reflectors, rear fender, helmet lock, passenger footpegs and brackets, chain guards, radiator fan(s) and wiring.

c) **FRAME:** Frames must remain stock except for the following: crash bumpers/frame sliders may be installed; frame brackets/spools may be added to permit the use of stands; aftermarket chain guards/"shark fins" may be added; frames may be polished, painted or powdercoated, providing the VIN remains visible and readable. Subframes may be modified. Machines equipped with an OEM bolt-on subframe may replace the subframe with an OEM or aftermarket unit in steel or aluminum only.

d) **ENGINE**
   1. Up to 0.040" overbore is allowed only on machines with OEM cast-iron cylinder liners. Only OEM pistons and rings may be used. There is no allowance for overbore on any other machines.
   2. Cam sprockets may be modified or replaced. Cam-chain tensioners may be modified or replaced.
   3. Cylinder head, cylinder and crankcase gasket surface may be machined for increased compression. All other surfaces of the head, cylinder and crankcases must remain stock. Aftermarket gaskets may be used. Head and base gaskets do not have to conform to stock specifications.
   4. Valves must remain stock. Multi-angle or -radius valve jobs are permitted.
   5. Transmission must use stock OEM parts for that model and year. Shifter return or detent springs may be replaced. Electric shift devices (quick shifters) may be used.
   6. Sparkplugs, clutch plates, clutch springs, and oil filters may be replaced. An aftermarket slipper clutch may be fitted.

e) **BODYWORK**
  1. For motorcycles produced with full fairings, replica replacement bodywork may be used. If stock bodywork includes air ducting, it may be removed. If the ducting is retained, it must be stock or exact replica replacements and made of the same material as OEM.
  2. Solo seat cowlings are permitted. Replacement solo tail sections are permitted providing they conform to the shape and size of the stock bodywork. OEM seats may be removed and replaced by foam padding.
  3. Bodywork may be made of fiberglass, plastic, composite, or carbon fiber. Bodywork may be attached with non-OEM fasteners such as Dzus.
  4. For motorcycles produced without full fairings or with less than full fairings, replica replacement bodywork from any U.S.-legal production motorcycle may be used. All other rules as detailed above, apply.
  5. Fluid containment systems are required on all roadrace machines (see 9.3f).
  6. Number plates may be added to the rear seat section.
  7. Original instrument/fairing bracket may be replaced. No composite or carbon fiber brackets allowed.
  8. OEM fuel tank must be retained and used in the OEM location. Fuel cap may be replaced.

f) **TIRES:** Slicks, DOT or rain tires may be used.

g) **SUSPENSION**
  1. Rear shock(s) may be modified or replaced. All linkage must remain stock. (Suzuki TL models are allowed to use aftermarket linkage to allow for replacing the stock rotary shock with a standard-style shock.)
  2. Fork oil may be changed. Fork caps may be changed. Fork internals may be modified or replaced. Fork braces may be modified or added. Triple clamps may be modified or changed to alter the fork offset and/or to add a steering damper.

h) Captive wheels spacers may be added. Speedometer drive may be replaced with a spacer.

i) Steering dampers may be replaced or added.

j) **BRAKES:** Steel braided or Kevlar brake lines may be used. Brake pads may be changed. Brake rotors may be drilled. Brake rotors may be replaced but must remain the same size as OEM. No composite or carbon fiber rotors. Brake calipers must remain stock. Brake and clutch master cylinders may be replaced. Clutch slave cylinders may be modified or replaced.

k) **INDUCTION**
  1. Carburetor jets and needles may be replaced. Resizing of air-metering holes in CV carbs is allowed. Throttle slide and return springs may be replaced. Fuel lines, vent lines and fuel filters may be replaced.
  2. All components in the fuel-injection system must remain standard except the electronic control modules, which may be modified or replaced. Add-on ignition/injection modules, such as Power Commanders, may be used.
  3. OEM airbox systems may be removed. Gen 1 SV650s (1999-2002) may use flat slide carburetors. Air filters may be replaced. Airbox drains must be sealed. Crankcase vent hose must remain routed to the airbox. Crankcase breathers may be modified or replaced. If the airbox is removed, the crankcase vent must be routed to a 120 ounce, leakproof catch can.

l) **EXHAUST:** Complete exhaust system may be replaced. Insulating pipe wrap is permitted. See rule 9.3h.
m) **FINAL DRIVE:** Final drive sprockets and chain may be replaced. Chain size may be altered. Sprocket carrier may be replaced. Machines originally equipped with a belt final drive may change to a chain-drive system.
n) **MISCELLANEOUS**
1. Rider footpegs and brackets may be modified or replaced. Shift lever, rear brake lever and linkage may be modified or replaced.
2. Handlebars may be modified or replaced.
3. Instruments, instrument brackets, switches and associated cables/wiring may be removed or replaced. Unused wires may be trimmed from the wiring harness, but the original OEM harness may not be replaced.

■ SECTION 10 - REQUIREMENTS FOR ROAD RACING CLASSES

MISSION STATEMENT: AHRMA's mission is to recreate and preserve the vintage era of road racing, including the sights, sounds, smells and camaraderie. Many consider the 50-year time span – from the 1930s to the mid-'70s – the golden age of road racing. We recognize that the oldest of these motorcycles are the least available; therefore, only small numbers are likely to participate in most events, and some events may have no examples. However, AHRMA is committed to maintaining a venue to showcase these early motorcycles, no matter how few.

Vintage roadrace classes are broken down into five basic groups:

a) **Grand Prix:** Period GP racers and appropriately modified street machines from 1968 and earlier. Classes include 200 GP Plus, 250 GP, 350 GP, 500 Premier.
b) **Formula:** Purpose-built race machines and GP-kitted street bikes built up to 1972. Classes are Formula 125, 250, 500 and 750cc, plus Formula Vintage.
c) **Classic:** AHRMA's earliest machines, from the Pre-War period up to about 1960, represented by Pre-1940 Grand Prix, Class C, Classic Sixties and Classic Sixties 650.
d) **Sportsman:** Racing motorcycles through 1972 based on street motorcycles or with special dirt track frames. Three classes for machines with 350, 500 or 750cc engines.
e) **Novice Historic Production:** Entry-level classes designed for a beginning vintage race enthusiast to compete on comparable, near-stock machines. Classes for Lightweight and Heavyweight, 1972-and-earlier machines.

10.1 PERFORMANCE INDEX

When a motorcycle is demonstrably faster or slower than others in its displacement group it may, at the discretion of the review committee, be assigned to another class.

10.2　GRAND PRIX: 500 Premier, 350 GP, 250 GP, 200 GP Plus

Fully GP-kitted motorcycles built prior to December 31, 1968. Only four-strokes in 500 Premier; two-strokes are permitted in 350, 250 and 200 GP. Drum brakes only. Fairings are encouraged but not mandatory. Unless specified otherwise, engine modifications are not limited as long as period components are used, and class displacement is not exceeded.

Each of the above classes has its own eligibility listing, requirements, and restrictions. All of these classes must also comply with rules 10.2.6.a-l. Please note that in some cases those machines listed with an asterisk (*) will have special instructions listed below. If for some reason your machine does not comply with the year cutoffs and is not listed in the class as eligible, you must submit an Eligibility Request Form at least 10 days before an event in which you intend to compete (see section 19.10).

10.2.1　500 PREMIER

Any fully GP-kitted 500cc OHV/OHC or 750cc sidevalve four-strokes built before December 31, 1968, and like design. Among the eligible machines are:

- Benelli, "works" fours
- Bianchi 500 "works" twin
- BMW Rennsport
- BSA 500cc twin or single "works" or replica, BSA B50 permitted as both a single "works" or replica and like design
- Dick Mann frame with G50 or other period engine
- Ducati 450 single
- Ducati 500cc bevel-gear V-twin "works" racer and accurate replicas
- ESO 500 single
- Gilera
- Harley-Davidson KR roadracer
- Honda CR450 roadracer
- Honda-Drixton 450
- Honda RC181 4-cylinder (no replicas)
- Jawa "works" twin
- Jawa 500 single
- Linto
- Matchless G50
- McIntyre Special and replica, G50 powered
- Moto Guzzi single, twin and V8
- MV triple
- MV four, early wide-angle head (pre-1973 era)
- Norton Dominator Daytona 500 or replica
- Norton Manx
- Paton twin (8-valve Paton twin not legal for 500 Premier)
- Rickman GP road racing frame, powered by G50 or other period engine
- Royal Enfield, including India-built models.
- Seeley frame with G50 or other period engine
- Triton

- Triumph 500cc twin "works" or replica; Weslake four-valve heads permitted
- Velocette Thruxton and Venom Clubman
- Vincent Grey Flash or replica
- Weslake (Nourish) pre-unit engines

Note: Honda CB/CL/SL 350 twins are not eligible for this class. See 350 Sportsman or Formula 250.

10.2.2 **500 GRAND PRIX:** Combined with 500 Premier (10.2.1)

10.2.3 **350 GRAND PRIX**
Any of the following types of fully GP-kitted motorcycles built before December 31, 1968, and like design: 350cc OHV/OHC four-stroke; 350cc air-cooled single-cylinder two-stroke; 250cc liquid-cooled, single-cylinder two-stroke; 250cc air-cooled twin-cylinder two-stroke. Among the eligible machines are:

- Aermacchi 350 four-stroke single roadracer
- AJS 7R
- Bianchi "works"
- Benelli twin "works" roadracer and fours
- BSA 350 OHV single
- Bultaco 250 liquid-cooled single, round cylinder type only
  Note: Bultaco AJR replicas are not allowed
- Ducati 350 narrow- and wide-case
- Gilera
- Harley-Davidson ER/CRTT four-stroke roadracer
- Honda CR77 "works" or replica, CB77 fully race-kitted.
- *Note: The CB350F is not eligible for this class.*
- Jawa "works" twin roadracer
- Kawasaki A1R (not A7RA) twin, maximum 250cc
- McIntyre Special and replica, 7R powered
- Moto Guzzi single
- Moto Rumi "works" or replica
- MV triple
- MV four, early wide-angle head (pre-1973 era)
- MZ "works" 250 twin
- Paton twin
- Rickman GP road racing frame, powered by H-D ER/CRTT or AJS 7R
- Seeley 7R, or other period engine
- Suzuki X6 with racing exhaust
- Triumph Tiger 80, 90 350cc twin
- Yamaha; TD1C, TD2, TD2B, RD56/TD1 "works special" /YZ607, maximum 30mm carburetors.

Note: Honda CB/CL/SL 350 twins are not eligible for this class. See 350 Sportsman or Formula 250.

10.2.4 **250 GRAND PRIX**
Any of the following types of fully GP-kitted motorcycles built before December 31, 1968, and like design: 250cc OHV/OHC four-stroke; 250cc air-cooled single-cylinder two-stroke; 175cc liquid-cooled, single-cylinder two-stroke; 175cc air-cooled twin-cylinder two-stroke. Among the eligible machines are:

- Aermacchi 250 four-stroke single roadracers
- AJS 250 Stormer
- Benelli 250 four-stroke single roadracer
- Bridgestone 175cc twin
- Bridgestone 200cc, maximum 24mm carburetors
- BSA B25 & C15 single
- Bultaco Metralla round or square cylinder allowed.
- Bultaco TSS air-cooled single (round cylinder type only)
- Bultaco TSS 250cc liquid-cooled singles
- Cotton Conquest or Telstar
- CZ single "works" replica
- Ducati MkI, Diana, MkIII, F-3, narrow and wide case
- Greeves Silverstone
- Harley-Davidson CRTT four-stroke roadracer
- Honda CR72 "works" or replica, CB72 fully race-kitted
- Honda "works" four or six
- Montesa Impala
- Moto Rumi "works" or replica
- Motobi production racers
- NSU Sport Max
- Ossa 250 single
- Parilla production racer
- Rickman GP road racing frame powered by H-D CRTT
- Suzuki X6 with OEM street exhaust and silencers
- Triumph Tiger 70, TR25W/T25T/T25SS singles
- Villiers Starmaker-powered machines
- Yamaha CS3 and CS5

10.2.5 **200 GRAND PRIX PLUS**

This class combines a variety of engine designs and displacements, based on an index of performance. Eligible machines are listed below by make, model, displacement, and individual restrictions. Like-design models also are permitted. The class limit displacement as noted for each model may be increased by boring up to the maximum allowable overbore (see rule 9.7.2c).

- Aermacchi/H-D 250cc long-stroke (66mm bore x 72mm stroke) and 250cc short stroke (72mm bore x 61mm stroke), original backbone chassis, maximum 30mm carburetor (i.e., up to 1966)
- AJS/Matchless 250cc pushrod single, maximum 30mm carburetor
- Ariel Arrow 250cc twin, original frame and forks, one 32mm or smaller carburetor
- Benelli/Motobi production racers pushrod single up to 250cc, maximum 30mm carburetor
- BMW R26 250cc single, maximum 30mm carburetor
- Bridgestone 175cc twin, maximum 22mm carburetors
- BSA/Triumph 250cc single, maximum 30mm carburetor
- Bultaco 125cc liquid-cooled TSS (round barrel only)
- Bultaco 175cc air-cooled single (round barrel only), maximum 30mm carburetor
- Bultaco 200cc air-cooled single, maximum 4-speed, maximum 28mm carburetor
- Ducati 125, 160, 175, 203cc single (all allowed 203cc, plus overbore)
- Hodaka 125cc
- Honda CR110 (CR93)
- Honda CB/CL 160, 175cc twin, including later CB/CL175 vertical engine (all allowed 200cc)
- Honda CA/CB 125, 160cc twin (allowed 200cc)
- Indian Arrow 250cc single, maximum 30mm carburetor
- Maico RS 125cc, maximum 30mm carburetor
- Moto Guzzi 250cc pushrod, maximum 30mm carburetor
- MV 200cc "works" or replica single or twin
- MV Augusta 250cc pushrod, maximum 30mm carburetor
- Norton 250cc pushrod twin, maximum 30mm carburetor
- Ossa 175cc, maximum 30mm carburetor
- Parilla 250cc pushrod, maximum 30mm carburetor
- Parilla 200cc production racer
- Puch/Allstate 250cc split single, maximum one 32mm carburetor
- Rumi 125cc flat twin
- Suzuki X5, T200, GT185, maximum 22mm carburetors
- Triumph 200cc T20 Tiger Cub, maximum 250cc with allowable overbore; maximum 30mm carburetor
- Villiers-based 250cc two-strokes (series 31A to 37A engines) such as Cotton, DMW, Greeves, maximum 32mm carburetor
- Yamaha AS1 125cc twin (pre-1968), cast iron cylinders only
- Yamaha CT1 175cc single (no Noguchi engine components), maximum 30mm carburetor
- Yamaha YCS1 180cc twin (pre-1969), maximum 22mm carburetors; CS3 and CS5 (195cc) cylinders may be used on standard bore only, no overboring allowed
- Yamaha CS3 and CS5 195cc twin, maximum 22mm carburetors. Must retain standard cylinder bore, no overboring allowed

10.2.6 REQUIREMENTS AND MODIFICATIONS FOR GRAND PRIX CLASSES

a) All GP-class motorcycles must be fully GP-kitted, with no lights, no starting mechanisms, no street equipment, or associated brackets (factory-welded brackets may be retained if desired), low narrow handlebars (maximum width 32 inches). **Fairings are encouraged.**
b) Frame may be changed to racing type, though must be period type and style. (See rule 9.7.3)
c) Front forks may be changed, though must be period type and style. "Ceriani-type" may be no larger in diameter than 35mm, unless supplied as OEM on that motorcycle.
d) Period retrofit gearboxes are permitted (e.g., Quaife, Schafleitner). Maximum six speeds unless otherwise stated.
e) Front disc brakes are prohibited. Rear disc brakes are permitted but must be period equipment.
f) Magnesium engine cases are allowed in 500 Premier.
g) The number of valves in the cylinder head may not be increased or decreased from stock.
h) No more than one carburetor per cylinder. Gardner carburetors are permitted.
i) All modifications must be consistent with the spirit of the class and period.
j) Appearance and workmanship of a reasonable standard shall be enforced.
k) Two-strokes must use silencers.
l) Maximum rim width is WM3 (2.15 inches) in all GP classes

Note: See requirements of all road racing motorcycles in Section 9.

10.3 FORMULA: Formula 750, Formula 500, Formula 250, Formula 125, Formula Vintage

10.3.1 FORMULA 750:

Fully GP-kittedtwo-stroke and four-stroke machines up to four cylinders, manufactured as 600-750cc and built prior to December 31, 1972, and like design.

Among the eligible F750 motorcycles are:

- BSA Rocket 3 & Triumph Trident "works" roadracers or replicas
- BSA Rocket 3 & Triumph Trident "production" racer (i.e., Slippery Sam)
- BSA "A-series" twins "production racer"
- BMW "works" (pre-'75 season)
- Ducati "works" V-twins (pre-NCR)
- Honda CR & RC750 roadracers (with factory kit in stock frame and unmodified swingarm), single-cam type
- Harley-Davidson XR750, iron and alloy motors, roadrace or dirt track frames
- Kawasaki H2 and H2R (specific two-stroke exception, one-year probationary period)
- Laverda SFC
- Moto Guzzi V7 Sport
- MV, street-based 750 fours
- Norton "FIM" production racers
- Norton "John Player" replica street machines
- Norton "works" JPS racers
- Norton 750 twins "production racer" (later castings permitted)
- Rickman Honda 750
- Rickman frames with various eligible engines
- Seeley frames with various eligible engines
- Suzuki GT750 and TR750 (specific two-stroke exception, one-year probationary period)
- Triumph twins "production racer"
- Yamaha XS650

Any Formula 500-legal motorcycle may "bump up" to Formula 750.

10.3.1A REQUIREMENTS AND MODIFICATIONS FOR F750

a) Every effort must be made to duplicate the original "works" appearance.
b) Fairings are encouraged, at minimum a quarter-fairing.
c) "Works" frames are allowed where appropriate, plus frames by Trackmaster, Champion, Seeley and Rickman are permitted.
d) <u>Floating</u> disc brakes are allowed, maximum 12-inch diameter, with two-piston calipers).
e) Front forks with hydraulic anti-dive or external reservoirs are not permitted. Forks may be no larger than 38mm, unless supplied as OEM on that motorcycle.
f) Weslake four-valve conversions for twins are allowed, as are Nourish-Weslake twin-cylinder engines.
g) Appearance and workmanship of a reasonable standard shall be enforced.
h) Modifications must be consistent with the spirit of the class.

i) Maximum rim width: front, 2.5 inches (WM-4); rear, 3.0 inches (WM-5), except H-D XR750s, which are permitted to use a WM6 (3.5 inches) when fitted with original Morris Magnesium wheels. No Astralite wheels.

j) Keihin CR Special carburetors are allowed, maximum 31mm for four-cylinders, 34mm for triples and 39mm for twins.

Note: See requirements of all road racing motorcycles in Section 9.

10.3.2 FORMULA 500

Two-strokes and certain four-strokes to 500cc. All motorcycles must be fully GP-kitted. The cutoff date is December 31, 1972. Like-design models are also permitted.

Among the eligible motorcycles are:

- Bridgestone 350 Daytona GTR
- HD RR/Aermacchi 250
- Honda SOHC fours to 550cc, DOHC twins to 550cc
- Kawasaki H1R, H1RA
- Kawasaki 350 A7R, A7RA
- JML (Kimtab 429) with wire wheels
- Suzuki 500 Titan factory racer, GT380 and GT550
- Yamaha RD350 and RD400 (air-cooled models only), TR2, TR3 and R5-based TR replicas
- Yamaha TX500, TX500A
- Yamaha TZ250 Twin Shock

10.3.3 FORMULA 250

Two-stroke twins up to 250cc, two-stroke singles to 360cc, four-stroke singles to 350cc, Honda CB350 twins and Honda CB350F fours. All motorcycles must be fully GP-kitted. The cutoff date is December 31, 1972. Like-design models also are permitted.

Among the eligible motorcycles are:

- Bridgestone 175, 200
- Bultaco, pre-1973 up to 360cc
- Bultaco, 350cc AJR replicas
- Can-Am, pre-1973 250 (57.5 mm stroke, aluminum, or magnesium cases)
- H-D/Aermacchi, pre-1973 (two- and four-stroke)
- Honda CB350K twin, CB350 four, CB400F four with original stroke and bore (.040" overbore permitted)
- Kawasaki A1R, 350 Bighorn single, F5, F9, S1
- Maico 175cc air-cooled single
- Montesa, pre-1973 up to 360cc
- Ossa, pre-1973 250
- Suzuki 250 X6, GTX, GT, T250, T200
- Yamaha RD125, RD200, RD250, TD2, TD2B, TD3, TA250, TA125, RD56/TD1 "works special"

10.3.4 **FORMULA 125**
Air-cooled, <u>2-stroke</u>, twin-shock, steel-framed Grand Prix motorcycles up to 125cc, plus certain GP-kitted street and enduro machines. Major components (and modifications) must be consistent with those used in the 1960s and '70s.

The following motorcycles are eligible for this class; if not included on this list, approval must be obtained from the Vintage Roadrace Rules & Eligibility Committee:

- Bridgestone 200cc twin
- Bultaco, up to 200cc
- Can-Am 125, 175
- <u>Derbi 125</u>
- Honda MT125, MT125R, 200cc four-stroke twin
- Husqvarna 175, 1975-'82
- Kawasaki F7
- Maico RS125
- Montesa, up to 175cc
- <u>MZ 125cc</u>
- Ossa, up to 175cc
- Suzuki GT185, TS125/185
- Yamaha TA125, AT1/2/3, DT125, RD125
- Yamaha YCS1, CS3/5, CT1/2/3, DT175, RD200

Maximum carburetor or restrictor plate size for 175cc singles is 34mm; maximum carburetor or restrictor plate size for 180-200cc two-stroke twins is 22mm. (See rule 9.7.14b).

<u>GP200 race bike can bump up to Formula 125 only if compliant with the above rules.</u>

10.3.5 **FORMULA VINTAGE**
Eligible motorcycles include any 500 Premier, Formula 500, Formula 750, or Sportsman 750 machine.

Additionally, the following motorcycles, up to model-year 1982 (and like design, except where specifically noted) are eligible:

- Honda CB550 four-cylinder
- Kawasaki H2R 750, KR750
- Suzuki RG500, through 1987
- Suzuki GT750, TR750
- Yamaha RZ350, all years, including Canadian and Brazilian models
- Yamaha RZ500, through 1987
- Yamaha TZ250, through 1984
- Yamaha TZ350, TZ500, TZ750

a) Frames must be of period-design tubular steel, or OEM street-based aluminum frames (e.g., RG500) from specifically-allowed motorcycles. There is no displacement limit on 250/350cc-based twins. Wheels, forks, and brakes to follow Vintage Superbike Heavyweight rules.
b) Modern treaded tires and slicks allowed. Rain tires allowed.

Note: If you believe a machine would fit into this class but is not listed, please submit an Eligibility Request Form (see section 19.10).

10.3.6 **REQUIREMENTS AND MODIFICATIONS FOR FORMULA 125/250/500**
a) All machines must be no-compromise Grand Prix racers (i.e., clip-on, or low, narrow handlebars; no lighting equipment or related brackets, except that factory-welded brackets may be retained if desired; no street equipment of any kind, including brackets). Electric starters allowed if originally equipped.
b) All machines must be equipped with racing exhaust systems; silencers are required. See rule 9.3h.
c) Any drum brakes (front or rear) of the period are permitted.
d) One front rigid-mounted steel disc brake may be used on F125 and F250 machines, and two front rigid-mounted steel discs on F500 machines. Calipers must be period type with a maximum of two pistons. Late-model alloy types are prohibited.
e) **Rims:** *Formula 500*: Wheel rim diameter must be at least 18-inches and not exceed WM3 (2.15 inches) front and WM5 (3.00 inches) rear. *Formula 250*: Wheel rim diameter must be at least 18-inches and not exceed WM3 (2.15 inches) front and WM4.5 (2.75 inches) rear. *Formula 125*: Wheel rim width must not exceed WM3 (2.15 inches) front or rear.
f) All engines may use Keihin CR Special carburetors in all Formula classes. Maximum 26mm for CB350/400 fours in Formula 250 and Formula 500.
g) Front forks may be changed, though must be period type and style. "Ceriani-type" may be no larger in diameter than 38mm, unless supplied as OEM on that motorcycle.

10.4 CLASSIC: Class C, Class C Handshift, Pre-1940 GP, Classic Sixties

10.4.1 **CLASS C**
This class is intended for AMA "Class C" motorcycles and other for-sale, production-based machines of the period that existed up to and including 1951. Like-design models also are permitted. **Class C Handshift** is a championship class scored separately from, but run together with, Class C. 750cc sidevalve (45.7 cu. in.), 500cc OHV/SOHC/DOHC (30.5 cu. in.), plus .080" overbore. All major components must be OEM parts that existed prior to 1951, or accurate, detailed replicas of the same parts using the same type materials and technologies, unless specifically noted below. The burden of authenticating is upon the rider. Press clippings and photos with identifiable date may be helpful. There are no restrictions on internal modifications, except the stroke may not be changed from the original specifications and the bore may not exceed the .080" overbore limit.

10.4.1A **REQUIREMENTS AND MODIFICATIONS FOR CLASS C**
a) All 750cc machines must use handshift gearboxes.
b) Norton swingarm or Featherbed frames are not permitted.
c) Hydraulic dampers may be used in place of springs on springer or girder forks as a safety measure. It is strongly encouraged that such damper units be "camouflaged" (e.g., springs painted flat black) to give more of a period appearance. Hydraulic rear dampers are prohibited unless such units were original equipment on that particular model of motorcycle.

- d) All machines must use the OEM or period carb. If these carburetors are not available, machines are limited to the following:
    1. **Single-cylinder/single carb:** Dell'Orto SS1, Amal GP or Amal Monobloc to 32mm (1-1/4"). Amal Mk1 Concentric (600, 900 or 1000 series) to 34mm (1-5/16").
    2. **Twin-cylinder/single carb:** Dell'Orto SS1, Amal GP or Amal Monobloc to 30mm (1-3/16"). Amal Mk1 Concentric (600 or 900 series) to 32mm (1-1/4").
    3. **Twin-cylinder/twin carb:** Dell'Orto SS1, Amal GP, Amal Monobloc or Amal Mk1 Concentric (600 or 900 series) to 28mm (1-1/8"), Bing Type 53 26mm.
    4. **750cc sidevalve machines** must use one OEM or exact replica butterfly-type carburetor or abide by the above single-carburetor rule.
- e) Wheels and brakes: Minimum wheel diameter is 16 inches. Maximum rim width is WM3 (steel or alloy). Wider steel rims are acceptable if they were provided as original equipment on that model. Wire-spoke wheels and drum brakes are required on both wheels. Brakes must be OEM equipment. Or, if changed, brakes must be single-leading/single-trailing shoe type. Maximum brake diameter is 8.75 inches, and maximum shoe width is 1.75 inches.
- f) Machines must use OEM or period type transmissions of no more than four speeds. 750cc sidevalve machines must use a three-speed transmission.
- g) Safety bars, stands, lights and mufflers must be removed.
- h) Fairings or streamlining are not permitted. The front number plate must be parallel with the front fork angle.
- i) Total-loss oiling is not permitted. Any machine with a non-recirculating oiling system must be equipped with unbreakable catch bottles and/or a "select pad" diaper system of sufficient capacity. **Oil must not be deposited on the track**.
- j) Triumph pre-unit 500cc twins may use 650cc crankshaft but must not exceed .030" overbore.
- k) The throttle must be self-closing, and each machine must have a handlebar-mounted kill switch. See rule 9.7.8.i.

10.4.2 PRE-1940 GRAND PRIX

This class is intended for 1940 and earlier GP and modified street machines, up to and including 500cc OHV and OHC, or 750cc sidevalve machines. Like-design models also are permitted. All major components must be OEM parts that existed prior to 1941, or accurate, detailed replicas of the same parts using the same type materials and technologies, unless specifically noted below. The burden of authenticating is on the rider. Press clippings and photos with identifiable dates may be helpful. There are no restrictions on internal modifications. However, the bore may not be increased more than .080".

10.4.2A REQUIREMENTS AND MODIFICATIONS FOR PRE-1940

- a) All machines must use the OEM or period carb. If these carburetors are not available, machines are limited to the following:
    1. **Single-cylinder/single carb:** Dell'Orto SS1, Amal GP or Amal Monobloc to 32mm (1-1/4"). Amal Mk1 Concentric (600, 900 or 1000 series) to 34mm (1-5/16").
    2. **Twin-cylinder/single carb:** Dell'Orto SS1, Amal GP or Amal Monobloc to 30mm (1-3/16"). Amal Mk1 Concentric (600 or 900 series) to 32mm (1-1/4").

- 3. **Twin-cylinder/twin carb:** Dell'Orto SS1, Amal GP, Amal Monobloc or Amal Mk1 Concentric (600 or 900 series) to 28mm (1-1/8"), Bing Type 53 26mm.
- 4. **750cc sidevalve machines** must use one OEM or exact replica butterfly-type carburetor or abide by the above single-carburetor rule.

b) Wheels and brakes: Minimum wheel diameter is 16 inches. Maximum rim width is WM3 (steel or alloy). Wider steel rims are acceptable if they were provided as original equipment on that machine. Wire spoke wheels and drum brakes are required on both wheels. Brakes fitted as standard equipment may be used, or they may be updated to Class C specification.

c) Gearboxes must not have more than four speeds.

d) Safety bars, stands, lights and mufflers must be removed.

e) The throttle must be self-closing, and each machine must have a handlebar-mounted kill switch. See rule 9.7.8.i.

f) Fairings and streamlining are not permitted. Front number plates must be parallel with the front fork angle.

g) Total-loss oiling is not permitted. Any machine with a non-recirculating oiling system must be equipped with unbreakable catch bottles and/or a "select pad" diaper system of sufficient capacity. **Oil must not be deposited on the track.**

h) OEM superchargers are permitted (see rule 9.7.2.b).

i) Hydraulic dampers may be used in place of springs on springer or girder forks as a safety measure. It is strongly encouraged that such damper units be "camouflaged" (e.g., springs painted flat black) to give more of a period appearance. Hydraulic rear dampers are prohibited unless such units were original equipment on that particular model of motorcycle.

j) Indian Big Base Scout crankcases may be used in rebuilds of Pre-40 Indians.

10.4.3 CLASSIC SIXTIES

This class is intended for **1960s-era and earlier "Grand Prix" and "Clubman" racers** (and later machines of like design), 350cc/500cc OHV and OHC or 750cc sidevalve machines. All major components must be OEM parts that existed in that era, or accurate, detailed replicas of the same parts using the same type materials and technologies. The burden of authenticating is upon the rider. Press clippings and photos with identifiable dates may be helpful.

Among the eligible machines are:

- AJS 7R
- BSA Gold Star, up to DBD
- BSA A7 twin
- Gilera Saturno
- Harley-Davidson KR750 (no "lowboy" frames), with stock exhaust only
- Matchless G50
- Matchless G45 and accurate replicas
- Norton Daytona Dominator 500
- Norton Manx
- Norton International
- Royal Enfield Bullet built in India, four-speed; five-speed models permitted only if the transmission is mechanically limited to four speeds
- Triton (pre-unit 500 Triumph engine in Norton Featherbed frame)
- Triumph T100 pre-unit
- Triumph T100 unit-construction. Triumph unit-construction twins are intended as entry level.
- Velocette Thruxton and Venom Clubman
- Velocette KTT and KSS
- Vincent Grey Flash

10.4.3A CLASSIC SIXTIES 650

This class intended for 1960s-era 650cc OHV or 883cc sidevalve machines and like design. All requirements under rule 10.4.3 apply.

Among the eligible machines are:

- All non-unit British 650cc OHV machines.
- All European 650cc OHV machines
- Triton (Triumph engine in a Norton featherbed frame)
- Unit-construction BSA A65, up to 650cc, in Clubman trim
- Unit-construction long-rod Triumph TR6/T120, up to 650cc, in Clubman trim
- Harley-Davidson KH 55-cubic inch sidevalve
- Kawasaki W1

Note: Unit construction British machines may not use 1971-later OEM oil-bearing frames.

10.4.3.B REQUIREMENTS AND MODIFICATIONS FOR CLASSIC SIXTIES

a) The maximum cylinder overbore is .080" for singles and .060" for twins.
b) The stroke must remain stock.
c) All machines must use period-type carbs or Amal MkI Concentric (600, 900 or 1000 series) except eligible sidevalve machines, which may use one (1) Mikuni round-slide carb. BSA A65 and Triumph unit 650s in Classic Sixties 650 are restricted to 32mm carburetors, maximum one per cylinder.

d) Gearboxes must be mechanically restricted to four speeds.
e) Primary drive may be original-type chain, with chain guard (oiler must not operate). Belt conversions are encouraged but must be fully enclosed and hidden from view (see rule 9.7.2.j).
f) Oil must not be deposited on the track.
g) Brakes must of the period (i.e., two-shoe-type drum). Later-model BSA and Triumph drum brakes are allowed. (Manx Norton may use original four-shoe, seven-inch front brake). Minimum wheel diameter is 18 inches; maximum rim width is WM3 (2.15-in). OHC machines must use minimum 18-inch wheels, front and rear.
h) Forks and rear shocks (or rigid rear end) must be of the period. Ceriani forks are prohibited.
i) All machines must be GP or Clubman racers in essentially factory-standard trim consistent with the period.
j) Throttles must be self-closing. A handlebar-mounted kill switch is encouraged. See rule 9.7.8.i.
k) Fairings or streamlining are not permitted, except for original fork-mounted number plate-cowlings. The front number plate must be parallel with the front fork angle.
l) All machines must use period-style low exhausts only. Pipes must pass below the gearshift spindle. Velocettes may use a higher, OEM racing configuration exhaust. Twins must use two separate exhaust pipes (no two-into-one exhausts).

Note: Classic Sixties classes are run together but scored separately.

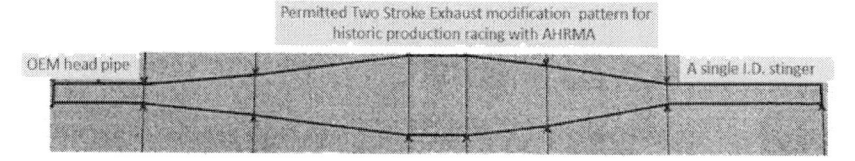

10.5 SPORTSMAN

Sportsman classes are open to four-stroke motorcycles, built by a recognized motorcycle manufacturer for street use up to December 31, 1972. Like-design models also are permitted. Classes are 350, 500 and 750cc.

10.5.1 Among the eligible **Sportsman 350** motorcycles are:
- BSA, all models up to 350cc
- Ducati, all four-stroke models up to 350cc
- Harley-Davidson, all four-stroke models up to 350cc
- Honda, all four-stroke, maximum two-cylinder, street models up to 350cc built prior to December 31, 1972
- Norton, all street models up to 350cc
- Triumph, all street models up to 350cc

10.5.2 Among the eligible **Sportsman 500** motorcycles are:
- BMW R50/5
- BSA, all 500cc models
- Ducati singles to 500cc
- Honda 450 up to December 31, 1972
- Moto Guzzi 500cc up to December 31, 1972
- Norton, all 500cc street models
- Triumph, all 500cc models

10.5.3 Among the eligible **Sportsman 750** motorcycles are:
- BMW R75/5
- BSA, all 650/750
- Ducati 750 round case Sport or GT (no Desmos)
- Honda CB750 SOHC, limited to 28mm non-smoothbore carburetors
- Laverda (SFC must compete in Formula 750)
- Moto Guzzi V-7 Sport or 750 S
- Norton, all 650/750 models (except short-stroke)
- Triumph, all 650/750
- Yamaha XS650, including 750-kitted

10.5.4 **REQUIREMENTS AND MODIFICATIONS FOR SPORTSMAN**
- a) The frame must be a pre-'73 production type (period tubing type). Frames by Trackmaster, Champion and Rickman are permitted; "Rob North" or Rickman **roadrace** types are not.
- b) The production street engine must be used.
- c) The piston stroke **may not** be changed.
- d) Weslake cylinder heads, or any other than stock, are **not** permitted. However, it is permissible to use a twin-carb head if it will interchange with no modifications (e.g., Triumph TR6 and T120).
- e) Exhaust pipes may be changed or moved for more ground clearance. TT pipes are allowed.
- f) Wheel rim diameter must be at least 18 inches and cannot exceed WM3 (2.15 inches) front and WM4 (2.5 inches) rear. WM4 (2.5 inches) front rims and WM5 (3.0 inches) rear rims are permitted on 750s only.
- g) Gearboxes may have up to five ratios.
- h) 350 and 500 Sportsman machines must use drum brakes.
- i) No fairings or streamlining allowed on Sportsman motorcycles.
- j) Sportsman 750 machines may use one front disc brake; period-type floating steel disc, maximum diameter 12 inches, two-piston caliper. Sportsman 750 machines may use a period-type rear drum brake or floating rear disc with a two-piston caliper.
- k) Front fork stanchions must be no larger than 38mm unless supplied as OEM on that motorcycle. Forks with external adjusters are prohibited. All forks must be of the period, or like design.
- l) **Note:** See requirements of all road racing motorcycles in Section 9.

10.6 NOVICE HISTORIC PRODUCTION

Novice Historic Production is open to production street machines built up to 1978-model-year, as determined by the frame and major component parts, and like design. Machines must use original unmodified, OEM frame, swingarm, fork and handlebar mounts. Unnecessary tabs and brackets may be removed, but gusseting (no strengthening) can be added; no geometry may be altered. Gas tank, seat pan and fender must be OEM, equivalent, or replica replacements. Fenders must be untrimmed. Engines must be original OEM bore and stroke, regardless of displacement (plus allowable overbore, as described in rule 9.7.2.c).

All engine and transmission components and assemblies must maintain OEM dimensions and limits. Aftermarket parts are allowed only if they are a direct replacement for the originals. Modifications for reliability (e.g., starter removal or ignition replacement) or to resolve non-performance issues (e.g., cam chain tension or oil pressure) are permitted. Classes are Lightweight (four-strokes up to 500cc, 250cc two-strokes and specific 350cc two-strokes listed with an asterisk (*) below) and Heavyweight (four-strokes up to 750cc and 350-500cc two-strokes); three- or four-cylinder DOHC machines are not allowed.

10.6.1 RIDER ELIGIBILITY

This class is intended for novice and returning non-professional veterans, not seasoned racers. At the referee's discretion, riders who are obviously too fast for the Novice Historic Production class may be moved to a more appropriate class, such as Sportsman. This does not exclude Historic Production riders from racing another bike eligible for any other class. See section 3.4.

10.6.2 Eligible Novice Historic Production Lightweight motorcycles include:
- Aermacchi/Harley-Davidson 350
- BMW R50
- Bridgestone 350cc twin*
- BSA A50, B50
- Bultaco 250 Metralla
- Ducati 450
- Honda 350 two- and four-cylinder
- Honda 400 four-cylinder
- Honda 450 two-cylinder, must use OEM CV carbs or replacements no larger than 28mm
- Kawasaki A1 250cc, A7 338cc twin*
- Moto Guzzi 500
- Suzuki T250, X-6 and T305 twin*
- Triumph 500
- Yamaha 250 (up to RD250)

10.6.3 Eligible Novice Historic Production Heavyweight motorcycles include:
- BMW R75/5
- BSA, all 650/750, two- or three-cylinder
- Ducati 750 round-case Sport or GT (no Desmos)
- Honda 750 four-cylinder
- Honda 500T two-cylinder
- Kawasaki 500 two-stroke
- Laverda SF750 (SFC must compete in Formula 750)
- Moto Guzzi 750 (V7 Sport must compete in Formula 750 or Sportsman 750)
- Norton, all 650/750 (except short stroke)
- Suzuki 500 two-stroke
- Triumph, all 650/750 with two-valve head; two- or three-cylinder
- Yamaha R5 and RD350/400 air-cooled two-stroke

10.6.4 **REQUIREMENTS AND MODIFICATIONS FOR HISTORIC PRODUCTION**
   a) **CARBURETORS:** Must be OEM and same type (i.e., if originally CV, must use CV), no larger than the original OEM bore size. (Restrictors may be introduced to ensure parity of performance.) Air intake: Airboxes and/or air filters may be removed. No performance-increasing devices may be added (velocity stack, scoops, etc.) Aftermarket foam or mesh-type air filter(s) may be added.
   b) **EXHAUST SYSTEMS:** Four-stroke engines must have the same number of pipes as provided on that motorcycle, (i.e., two-into-two, four-into-four, or three-into-two for three-cylinder engines). Exhaust pipes may be aftermarket, may be tucked or raised for ground clearance, and must have effective silencers. Two-stroke engines may use production street exhausts from the time period, any manufacturer. Expansion chambers are allowed provided they are constructed in keeping with the vintage design scheme shown as illustrated. The system will be constructed with a constant diameter chamber then tapering to constant diameter head and tail pipes of OEM dimensions. The attached silencer will limit sound to 103dB.
   c) **BRAKES:** Front and rear may be upgraded to Sportsman 750 specifications in the Heavyweight class only. Lightweight-class machines must use OEM brakes as fitted on that make and model year.
   d) **RIM SIZES:** Replacement rims must be the same diameter and material as OEM. Maximum allowable rim widths are WM3 (2.15 inches) front and WM4 (2.5 inches) rear.
   e) Sidestands and centerstands must be removed.
   f) **CONTROLS AND FOOTRESTS:** Controls: Handlebars must bolt to the stock locations. Clubman bars are allowed. Footrests may be trimmed down or raised for ground clearance; rearsets may be used.
   g) Lighting equipment must be removed or taped over to the tech inspector's requirements.
   h) **FAIRINGS AND BODYWORK:** Fairings of any type are not allowed. Gas tank, seat and fenders must be OEM equipment or period replacements. No modern "GSXR-style" bodywork will be allowed.
   i) **SUSPENSION:** Front end must be period OEM of the same dimensions as stock. Springs may be replaced. Shocks must be straight body, no reservoirs, mounted in the stock location(s).
   j) **NUMBER PLATES:** 10x12-inch rectangular, white background with red numbers. See rule 9.5.
   k) Specialty machines such as Rickman, Dunstall are not eligible.

l) Historic Production bikes are not allowed to bump up into any other AHRMA class.
m) Except as noted above, rules 9.3, 9.4 and 9.7 apply.

10.7 BRITISH EUROPEAN AMERICAN RACING SERIES (BEARS®)

BEARS® is open to two-cylinder pushrod machines built up to December 31, 1968. Like-design models also are permitted. Eligible machines include:
- BMW, all 1971 and earlier twins up to 750cc
- BSA, all 650/750 twins
- Harley-Davidson KR750
- Harley-Davidson Sportsters with iron cylinder head, up to 1000cc (like-design through 1985; drum brakes required)
- Moto Guzzi, all pre-1969 twins
- Norton, all 650/750 twins
- Triumph, all 650/750 two-valve twins

10.7.1 All machines compete under Formula 750 rules (see 10.3.1A).

10.8 VINTAGE SUPERBIKE

MISSION STATEMENT: AHRMA's mission is to recreate and preserve the look and feel of this important era of U.S. road racing and to showcase these unique machines. While Superbikes were based on the same production bikes available in the showroom, period performance parts are extremely rare or even unavailable; therefore, a limited amount of modern replacement parts are allowed in the interest of safety, cost containment and competition.

10.8.1 These rules have been designed with the following intent:
a) All motorcycles competing in these classes shall be as visibly close to "production" motorcycles as possible. All eligible motorcycles shall be based on street-legal models which were available for sale in the United States and/or Canada.
b) Allow the tuner to have more influence over the performance of the motorcycle by eliminating the need for special frames, suspension systems and "state of the art" components to be developed or purchased.
c) To provide racing classes with equipment available through normal commercial channels, and in adequate quantities.
d) Provide interest to aftermarket suppliers and sponsors.
e) Provide a very distinct look and appearance from the other motorcycles competing in AHRMA events with strict bodywork requirements.

10.8.2 **REQUIREMENTS AND MODIFICATIONS FOR VINTAGE SUPERBIKE**
a) **GENERAL**
1. Model year cutoff is 1982, or like design (see definition in Section 2). Exception: The model-year cutoff for Kawasaki GPz550 is 1981.
2. Engines and frames must be from the same model.
3. All street equipment must be removed (turn signals, centerstands and sidestands, mirrors, horn, helmet lock, passenger pegs, etc.). Headlight shell must be retained. Taillight and license plate bracket must be removed.

4. All motorcycles are to use three green number plates, 10x12-inches in size, with white numerals not less than seven inches in height with a minimum of one-inch stroke width. Standard block-type numerals, without serifs, must be used. Visibility must not be blocked by rider's foot or leg while racing. See section 9.5.
5. Competitors in the Vintage Superbike classes must comply with all applicable parts of Sections 1 through 9 of the AHRMA Handbook.

b) **ENGINE**
1. All engines must use OEM crankcases, cylinders, and heads from the period 1982 and earlier.
2. Allowed displacement may be arrived at in any manner (i.e., stroker and sleeve kits are legal). Aftermarket "big block" kits are not allowed (See 1. above).
3. All round-slide carbs are allowed (Keihin CR, Dell'Orto, Mikuni "smooth bore" and like design). Flat-slide carbs are not allowed. Pumper carbs may be used, but the pumper mechanism must be disabled. Four-valve-per-head 1025cc four-cylinders may use carburetors up to 29mm, and two-valve-per-head 1025 four-cylinders may use carburetors up to 31mm or the stock constant-velocity carburetors that were original equipment on that machine.
4. Any exhaust system design is allowed. However, all exhaust systems must be equipped with an effective silencer. Open pipes and reverse cone megaphones are **not** silencers. All exhaust systems must include sound-attenuation material or devices. Modern canister-type silencers are not allowed. Period-style exhaust systems are encouraged. See rule 9.3.h.
5. Liquid-cooled or two-stroke engines are prohibited.

c) **CHASSIS AND FRAME**
1. Frame must be a production model built no later than 1982 (or like design).
2. Frame modifications are allowed (bracing or gussets allowed, steering head angle may be altered, shock location changed or altered, etc.), but welds and modifications must be of the highest quality and are subject to scrutiny at tech inspection.
3. Approved period aftermarket swingarms or accurate replicas are permitted. Shock location may be changed and OEM swingarm may be reinforced, shortened, or lengthened.
4. Standard shock configuration must be used, but shock(s) may be repositioned. Remote reservoir shocks are not allowed, although piggyback shocks are. BMW models may replicate factory Superbikes of the period.
5. Front forks must be of OEM or aftermarket origin, with stanchions no larger than 41mm in diameter. Anti-dive and external adjusters are allowed. Forks must be conventional type (no upside-down units).
6. Handlebars must be fitted to the original mounts and must not be below the top of the fork crowns. No Clubman bars or clip-ons, except when used as original equipment.

7. Any wheel diameter from 16-inch to 19-inch is allowed. Maximum rim width: 4.5-inch rear, 3.5-inch front. Wheels may be wire-spoked or mag-style in either alloy or magnesium. Modern alloy mag-type wheels are permitted. Cut/machined wheels (Performance Machine, etc.) are not permitted. However, Astralite and Comstar wheels are allowed. If uncertain as to the legality of certain wheels, please contact the Vintage Superbike Rules & Eligibility Committee with questions before making a purchase.
8. Only single- or two-piston brake calipers are allowed. Front and rear discs, floating or rigid mount of any material except carbon fiber, are allowed. "Wave" or petal-type rotors are not allowed.
9. Tire warmers are permitted. All racing tires are allowed including DOTs and slicks.
10. Airboxes and toolboxes may be removed or modified.
11. Fuel tank and bodywork must be as found on the same year and model of the production motorcycle on which the racer is based. Motorcycles must have original seat, which may be modified or recovered while retaining the stock seat pan. Motorcycles must have the front and rear fenders, side panels and front fairing as the original production model or accurate replicas. Fenders may be trimmed to fit tires. No tail sections may be added unless OEM on that model.
12. Only fairings that were furnished as standard equipment on the street model are allowed. Fairings must not extend below the fuel tank.
13. All motorcycles must use the OEM-appearing speedometer and tachometer housing (if so equipped). Speedometer and tachometer instruments are optional.

10.8.3 **CLASSES**
a) **HEAVYWEIGHT:** Unlimited displacement twins and pushrod triples, and displacement-limited fours and sixes (see chart).
b) **MIDDLEWEIGHT:** Unlimited displacement singles, with limited pushrod twins, OHC twins, pushrod triples, OHC fours, and aircooled rotary (see chart). The model-year cutoff for Kawasaki GPz550 is 1981.
c) **LIGHTWEIGHT:** Singles, twins and multis using performance indexes for smaller bikes (see chart).

10.8.4 All classes listed above are based upon an index of performance. If any model proves to be significantly faster than other models in its class, its performance may be restricted by limiting carburetor size, etc. If any model proves to be significantly slower than others in its class, it may be moved down to the next lower class.

10.8.5 Vintage-class motorcycles may not bump into Vintage Superbike classes.

VINTAGE SUPERBIKE (10.8.3)

CLASS	ENGINE TYPE	EXAMPLES	DISPLACEMENT LIMIT (cc)
HEAVYWEIGHT	Pushrod twin	H-D Sportster, XR1000; BMW twins; Moto Guzzi	Unlimited
	Pushrod triple	Triumph Trident; BSA Rocket 3	Unlimited
	OHC twin	Yamaha XS650/750, XV750/920	Unlimited
	6-cylinder DOHC *Unrestricted intake*	Honda CBX (early & Pro-Link)	1047 stock bore
	4-cylinder OHC 2v *Unrestricted intake*	Kawasaki KZ900 (Z1), KZ/GPz750; Suzuki GS750; Honda CB750 SOHC, CB750 Nighthawk	931
	4-cylinder DOHC 4v	Honda CB750 DOHC; Suzuki GS750-4v	931
	4-cylinder restricted	Honda CB900F; Yamaha 900 Seca; Kawasaki KZ1000, GPz1100*, ELR; Suzuki GS1000-2v, GS1000S Katana, GS1100*	1025
MIDDLEWEIGHT	Pushrod twin	Moto Guzzi; Norton 850; Triumph twins; BMW R65, R75, R80	890
		Harley-Davidson Ironhead XL Sportster (must use stock intake manifold; no XRs)	1050
	OHC twin	Yamaha XS650/750, XV750	790
	Pushrod triple	Triumph Trident; BSA Rocket 3	790
	4-cylinder OHC	Kawasaki KZ/GPz550, KZ650; Suzuki GS500/550/650; Yamaha Maxim/Seca 550-650	685
LIGHTWEIGHT	Single-cylinder 2v	Yamaha SR/TT/XT500	590
	Single-cylinder 4v	Honda FT500	510
	Pushrod twin	BMW	650
	Multi-cylinder	Honda CB350-4, CB400-4	424
	OHC twin	Yamaha XS400; Suzuki GS400-450; Kawasaki KZ400-440; Honda CB450T Hawk	470

Class displacement limits shown above are absolute, including overbores. **NO additional overbore is allowed.**

*GPz1100, GS1100, XS1100 fours may be used but must displace less than 1025cc and use 29mm restricted or stock OEM carbs.

page 62   2024 AHRMA HANDBOOK_REV 2024.02.23

10.9 NEXT GEN: Next Gen Superbike, Next Gen Superbike 2, Next Gen Superbike 3, Next Gen Superbike Lightweight, Next Gen Superbike Middleweight

MISSION STATEMENT: AHRMA's mission with this class is to recreate and preserve the look and feel of this popular era of U.S. Superbike racing. Based on production machinery available on the dealer showroom floor, these motorcycles were modified within a set of rules that kept the machines looking relatively stock but allow a dramatic increase in their performance. AHRMA rules in this class follow that same theme but allow modern upgrades where appropriate in the interest of safety, cost containment, and competition.

These rules have been written with the following intent:

a) All machines competing in these classes shall be as visibly close to top-level Superbikes of the time period as possible. Period-appropriate paint schemes, replicas of period race team bikes, etc., are all encouraged.
b) Period-appropriate modifications/accessories are encouraged. Select modern upgrades are allowed, but they must maintain the general look and feel of the time period.
c) To provide a very distinct look and appearance from the other motorcycles competing in AHRMA events. To that end, strict bodywork and craftsmanship requirements will be enforced.

10.9.1 NEXT GEN SUPERBIKE

Among the eligible machines are:

- Ducati 851, 888
- Honda VF700F, VF750F, VFR700F, VFR750F, RC30
- Kawasaki GPz750 (1983-'87), ZX7/ZXR750/ZX750R (1989-'92)
- Suzuki GS700E/GS700ES/GS750E/GS750 ES ('83-'85); GSXR750/GSXR750R ('85-'92, non-liquid-cooled)
- Yamaha FZ750/FZR750R/FZR750RR ('85-'92)
- Norton F1/F1-Sport
- Buell RR1000/1200

10.9.1.1 REQUIREMENTS AND MODIFICATIONS FOR NEXT GEN SUPERBIKE

a) **GENERAL**
1. Engines, frame, swingarm, and bodywork must be from the same make and model (see rules for specific allowances.)
2. AHRMA's "like design" rule does not apply in this class: Any and all exceptions will be specially called-out in the rules.
3. All street equipment must be removed (turn signals, centerstands and side-stands, mirrors, horn, helmet lock, passenger pegs, etc.)
4. All motorcycles are to use three white number plates/backgrounds of approximately 10x12-inches, with one plate/background on the front center fairing of the motorcycle, and one on each side of the rear tail section, behind the rider. Number plates/backgrounds shall not be placed anywhere else on the motorcycle. Numerals shall be black at least seven-inches tall, block-style, without serifs, with a stroke width of one-inch and legible. See section 9.5 for additional number requirements.
5. Competitors must comply with all applicable parts of Sections 1 through 9 of the AHRMA Handbook.
6. All work and modifications must be performed to a high standard of fit, finish, and craftsmanship.

b) **ENGINE**
1. Four-cylinder machines must retain stock stroke. Stock bore may be increased up to 2.0mm (.080").
2. Twin-cylinder machines may alter stroke and/or bore to increase displacement up to class limit of 1000cc. Pushrod twins may have unlimited displacement (same as BOT1 rules).
3. Engine must be from the same year, make and model as the frame. Updated/ backdated parts available during the period (1985-'92) are allowed. "Ducati may update engine cases only beyond the period.
4. The use of race-type crankcase covers, or welded/braced OEM covers, is allowed and encouraged, for safety purposes.
5. Bike must use carburetors or fuel injection, as fitted OEM. Carbs may be replaced with any style/size of carbs. Fuel injection may be modified. Shower-type fuel injection is prohibited.
6. Motorcycles must remain naturally aspirated.
7. Period-style exhaust required. No "shorty," "MotoGP-style," or under-seat exhausts allowed. All exhaust systems must be equipped with an effective silencer; open pipes or open megaphones are not allowed. See Rule 9.3.h.
8. No electronic traction-control or telemetry allowed.

c) **CHASSIS AND FRAME**
1. Frame must be from a production motorcycle listed under "Approved Motorcycles."
2. Frames may be braced/strengthened but must otherwise remain unmodified or altered in any way other than unused street brackets/tabs may be removed. Frames may be painted, coated, or polished. Bolt-on subframes may be modified or altered.
3. Swingarm must be from the same year, make, and model as the frame. Bracing is allowed using round or rectangular aluminum tubing only. Bracing may not be "sheeted" or enclosed. Period aftermarket or OEM racing kit swingarms are allowed.
4. Rear shock can be replaced or modified but cannot be repositioned. Suspension rockers, linkage, etc., may be replaced.
5. Front forks may be either conventional or upside-down type, regardless of which style was fitted by the OEM. Triple clamps may be modified or replaced.
6. No restrictions on wheel size/style, although period-appropriate appearance is required. Carbon fiber wheels are not allowed unless equipped from the factory (Britten V1000).
7. Rotors must be conventional steel. Perimeter brakes allowed if they were OEM.
8. No radial-mount calipers allowed. No perimeter (i.e., Buell-style) calipers allowed, unless fitted OEM. No other restrictions on number, size, or style of caliper allowed.
9. No restrictions on tires. Slicks, DOT, or rain tires may be used.
10. Tire warmers may be used.

d) **BODYWORK**
1. Fuel tank and bodywork must be OEM or accurate street or race replicas, from the same year, make, and model of the frame. Material/construction of bodywork is unrestricted.
2. Rear fender may be removed.

3. Oil-retention belly pan must be used (see rule 9.3.f).
4. Machines will not pass tech with bodywork removed or missing.
5. Machines will not pass tech with unpainted bodywork, bodywork in primer, or damaged bodywork.
6. Period OEM paint schemes, or period racing team paint schemes are strongly encouraged.

10.9.2 NEXT GEN SUPERBIKE 2
Among the eligible machines are:
- Aprilia RSV Mille, Mille R, Mille SP and Replicas (Haga and Edwards). Bikes are limited to first generation Mille only.
- Ducati 851, 888 with 996 engine; Ducati 916, 916SP, 916 Corsa and 916R; Ducati 996, 996S, 996SPS, 996RS. All Ducati motorcycles must use Desmoquattro engines only, no Testastretta engines, heads, or components. Ducati 748, 748R, 748RS may compete, provided engine capacity has been increased by modifying bore and/or stroke to a maximum of 996cc.
- Honda RC45, RC51 SP1, RC51 SP2
- MV Agusta F4 750 ORO, S, S 1+1, SPR, 1999-2004. 750cc models
- Kawasaki ZX7R, ZX7RR models included are L, M, N and P1-P7
- Suzuki GSX-R750 models N-X (SRAD), TL1000R
- Yamaha R7, YZF750R, YZF750SP

Approved motorcycles must have been available for sale in North America.

10.9.2.1 REQUIREMENTS AND MODIFICATIONS FOR NEXT GEN SUPERBIKE 2
a) **GENERAL**
1. Engine, Frame, swingarm and bodywork must be from the same make and model.
2. AHRMA's "like design" rule does not apply. Exceptions will be written in the rules.
3. All street equipment must be removed.
4. All motorcycles are to use three white number plates/backgrounds of approx. 10"x12", with one on the front center of the fairing and one on each side of the rear tail section, behind the rider. Number plates/backgrounds shall not be placed anywhere else on the motorcycle. Numerals shall be black, at least 7" tall, block style, without serifs, with a stroke width of one inch and legible. See section 9.5 for additional requirements.
5. Competitor must comply with all applicable parts of sections 1-9 of the AHRMA Handbook.
6. All work and modifications must be performed to a high standard of fit, finish, and workmanship.

b) **ENGINE**
1. All machines must retain stock bore and stroke, except Ducati 748 (see approved motorcycle list).
2. Engines must be from the same make and model as the frame. All manufacturer engines should be period correct (see approved motorcycle list). Engine parts may be updated only if they are directly interchangeable.
3. The use of race-type crankcase covers or welded/braced OEM covers is allowed and encouraged, for safety purposes.

4. Bikes must use fuel delivery type as fitted from the factory. OEM carburetors may be replaced with any style or carb size. Fuel Injection systems may be modified, both programming and throttle body size.
5. Motorcycles must be naturally aspirated.
6. Motorcycles must have period-style exhaust.
7. No electronic traction control, wheelie control or telemetry allowed. Quick shifters and lap timers are allowed.

c) **CHASSIS AND FRAME**
1. Frame must be from a production motorcycle listed under the "approved motorcycles" list.
2. Frames may be braced and strengthened to period modifications only. Brackets and tabs for street equipment may be removed. Frames may be polished, painted, or coated. Subframes may be modified or altered.
3. Swingarms must be from the same make and model as the frame. Bracing is allowed using round or rectangle aluminum tubing only. Bracing may not be "sheeted" or enclosed. Period aftermarket or OEM kit swingarms are allowed.
4. Rear shock may be replaced or modified but cannot be repositioned. Suspension rockers, linkage etc. may be replaced or modified.
5. Front forks may be replaced with kit (Ohlins or equivalent) forks. They can be conventional or upside down. Replacement forks must be of the period. No later model forks allowed; no gas-charged forks allowed.
6. No restrictions on wheel size, although period-appropriate appearance is strongly encouraged. Carbon fiber wheels are not allowed.
7. Carbon rotors are not allowed. "Wave" or "petal" rotors are allowed. Perimeter rotors are not allowed.
8. Radial calipers allowed. No perimeter calipers allowed.
9. No restrictions on tires – slicks, DOT, or rain tires are allowed. Tire warmers may be used.

d) **BODYWORK**
1. Fuel tank and bodywork must be OEM or accurate street or race replicas, from the same make and model of the frame. Material construction of bodywork and tank is unrestricted.
2. Rear fender may be removed.
3. Oil-retention belly pan must be used (see rule 9.3.f).
4. Machines will not pass tech with unpainted bodywork, bodywork in primer or bodywork that is damaged.
5. Period OEM or race team paint schemes are strongly encouraged.

10.9.3 NEXT GEN SUPERBIKE LIGHTWEIGHT

MISSION STATEMENT: To provide a lightweight class to showcase what was raced in the '80s through the early '90s. This will be a world market class based on an index of performance. If a motorcycle is proven to be demonstrably faster than the competition, it can be mechanically limited or bumped to another class immediately. This class will be limited to period modifications.

Among the eligible machines are:

- 1988 Bimota YB7 400cc
- 1985-1987 Cagiva Alazzurra 650cc
- 1980-1984 Ducati TT2 597cc
- 1979-1983 Ducati Pantah 500cc, 600cc and 650cc
- 1989-1992 Honda VFR400 through NC30
- 1989-1994 Honda CBR400 NC23 and NC29
- 1989-1990 Honda CB-1
- 1988-1991 Honda Hawk NT650
- 1983-1985 Honda VF500F
- 1987-1993 Honda NSR250 MC18 and MC21
- 1988-1992 Kawasaki KR1 and KR1S. KR1R is not eligible.
- 1987-2009 Kawasaki EX500
- Laverda Zeta 500 Twin
- 1985-1989 Suzuki GSX-R400
- 1989-1997 Suzuki GSF400 Bandit
- 1988-2000 Suzuki GS500E/F
- 1989-1993 Suzuki RGV250 VJ21
- 1986-1988 Yamaha FZ600
- 1986-1990 Yamaha TZR250 up to 3MA
- 1986-1994 Yamaha FZR400 up to 3TJ7
- 1983-1985 Yamaha RZ350
- 1980-1983 Yamaha RD250/350LC
- 1973-1985 Yamaha TZ250/350
- 1986 Yamaha SRX600
- 1984-1991 Yamaha FJ600

10.9.3.A REQUIREMENTS AND MODIFICATIONS FOR NEXT GEN SUPERBIKE LIGHTWEIGHT

a) GENERAL
1. Engine, frame, and bodywork must be from the same make and model, see section "C" chassis and frame.
2. AHRMA's "like design" rule does not apply. Exceptions will be written in the rules.
3. All street equipment must be removed.
4. All motorcycles are to use 3 (three) white number plates/backgrounds of approx. 10"x12", with one on the front center of the fairing and one on each side of the rear tail section, behind the rider. Number plates/backgrounds shall not be placed anywhere else on the motorcycle. Numerals shall be black, at least 7" tall, block style, without serifs, with a stroke width of one inch and legible. See section 9.5 for additional requirements.
5. Competitors must comply with all applicable parts of sections 1-9 of the AHRMA handbook.
6. All work and modifications must be performed to a high standard of fit, finish, and workmanship.

7. 250cc 2-stroke GP replica machines (TZR, NSR, RGV, etc..), are limited to Supersport modifications, see 9.8.1.
8. Eligible machines in this class can be from any market in the world.

b) **ENGINE**
1. All machines must retain stock stroke. Bore may be increased to 2.0mm over; Kawasaki EX500 bore may be increased to allow 675cc max.
2. Engines must be from the same make and model as the frame. All manufacturer engines should be period correct. OEM parts may be updated only if they are directly interchangeable and have no performance advantage. Superbike rules apply to engines unless otherwise specified. The Yamaha RZ must use OEM RZ350 or Banshee cylinders. No aftermarket Banshee cylinders allowed (Cheetah, Driveline, etc.). Yamaha RZ may use "cool head."
3. The use of race type crankcase covers or welded/braced OEM covers is allowed and encouraged, for safety purposes.
4. Bikes must use fuel delivery type as fitted from the factory. OEM carburetors may be replaced with any style or carb size.
5. Motorcycles must be naturally aspirated.
6. Airbox modifications allowed for all machines except GP replica machines which must run under Supersport rules, see 9.8.1.
7. Motorcycles must have period style exhaust. All exhaust systems must be equipped with an effective silencer; open pipes or open megaphones are not allowed. See rule 9.3.h.
8. No electronic traction control, wheelie control or telemetry allowed. Quick shifters and lap timers are allowed.

c) **CHASSIS AND FRAME**
1. Frame and engine must be from the same model with the following exceptions: Yamaha TZ250 and TZ350's can use steel replacement frames. Examples are, Harris, Spondon, Seely, Nico Baker, Rob North etc. No aftermarket aluminum chassis are allowed.
2. Frames may be braced and strengthened to period modifications 66 only. Brackets and tabs for street equipment may be removed. Frames may be polished, painted, or coated. Subframes may be modified or altered.
3. Period swingarm conversions are allowed. Swingarms used in conversions must be pre 1992 model year. Bracing is allowed using round or rectangle aluminum or steel tubing only. Bracing may not be "sheeted" or enclosed. Period aftermarket swingarms are allowed. In the case of the aftermarket frames listed in C.1, if a swingarm is not part of the aftermarket frame the stock swingarm from that motorcycle must be used.
4. Rear shock(s) may be replaced or modified but cannot be repositioned. Suspension rockers, linkage etc. may be replaced or modified.
5. Forks may be replaced with other period units. Forks must be of the conventional right side up type.
6. No restrictions on wheel size, although period-appropriate appearance is strongly encouraged. Carbon fiber wheels are not allowed.
7. Rotors must be conventional steel. Petal rotors are prohibited. Perimeter brakes allowed if they were OEM.
8. Calipers must be axial style.
9. No restrictions on tires, Slicks, DOT, or rain tires are allowed. Tire warmers may be used.

d) **BODYWORK**
  1. Fuel tank and bodywork must be OEM or accurate street or race replicas. Material construction of bodywork and tank is unrestricted. Bodywork design must be of the period. Bodywork for motorcycles that do not have OEM full fairings are limited to bodywork used prior to 1992.
  2. Rear fender may be removed.
  3. Oil retention belly pan must be used on all machines. (See rule 9.3.f)
  4. Machines will not pass tech with unpainted bodywork, bodywork in primer or bodywork that is damaged.
  5. Period OEM and Race Team paint schemes are strongly encouraged.
  6. For more information contact any member of the next gen superbike rules and eligibility committee.

10.9.4 **NEXT GEN SUPERBIKE MIDDLEWEIGHT**
MISSION STATEMENT: To provide a middleweight class to showcase what was raced in the late '80s through the early '90s. This class will be limited to period modifications.

Among the eligible machines are:

- 1986-1988 Ducati Paso (750)
- 1989-1991 Ducati 750 Sport
- 1992-1997 Ducati 750SS
- 1987-1998 Honda CBR600F and CBR600F2/F3
- 1985-1987 Honda NS400R
- 1985-1994 Kawasaki GPZ600R through ZX600E2
- 1985-1991 Moto Guzzi LeMans 850
- 1992-1993 Suzuki GSX-R600
- 1988-1991 Suzuki GSX600 F-M
- 1985-1987 Suzuki RG500, RG400
- 1989-1999 Yamaha FZR600
- 1988-1992 Yamaha FZR400 with FZR600 engine
- 1984-1986 Yamaha RZ500

10.9.4.A **REQUIREMENTS AND MODIFICATIONS FOR NEXT GEN SUPERBIKE MIDDLEWEIGHT**
  a) **GENERAL**
  1. Engine, frame, and bodywork must be from the same OEM make and model, see section "c" chassis and frame.
  2. AHRMA's "like design" rule does not apply. Exceptions will be written in the rules.
  3. All street equipment must be removed.
  4. All motorcycles are to use three white number plates/backgrounds of approximately 10"x12," with one on the front center of the fairing and one on each side of the motorcycle. Numerals shall be black, at least 7" tall, block style, without serifs, with a stroke width of one inch and legible. See section 9.5 for additional requirements.
  5. Competitor must comply with all applicable parts of sections 1-9 of the AHRMA handbook.
  6. All work and modifications must be performed to a high standard of fit, finish, and workmanship.

b) **ENGINE**
1. All engines must retain stock stroke. Bore may be up to 2.0mm over. Engines can be built to superbike specs.
2. Engines must be from the same OEM make and model as the frame. All manufacturer engines should be period correct. Engine parts may be updated only if they are directly interchangeable and have no performance advantage.
3. The use of race type crankcase covers or welded/braced OEM covers is allowed and encouraged.
4. OEM carburetors may be replaced with any style or carb size.
5. Motorcycles must be naturally aspirated.
6. Motorcycles must have period style exhaust. See rule 9.3.h.
7. No electronic traction control, wheelie control or telemetry allowed. Quick shifters and lap timers are allowed.

c) **CHASSIS AND FRAME**
1. Frame and engine must be from the same OEM model with the following exception, Yamaha FZR400 frame with period FZR600 motor swap.
2. Frames may be braced and strengthened to period modifications only. Brackets and tabs for street equipment may be removed. Subframes may be modified or altered.
3. Period swingarm conversions are allowed. Swingarms used in conversions must be pre 1992 model year. Bracing is allowed using round or rectangle aluminum or steel tubing only. Bracing may not be "sheeted" or enclosed. Period aftermarket swingarms are allowed.
4. Rear shock may be replaced or modified but cannot be repositioned. Rockers, linkage etc. may be replaced or modified.
5. Forks must be of the conventional right side up type. Ducati 750SS retains OEM forks only.
6. No restrictions on wheel size. Carbon fiber wheels are not allowed.
7. Calipers must be axial style.
8. No restrictions on tires.

d) **BODYWORK**
1. Fuel tank and bodywork must be OEM or accurate street or race replicas. Material construction of bodywork and tank is unrestricted. Bodywork OEM full fairings are limited to bodywork used prior to 1992.
2. Rear fender may be removed.
3. Design must be of the period. Bodywork for motorcycles that do not have Oil retention belly pan must be used on all machines. (See rule 9.3.f)
4. Machines will not pass tech with unpainted bodywork, bodywork in primer or bodywork that is damaged.
5. Period OEM and Race Team paint schemes are strongly encouraged.

10.9.5 **NEXT GEN SUPERBIKE 3**
10.9.5.A **REQUIREMENTS AND MODIFICATIONS FOR NEXT GEN SUPERBIKE 3**
Approved motorcycles must have been for sale in North America
Among the eligible machines are:

- All Next Gen 2 models
- Aprilia RVS1000R, RSV100R Factory 2004-2006
- Bimota models 1988-2006: SB6, SB6R, SB7, SB7R, SB*, SB8R, YB6, YB8, YB9, YB10, YB11
- Ducati 996 and 998, all models including Corsa and RS
- Ducati 999, all models including the S, R, RS and FO, 2003 to 2006
- MV Agusta F4 1000 models, 1998 to 2006
- Honda models: CBR900RR, CBR919RR, CBR929RR, CBR954RR and CBR1000RR 1992 to 2005
- Kawasaki ZX10R 2004 to 2005
- Kawasaki ZRX (1100 and 1200)
- Kawasaki ZX7 Muzzy Raptor 96-03 (replicas are eligible)
- Suzuki Bandit 1200 (air-cooled)
- Suzuki GSX-R750 2000 to 2004
- Suzuki GSX-R1000 2001 to 2004
- Suzuki GSX-R1100 (all years)
- Yamaha YZF-R1, YZF-R1 LE 1998 to 2006
- Yamaha FZ1 (all years)
- Yamaha R7 with period YZF-R1 Motor 1999

10.9.5.B **REQUIREMENTS AND MODIFICATIONS FOR NEXT GEN 3**
a) **GENERAL**
   1. Engine, frame swingarm and bodywork must be from the same make and model.
   2. AHRMA's "Like Design" rule does not apply. Exceptions will be written in the rules.
   3. All street equipment must be removed.
   4. All motorcycles are to use three white number plates/backgrounds of approximately 10"X12," with one on the front center of the fairing and one on each side of the motorcycle. Numerals will be black, at least 7" tall, block style without serifs, with a stroke width of one inch and legible.
      See Section 9.5 for additional requirements.
   5. Competitor must comply with all applicable parts of Sections 1-9 of the AHRMA Handbook.
   6. All work and modifications must be performed to a high standard of fit, finish and workmanship.

b) **ENGINE**
   1. All machines must retain stock bore and stroke.
   2. Engines must be from the same make and model as the frame. All manufacturer engines should be period correct (see approved motorcycle list). Engine parts may be updated only if they are directly interchangeable
   3. The use of race-type crankcase covers or welded/braced OEM covers is allowed and encouraged, for safety purposes.
   4. Bikes must use fuel delivery type as fitted from the OEM. Carburetors may be replaced with any style or carb size.
   5. Engines must be naturally aspirated.

6. Motorcycles must have period-style exhaust.
7. Only 2000 to 2006 era electronic traction control, wheelie control or telemetry are allowed. Quick shifter and lap timers are allowed.
8. Period components and superbike engine modifications are allowed.

c) CHASSIS AND FRAME
1. Frame must be from a production, period aftermarket or factory-built race motorcycle listed under the "approved motorcycle" list.
2. Frames may be braced and strengthened to period modifications. Brackets and tabs for street equipment may be removed. Frames may be polished, painted or coated. Subframes may be modified or altered.
3. Swingarms must be purpose built for the same make and model as the frame. Bracing is allowed using round or rectangle aluminum tubing. Bracing may not be "sheeted" or enclosed. Period aftermarket or OEM kit swingarms are allowed.
4. Rear shock may be replaced or modified but cannot be repositioned. Suspension rockers, linkage, etc., may be replaced or modified.
5. Front forks may be replaced with kit (Ohlins or equivalent) forks. They can be conventional or upside down. Replacement forks must be of the period, no later model forks allowed. Period gas-charged forks are allowed.
6. No restrictions on wheel size, although period-appropriate appearance is strongly recommended. Carbon fiber wheels are not allowed.
7. Carbon rotors are not allowed. "Wave" or "petal" rotors are allowed. Perimeter rotors are not allowed.
8. Radial calipers are allowed. No perimeter calipers allowed.
9. No restrictions on tires. Slicks, DOT, or rain tires are allowed. Tire warmers may be used.

d) BODYWORK
1. Fuel tank and bodywork must be OEM or accurate street or race replicas from the same make and model of the frame. Material construction of tank and bodywork is unrestricted.
2. Rear fender may be removed.
3. Oil retention belly pan must be used. See Section 9.3.f.
4. Machines will not pass tech inspection with unpainted bodywork or bodywork in primer or bodywork that is damaged.
5. Period OEM or race team paint schemes are strongly encouraged.

10.10 SIDECAR

MISSION STATEMENT: To preserve the rich and full history of the golden era of Sidecar road racing by maintaining a venue to showcase the types of road racing Sidecar outfits that made the sport an integral part of the historic Grand Prix experience and showcase types of sidecars which have historically been under-represented in modern road racing.

a) **SIDECAR OUTFITS:** Sidecar outfits shall comply with AHRMA definitions and requirements listed in sections 2. DEFINITIONS, 9.3 TECHNICAL INSPECTION, 9.4 LOCKWIRE REQUIREMENTS, 9.5 NUMBERS AND NUMBER PLATES, 9.7 MECHANICAL REQUIREMENTS FOR VINTAGE CLASSES and all other applicable AHRMA rules except as detailed below.

b) **DRIVER AND PASSENGER:** Drivers and passengers of Sidecar outfits shall meet all current AHRMA requirements listed in section 3.4 RIDER ELIGIBILITY and 9.1 RIDER ELIGIBILITY. Passenger must be 18 years of age with an AHRMA race membership, a working knowledge of the Sidecar outfit and an understanding of AHRMA/racetrack rules. Passenger may wear leather high-top footwear that covers the ankle and is duct-taped to the bottom edge of the leather pants.

c) **ROADRACE PROCEDURES:** All roadrace procedures in Section 3.6 are applicable. The Sidecar Team consists of the driver, the passenger (co-pilot) and the Sidecar outfit. The Sidecar Team must start and finish together. If in the event either the driver and/or passenger (co-pilot) is ejected from the Sidecar outfit, the Sidecar Team will be immediately black-flagged and treated as a crashed vehicle for scoring purposes. In the event of a stall at the starting grid the Sidecar Team may pull to the side and restart the outfit within 50 yards of grid position after all other outfits have left the grid. If unable to start, the Sidecar outfit it will be placed as to not obstruct any other competitors and the driver and passenger will remove themselves from the track. At no other time during the race will the driver and/or passenger be able to dismount the Sidecar outfit – this will be considered a crash or mechanical failure, and roadrace procedure protocol will be in place.

d) **SPORTSMANSHIP:** The Sidecar class is designed to be fun, safe, and competitive, and as such, good sportsmanship, honesty, and a sense of fair play should exist at all times. **It is important to recognize that all Sidecar classes may be on the track at the same time.** Driving maneuvers liable to hinder other Sidecars, such as premature direction changes, deliberate crowding or blocking or any other abnormal change of direction are strictly prohibited and shall be penalized, according to the importance and repetition of the offenses, at the sole discretion of the AHRMA Roadrace Director. The repetition of dangerous driving, even involuntarily, shall also be subject to penalty at the sole discretion of the AHRMA Roadrace Director, penalties shall range from verbal warnings to suspension.

e) **COMPETITIVE EQUALITY:** Any machine consistently demonstrating a significant power advantage shall be subject to restriction at the sole discretion of the AHRMA Roadrace Director.

10.10.1 **CLASSES**
   a) **VINTAGE SIDECAR (SC1):** Front-exit sidecars. Air-cooled, one- or two-cylinder, two- or four-stroke, built before December 31, 1967. Two-stroke 350cc maximum. Four-stroke, 650cc overhead valve and 750cc sidevalve maximum. Carbureted only. Fuel injection, supercharging and turbocharging are prohibited. No short-stroke engines permitted. Stock stroke length and stock bore with allowable overbore (see 9.7.2.c). Motorcycle-based powerplants only.

   b) **SUPER VINTAGE SIDECAR (SC2):** Front-exit sidecars. Air-cooled, one- or two-cylinder, two- or four-stroke engines, built before December 31, 1972. Two-stroke, 500cc maximum. Four-stroke, 750cc maximum. Carbureted only, 34mm maximum venturi. Fuel injection, supercharging and turbocharging are prohibited. Stock stroke with crankshafts phased as per the manufacturer's intent and stock bore plus allowable overbore with allowable overbore (see 9.7.2.c). Stock valve sizes. Motorcycle-based powerplants only.

   c) **LOST ERA SIDECAR (SC3):** Front- or rear-exit sidecars. Air-cooled, one-, two- or three-cylinder two-stroke, one-, two-, three- or four-cylinder four-stroke engines, built before December 31, 1977. Two-stroke, piston-port, or reed-valve, 550cc maximum. Four-stroke, 864cc maximum, two valves per cylinder. Altered stroke and/or re-phased crankshafts beyond the manufacturer's intent are permitted. Supercharging and turbocharging are prohibited. Stock bore plus allowable overbore must be within the maximum displacement allowed. Motorcycle- and snowmobile-based powerplants only.

   d) **FORMULA CLASSIC SIDECAR (SC4):** Front- or rear-exit sidecars. Motorcycle-based powerplants: Four-stroke twins (1300cc maximum, plus allowable overbore), four-stroke multis (1100cc, including overbore) or two-stroke (750cc, plus overbore). Automotive-based powerplants: Two-stroke (900cc, including overbore) or four-stroke (1300cc, including overbore).

10.10.2 **TECHNICAL REQUIREMENTS (Construction)**

10.10.2.1 **GENERAL DESIGN:** An outfit or Sidecar is a three-wheel vehicle leaving two tracks, with only the rear wheel driving and only the front wheel steering. The frame may be cut down or altered to provide either a sitting or kneeling position for the driver. The driver's point of contact with steering controls must be rigidly attached to front forks or other steering assembly. Center hub steering is prohibited.

10.10.2.2 **FRAME:** Steel tube frame construction only: No partial or entire frame stressed skin or monocoque construction. Sidecar chair must be rigidly affixed to cycle portion of the outfit by a minimum of four rigid mechanical or welded connections. Chair may be on the right or left of the cycle portion of the outfit. Outfit must be equipped with appropriate handholds for the passenger, including – but not limited to – a passenger handhold on the rear, outside of the outfit opposite the chair and to the back of the driver. All handholds are recommended of the closed-loop type. Any single projecting handholds must have a minimum 2" (50mm) diameter ball at the end.

10.10.2.3 **SWINGARM:** Swingarms must be of period design and materials. Single- or dual-shock configurations are allowed. Both 'sitter' and 'kneeler' designs are eligible.

10.10.2.4 **DRIVER POSITION & PASSENGER:** Driver must be positioned generally behind the engine. The driver and passenger in normal riding positions must be completely visible from above, with the exception of arms, legs, and feet. The driver must keep both hands in contact with the grips at all times and must be able to operate the clutch and front brake respectively unless intending to signal leaving the racing surface.

10.10.2.5 **STREAMLINING AND/OR BODYWORK:** The sidecar wheel, rear wheel, primary and secondary drives, and rear suspension shall be adequately protected to preclude the driver or passenger from becoming entangled. All streamlining and/or bodywork shall be consistent with applicable period. Period dustbin-style fairings are encouraged. Any downforce-generating devices and designs – including, but not limited to – airfoils, spoilers and ground-effect tunnels are prohibited. No part of the outfit may extend longitudinally more than 12" (305mm) forward of the front the front tire and/or rearward of the rear tire. Bodywork shall not impede the movement of the driver or passenger at any time. Streamlining and/or bodywork shall be detachable for tech inspection.

10.10.2.6 **BATTERY:** The battery must be mounted in such a way that neither the driver nor passenger can come into contact with the battery or its contents. The battery must be secured to the sidecar.

10.10.2.7 **ENGINE POSITION:** The engine must be behind the steering head and in front of the driver. The engine must be positioned in such a way that the centerline of the engine (the point midway between the centerline of outermost cylinders) shall not extend over 6.3" (160mm) from the centerline of the rear wheel. For longitudinal engines such as BMW or Moto Guzzi, substitute the center of gravity of the engine for the engine centerline. Drive must be transmitted through the rear wheel only.

10.10.2.8 **GEARBOX:** Applicable period components (or functionally accurate reproductions).

10.10.2.9 **OIL CONTAINMENT:** All oil containment systems shall comply with Section 9.3 TECHNICAL INSPECTION, subsection (f). A liquid-tight container around the bottom of the engine is required; oil-absorbing material shall be securely retained inside that container. All breather tubes from catch cans must be routed into the oil containment pan.

10.10.2.10 **OIL COOLERS:** Where fitted, oil coolers shall comply with Section 9.3 TECHNICAL INSPECTION, subsection (d). Coolers must be located so as to be generally visible to the driver and passenger in their operating positions. It is recommended that an oil pressure device be used to help prevent spillage

10.10.2.11 **FUEL SYSTEM:** The fuel tank must be securely fastened above the lower frame rails. No part of the fuel tank will be allowed below the frame rails. The fuel cap must securely close and not open by accident. The fuel tank should be located in such a place as to protect it from impact and/or be foam-filled to reduce spillage should a rupture occur. All fuel lines must be reinforced and positively anchored in such a way to protect them from impact. Fuel capacity shall be a maximum of 10.56 gallons (40 liters).

10.10.2.12 **CARBURETION:** For SC1/SC2, flat-slide or Lectron-type and injection-type carburetors are not permitted. "Power jet" and "pumper" type carburetors are not permitted unless the pumper mechanisms are removed and replaced with a block-off plate.

10.10.2.13 **EXHAUST:** All Sidecars must be fitted with a noise silencer or muffler. All pipes or exhausts terminating in a sharp edge must have a rolled edge added or a bull ring welded in place.

10.10.2.14 **SAFETY SWITCHES AND CUT-OUT (SHUT-OFF) DEVICES:** All outfits must be equipped with a functional "Master" switch mounted within reach of both the driver and passenger. The switch must be capable of stopping a running engine and turning off all other electrical systems. The switch plate and surrounding area must be labeled for identification by the driver, passenger, corner workers and other personnel. The mounting place of the switch and a 1" (25.4mm) square surrounding area shall be painted red. It is strongly recommended that an ignition cut-out be fitted to operate in the event that the driver leaves the machine. This ignition cut-out must interrupt the primary circuit and must be wired for the supply and return of the current. It must be placed as near to the center of the machine as possible and must be operated by a non-elastic cord of adequate length and thickness and be secured to the driver. A spiral cord (similar to telephone cord) of 39.37" (1000mm) maximum extended length is permitted.

10.10.2.15 **BRAKES:** All machines must have two independently operated braking systems.

10.10.3 **SC1 VINTAGE SIDECAR:** SC1 Sidecars are limited to front-exit outfits built before December 31, 1967, and outfits constructed after such date that are consistent in design and construction with outfits actually built in this classic period, subject to the following restrictions:

10.10.3.1 **ENGINES:** Air-cooled, one- or two-cylinder, two- or four-stroke, built before December 31, 1967. Two-stroke 350cc maximum. Four-stroke, 650cc overhead valve and 750cc sidevalve maximum. Carbureted only. Fuel injection, supercharging and turbo charging are prohibited. No short-stroke motors permitted. Stock stroke length and stock bore with allowable overbore (see 9.7.2.c). Motorcycle-based powerplants only.
Stock-phased crankshafts only. Examples:

- AJS 7R
- BMW R50/2, R50/5, R60/2, R60/5 w/OEM (stock) engine internals all gaskets must be in their original locations, maximum 26mm carburetors and four-speed gearbox
- Bridgestone 350
- Ducati bevel-drive single
- Honda CB/CL 450 w/OEM (stock) engine internals and OEM carburetors (K0 ONLY)
- Kawasaki 350 Avenger
- Matchless G50
- Norton Manx
- Suzuki T350
- Yamaha TR2, YM1, YDS5

10.10.3.2 **DIMENSIONS:** The front and rear wheel of the outfit shall be no more than 3" (76mm) out of line, measured center-to-center of the front and rear tires. The minimum track of the outfit shall be 32" (813mm), measured center-to-center of the sidecar tire and the furthest of either the front or the rear tire. The maximum track of the outfit shall be 44" (1118mm), measured center-to-center of the sidecar tire and the furthest of either the front or the rear tire. The maximum width of the outfit shall be 72" (1829mm). The minimum clearance of the front tire to the outfit shall be 1" (25mm). The front fork assembly and/or front wheel assembly shall not touch the streamlining and/or bodywork, regardless of the position of the handlebars. The minimum ground clearance of the outfit shall be 3" (76mm), measured over the entire length and width of the outfit, race ready, with driver, passenger, and fuel, and with the handlebars in the straight-ahead position. Any device, other than operational suspension travel, which could allow the ground clearance to be reduced during the course of the race, is prohibited.

10.10.3.3 **BRAKES:** Working brakes on front and rear wheel are mandatory; sidecar optional. All brakes are to be driver-operated only. Drum or single disc per wheel, provided that all disc brake components (disc rotor, caliper, and master cylinders) are components (or functionally accurate reproductions) actually available in the applicable period. Friction linings and pads are unrestricted.

10.10.3.4 **WHEELS & TIRES:** Front and rear wheels must be of wire-spoke construction; sidecar wheel may be of solid construction. No slicks or hand-cut tires. Wheels are to be minimum 15" (381mm) diameter front and rear, and minimum 8" (203mm) diameter on the sidecar. Tires' contact patch, measured with race-ready air pressures and fuel load, with driver and passenger on board, are to be a maximum 4.50" (114mm) on front and rear, and 4.80" (121mm) on the sidecar.

10.10.4 **SC2 SUPER VINTAGE SIDECAR:** SC2 Sidecars are limited to front-exit outfits built before December 31, 1972, and outfits constructed after such date that are consistent in design and construction with outfits actually built in the period, subject to the following restrictions:

10.10.4.1 **ENGINES:** Air-cooled, one- or two-cylinder, two- or four-stroke engines, built before December 31, 1972. Two-stroke, reed valve prohibited, 500cc maximum. Four-stroke, 750cc maximum.

All engines in this class are restricted to stock valve sizes and carb venturi diameter of 34mm. Carbureted only. Fuel injection, supercharging and turbocharging are prohibited. Stock stroke with crankshafts phased as per the manufacturer's intent and stock bore with allowable overbore (see 9.7.2.c). Stock valve sizes. Motorcycle-based powerplants only.

Examples:
- BMW, up to 750cc displacement, five-speed transmissions permitted.
- BSA 650
- Ducati bevel-drive 750
- Harley-Davidson Sportster 883 Iron-head (reduced to 750cc)
- Honda 450/500 twin
- Moto Guzzi 750
- Norton Commando 750 (850 sleeved to 750cc)
- Suzuki T500 (no TR500 components)
- Triumph 650/750
- Yamaha XS650, up to 750cc displacement (17-tooth front sprocket maximum)
- Yamaha TR3, R5

10.10.4.2 **DIMENSIONS:** The front and rear wheel of the outfit shall be no more than 3" (76mm) out of line, measured center-to-center of the front and rear tires. The minimum track of the outfit shall be 32" (813mm), measured center-to-center of the sidecar tire and the furthest of either the front or the rear tire. The maximum track of the outfit shall be 44" (1118mm), measured center-to-center of the sidecar tire and the furthest of either the front or the rear tire. The maximum width of the outfit shall be 72" (1829mm). The minimum clearance of the front tire to the outfit shall be 1" (25mm). The front fork assembly and/or front wheel assembly shall not touch the streamlining and/or bodywork, regardless of the position of the handlebars. The minimum ground clearance of the outfit shall be 3" (76mm), measured over the entire length and width of the outfit, race ready, with driver, passenger, and fuel, and with the handlebars in the straight-ahead position. Any device, other than operational suspension travel, which could allow the ground clearance to be reduced during the course of the race, is prohibited.

10.10.4.3 **BRAKES:** Working brakes on front and rear wheel are mandatory; sidecar optional. All brakes are to be driver operated only. Drum, dual disc, or single disc per wheel, provided that all disc brake components (disc rotor, caliper, and master cylinders) are components (or functionally accurate reproductions) actually available in the applicable period. Friction linings and pads are unrestricted.

10.10.4.4 **WHEELS & TIRES:** Front and rear wheels must be of wire-spoke construction; sidecar wheel may be of solid construction. No slicks or hand-cut tires. Wheels are to be minimum 15" (381mm) diameter front and rear, and minimum 8" (203mm) diameter on the sidecar. Tires' contact patch, measured with race-ready air pressures and fuel load, with driver and passenger on board are to be a maximum 5.0" (127mm) width on front, rear and sidecar.

10.10.5 **SC3 LOST ERA SIDECARS**

SC3 Sidecars are limited to front- or rear- exit, exit outfits built before December 31, 1977, and outfits constructed after such date that are consistent in design and construction with outfits actually built in the period, subject to the following restrictions:

10.10.5.1 **ENGINES:** Air-cooled, one-, two- or three-cylinder two-stroke, one-, two-, three- or four-cylinder four-stroke engines, built before December 31, 1977. Two-stroke, 550cc maximum. Four-Stroke multi cylinder two valve engines 864cc maximum. Altered stroke and/or re-phased crankshafts beyond the manufacturer's intent are permitted. Carburetors permitted. Fuel injection permitted as per manufacturer original application. Supercharging and turbocharging are prohibited. Stock bore plus allowable overbore must be within the maximum displacement allowed.

Examples:

- BMW R75
- BSA twins and triples
- Ducati bevel-drive 750
- Harley-Davidson Sportster "Ironhead" (1000cc max)
- Honda 750
- Kawasaki KZ750 twin, H1
- Moto Guzzi 750, 850
- Norton Commando 750
- Suzuki GS750, T500 (no TR500 components), GT380/550
- Triumph twins and triples
- Vincent 1000cc twins
- Yamaha XS650, XS750 triple, RD350/400

10.10.5.2 DIMENSIONS: May replicate those of either SC2 or SC4.

10.10.5.3 WHEELS & TIRES: May replicate those of either SC2 spoke wheels or SC4 type mag wheels. Minimum diameter of the inflated tire must be 15.7" (400mm). Slick tires are permitted. Wheel rims should be 10" (255mm) minimum, 13" (330mm) maximum diameter. Maximum tire width is 7" (177mm) for the front, rear and chair tire.

10.10.6 SC4 FORMULA CLASSIC SIDECARS: SC4 sidecars are limited to front- or rear-exit sidecars outfits built before December 31, 1981, and outfits constructed after such date that are consistent in design and construction with outfits actually built in the period, subject to the following restrictions:

10.10.6.1 ENGINES: Motorcycle-based powerplants: Four-stroke twins (1300cc maximum, plus allowable overbore), four-stroke multis (1100cc, including overbore) or two-stroke (750cc, plus overbore). Automotive-based powerplants: Two-stroke (900cc, including overbore) or four-stroke (1300cc, including overbore).

10.10.6.2 DIMENSIONS: Height: 31.5" (800mm) maximum overall.
- Passenger Platform: 31.5" by 11.8" (800mm by 300mm) minimum dimensions, measured (5.9" (150mm) above the platform.
- Wheelbase: 65" (1651mm) maximum.
- Minimum ground clearance is three inches, measured over the entire length and width of the outfit, race-ready, with driver, passenger, and fuel, and with the handlebars in the straight position. No device is permitted to reduce this clearance during the course of the race.

10.10.6.3 WHEELS & TIRES: The minimum diameter of the inflated tire must be 15.7" (400mm). Slick tires are permitted. Wheel rims should be 10" (255mm) minimum, 13" (330mm) in maximum diameter. Maximum tire width is 8" (203mm) for the front and 11" (254mm) for the chair and rear tire.

10.10.7 MODERN SIDECARS
10.10.7.1 US F1: Long wheelbase, 1000cc, per SRA rules.
10.10.7.2 US F2: Short wheelbase, 1000cc, per SRA rules.
10.10.7.3 TT1: Long wheelbase, 600cc, per FIM rules.
10.10.7.4 TT2: Short wheelbase, 600cc, per FIM rules.

10.11 EXHIBITION

Guidelines for *non-competitive exhibition or "rolling display" rides* are available from the AHRMA National office. Exhibition classes include, but are not limited to:

a) Moto LeMans: Any bike eligible for Formula 125 (10.3.4), 250 Grand Prix (10.2.4), or 200 Grand Prix Plus (10.2.5). Entry fee shall be the same as all other vintage road race classes. The start shall be a "Lemans" push start of the type previously used for CB160.
b) Formula Lightning Extreme
c) Big Wheel Sidecar

SOUND OF THUNDER / BATTLE OF THE TWINS ® / SOUND OF SINGLES ® / FORMULA LIGHTNING

MISSION STATEMENT: AHRMA's mission is to showcase single-, twin, three-cylinder and electric motorcycles which historically have been under-represented in modern road racing. The Battle of Twins concept was born in the late 1980s as modern Superbike racing became increasingly dominated by inline four-cylinder machines. BoT racing kept alive the thunderous roar of twin-cylinder machines from British, European, and American manufacturers. Sound of Singles racing features modern interpretations of the classic single-cylinder racebike, encompassing everything from production bikes to one-off custom-built machines.

10.12 SOUND OF THUNDER

10.12.1 **MACHINE ELIGIBILITY:** Eligible machines include one-, two- and three-cylinder four-stroke motorcycles, plus rotaries and two-strokes, based on an index of performance. All classes may be run together and scored separately as determined by the number of entries and track conditions. See section 9.8 for additional mechanical requirements:

- a) **SOUND OF THUNDER 1 (SoT1):** Open to the following types of machines:
  - Four-stroke singles of any displacement.
  - Four-stroke twins of any displacement.
  - Three-cylinder machines of any displacement.
  - Twin-rotor rotary engines.
  - Any Open Two-Stroke-class machine.
  - Turbocharging or supercharging permitted only on single-cylinder machines.
  - Engines and frames may be of any origin.

- b) **SOUND OF THUNDER 2 (SoT2):** Any AHRMA Sound of Singles or Motard machine; liquid-cooled twins to 900cc; unlimited air-cooled twins; triples up to 765cc; and two-strokes to 250cc are allowed.

- c) **SOUND OF THUNDER 3 (SoT3):** Harley-Davidson XR1200, pushrod OHV twin-cylinder machines to 1000cc, OHC two- or three-valve twins to 805cc, SOHC liquid-cooled V-twins up to 750cc (plus overbore), OHC liquid-cooled four-valve twins to 650cc. Pushrod OHV machines over 900cc must run under Supersport specifications (see (9.8.1). Suzuki SV650, Kawasaki 650R, Buell XB9R, Ducati 800SS and Monster limited to Supersport specifications (see 9.8.1); otherwise, must compete in SoT2. Thruxton Cup Challenge eligible machines may compete (see 10.14). Ducatis up to 750cc originally fitted with carburetors (e.g., 1991-98 750 Supersports and Monsters) must meet the mechanical requirements in 9.8 a) through m) only, with the additional requirement being they must use OEM or aftermarket carburetors. H-D XR1200 and Ducatis up to 805cc originally fitted with fuel injection (e.g., 750SSie, 800SS) must run under Supersport specifications (see 9.8.1). Machines originally equipped with 18" wheels may convert to 17" wheels.

- d) **SOUND OF THUNDER 4 (SoT4):** Any single or twin cylinder four-stroke production motorcycle up to 400cc sold in the U.S. with a street-legal VIN. The Ninja 400 is limited to Supersport specifications (see 9.8.1) otherwise it must compete in SOT3.

10.13 BATTLE OF TWINS®:

Open to unlimited-displacement air-cooled twins:

- a) **BOT 2**: Air-cooled OHC twins to 904cc; air-cooled OHV twins to 984cc
- b) **BOT 1:** Open to air-cooled twins 905cc-Open

10.14 THRUXTON CUP CHALLENGE:

This class is open to 865cc air-cooled Triumph Thruxtons and Harley Davidson XL883/1200 Sportsters and follows AHRMA Supersport rules (see 9.8.1) with the following exceptions:

a) Stock fuel tank, side covers, seat cowl and fenders must be retained in the stock location. Side covers may be modified or replaced if high-mount exhaust pipes are used. No additional fairings, bodywork, streamlining or ducting may be added.
b) Stock headlight shell must be retained in the stock location.
c) Stock gauges must be retained in the stock location. Speedometer may be removed.
d) Stock seat pan must be retained, although the padding and/or covering may be modified.
e) Inner rear fender may be removed.
f) Cylinders must be stock bore; no overbore allowed.
g) Electric shift devices (quick-shifters) are not allowed.
h) Secondary air system may be removed.
i) Rectangular or oval number plates may be used. Minimum 6" tall numbers may be applied to the front and rear cowl if so equipped. Sharkskin front number cowl is allowed.
j) Treaded racing tires required. No slicks or hand-cut slicks allowed. Rain tires may be used.
k) Updating and/or backdating of parts is allowed.
l) OEM triple clamps must be used. Thruxtons may update or backdate the OEM triple clamps to run either handlebars or clip-ons, at the rider's preference.

In addition to the above rules, the following rules apply specifically to the Harley Davidson XL883 and XL1200 Sportster:

1. May displace up to 1204cc using Harley-Davidson or Buell cylinders with a maximum bore of 3.5 inches. Aftermarket cylinders are not allowed.
2. OEM seat and rear fender may be replaced with an XR750-style one-piece seat/fender unit.
3. Gas caps and oil tank caps must be secured by either duct tape or lockwire.
4. All front fender rivets must be drilled out and replaced with nut-secured bolts.
5. Belt drive final drive may be replaced with conventional sprockets and chain.
6. Aftermarket air filter and/or aftermarket air cleaner may be used. No scoops or ducting allowed.
7. Aftermarket ignition modules are allowed.
8. The Harley-Davidson XR1200, or any of its components, is not allowed
9. Machines must meet all standards as noted in section 3.3, 9.3, 9.4, 9.5, and 9.8.
10. 18-inch front rims may be used with OEM hubs.
11. Handlebars or clip-ons may be used.

10.15 SOUND OF SINGLES®

10.15.1 **MACHINE ELIGIBILITY:** All competition classes are intended for single-cylinder motorcycles only. All classes may be run together and scored separately as determined by the number of entries and track conditions. See section 9.8 for additional mechanical requirements:

a) **SOUND OF SINGLES 1 (SoS1):** Unlimited displacement single cylinder four-strokes and unlimited-displacement two-stroke singles.

b) **SOUND OF SINGLES 2 (SoS2):** Liquid-cooled single-cylinder four-stroke machines to 450cc and liquid-cooled single-cylinder two-stroke machines to 300cc. Air-cooled single-cylinder four-stroke machines to 610cc and air-cooled single-cylinder two-stroke machines to 400cc. MZ Skorpions are permitted in Supersport spec (see 9.8.1); otherwise, see SoS1.

c) **SOUND OF SINGLES 3 (SoS3):** Single-cylinder machines with GP or Motard chassis as follows: Liquid-cooled two-strokes to 250cc; air-cooled two-strokes to 300cc; liquid-cooled four-strokes to 250cc and air-cooled four-strokes to 350cc. Single-cylinder machines with production chassis (with street-legal VIN) as follows: Liquid-cooled two-strokes to 300cc; air-cooled two-strokes to 350cc; liquid-cooled four-strokes to 375cc; air-cooled four-strokes to 400cc. All bikes must retain stock bore & stroke, stock frame (except the rear upper sub-frame may be removed and/or modified), and fork. Eligible machines include KTM 390RC and Duke.

d) **MOTARD:** Motocross, off-road, dual-sport and motard-specific single-cylinder machines including: two-stroke, liquid-cooled to 500cc; two-stroke, air-cooled unlimited; four-stroke, liquid-cooled to 570cc; four-stroke, air-cooled unlimited displacement. Machines must meet the requirements in Section 9.8, plus the following restrictions:
   1. No bodywork, fairings or streamlining may be added.
   2. Must use flat or upswept handlebars attached to the top triple clamp. Bars must be above the top of the upper triple clamp. Dropped, Clubman bars or clip-ons are not allowed.
   3. Footpegs may be relocated higher, but not further rearward, than the stock location.

10.16 OPEN TWO-STROKE:
Any two-stroke motorcycle is eligible, regardless of displacement, number of cylinders, frame type, cooling type, or date of manufacture. See Section 9.8 for additional mechanical requirements.

10.17 FORMULA THUNDER:
Open to all Next Gen Superbike, Sound of Thunder, Sound of Singles and Battle of Twins motorcycles.

10.18 FORMULA LIGHTNING

Open to any zero-emission motorcycle. Propulsion may be via flywheel, gravity, magnetism, battery, etc.

a) Battery-powered bikes must have a peak measured voltage of 125 volts maximum.
b) All electric wiring and connectors are to be substantially insulated, secure and circuit-protected to assure safety from damage, power leakage or short-circuiting. Areas of high voltage are to be protected from damage in case of a crash, and plainly marked to protect personnel such as corner workers, etc.
c) Electric bikes must have a light on the dashboard, visible to the rider, to indicate when the vehicle is powered on.

d) All racebikes shall have a plainly-marked, easily-accessed emergency disconnect switch on the handlebar (within reach of the rider with his/her hands on controls), plus a tether fastened to the rider that disconnects all sources of power should the rider become separated from the bike. A documented software/hardware function that disables motive power when the bike is horizontal can replace the tether.
e) Racebikes shall have an audible horn operated by a handlebar-mounted button.
f) All racebikes must conform to Handbook Sections 9.3, 9.4 and 9.8.

10.19 PHILLIP ISLAND CHALLENGE

Mission Statement: To allow entrants of Team USA to have a place to race and exhibit the machinery in preparation for the International Challenge held annually at the Phillip Island Classic, in Phillip Island, Australia. To provide machinery of large displacement vintage era engines to have an organization to race with that currently does not exist anywhere else.

All rules stated below pertain to all motorcycles including 4-stroke and 2-stroke machines

NOTE: 1 (one) year probation to evaluate for elimination starting with the 2025 racing season.

a) **PERIOD:** The period of machinery eligible includes all motorcycles engines up to and including the year 1984. Frames may be production, aftermarket, or custom, all built in a safe and workmanlike manner.
b) **ENGINE CAPACITY**: The following displacements are approved:
   1. 2-valve engines: 700cc to 1300cc
   2. 4-valve engines: 700cc to 1300cc
   3. Two-cylinder engines: 700cc to 1400cc
c) **WHEEL SIZE:** The following rim widths apply:
   1. Front wheel maximum rim width of 3.5 inch
   2. Rear wheel maximum rim width of 5.5 inch
d) **BRAKES:** The following restrictions apply:
   1. Two and four pot calipers are allowed
   2. Maximum brake rotor size of 340mm
   3. Wave rotors are NOT permitted
   4. Radial brake master cylinders are NOT permitted
e) **CARBURETORS:**
   1. Both round and flatslide carburetors are allowed
   2. Maximum carburetor bore size of 40mm
f) **FORKS:**
   1. Maximum tube diameter of 43mm
   2. Upside down forks are NOT permitted
g) **COOLING:**
   1. 4-stroke engines must be air cooled only
   2. 2-stroke engines can be either air or water cooled
h) **TIRES:** The use of the following is approved:
   1. DOT tires
   2. Slick tires
   3. Wet tires
   4. Tire warmers

i) **ELECTRONIC AIDS:** Electronic aids are NOT permitted other than ignition, i.e., no quick shifters or traction control.
j) **NUMBERS:** At least 7-inch-high numbers, block style, clearly visible and legible.
k) **BELLY PANS:** Mandatory on all bikes per AHRMA rule 9.3 (f).
l) **BODYWORK:** Must maintain the period vintage look. NO modern seat pans or fairings.
m) Examples of eligible machines and not limited to the following:
- Honda CB 750 to 1100, and CBX
- Yamaha TZ 750, Yamaha FJ Series Bikes
- Suzuki GS Series Bikes
- Kawasaki GPZ Series Bikes
- Other OEMs with similar configurations

*THESE RULES MAY OR MAY NOT MIRROR THE PHILLIP ISLAND CHALLENGE RULES. IT IS UPON THE RIDER TO BUILD ELIGIBLE MACHINERY FOR EACH RACE ORGANIZATION.

10.20 TWO-STROKE CLASSIC

MISSION STATEMENT: For Grand Prix or Factory road racing two-stroke 250/350cc motorcycles built from January 1974 through December 1984. Only genuine race bikes are allowed.

Among the eligible machines are any genuine 250/350cc Grand Prix two-stroke machine manufactured from 1973 through <u>1985 or replicas thereof.</u>

Examples are:
- Yamaha TZ250/350
- Kawasaki KR250/350
- Bimota TZ250/350
- Harris TZ250/350
- Maxton TZ250/350
- Armstrong-Rotax 250/350
- Nicco Baker TZ250/350

<u>Note:</u> 1 (one) year probation to evaluate for elimination starting with the 2025 racing season.

Requirements and Modifications for Two-stroke Classic

a) **GENERAL**
1. Only genuine race bikes <u>or replicas thereof</u> are allowed.
2. Like design does not apply to this class for motorcycle eligibility.
3. No replica parts are allowed unless they are exact copies of the originals.
4. All motorcycles are to use three white number plates. See section 9.5 for additional requirements.
5. Competitors must comply with all applicable parts of Sections 1-9 of the AHRMA Handbook
6. All modifications must be performed to a high standard of fit, finish and workmanship.

b) ENGINE
1. All engines must be single, parallel, or tandem twins. No v-twins allowed.
2. All engines must retain stock bore and stroke.
3. <u>Flat slide Power Jet type carburetors with mechanically-adjustable power jets allowed; no smart carbs or electrically-activated power jets allowed.</u>
4. Engines must be naturally aspirated.
5. <u>Reed valves allowed.</u>
6. <u>TZ750 373cc reed valve cylinders allowed on TZ350.</u>
7. Motorcycles must have period style exhaust. All exhaust systems must be equipped with an effective silencer, open pipes or open megaphones are not allowed. See rule 9.3.h.
8. No electronic traction control or quick shifters allowed. Lap timers are allowed.

c) CHASSIS AND FRAME
1. Frames must be steel or aluminum in round or square tube. No Deltabox allowed.
2. Frames may be braced and strengthened, period modifications only Subframes may be modified or altered.
3. Period swingarms allowed.
4. Rear shock may be replaced. Twin shock mounts may be repositioned.
5. Forks must be conventional non-inverted.
6. Wheel size requirements: 18 front, 18 rear; 17 front 18 rear; 16-inch wheels are allowed. Wheels must be of the period, spoke, mag, Astralite, etc.
7. Calipers must be axial-style, twin-piston. Dual rotors allowed.
8. No tire restrictions. Slicks, DOT, or rain tires allowed. Tire warmers permitted.

d) BODYWORK
1. Fuel tank and bodywork must be accurate replicas. Bodywork design must be of the period, 1974-1984.
2. Oil retention belly pan must be used on all machines. See rule 9.3.f.
3. Machines will not pass tech inspection with unpainted bodywork, bodywork in primer or bodywork that is damaged.
4. Period OEM and Race Team paint schemes are encouraged.

■ SECTION 11 - VINTAGE MOTOCROSS

MISSION STATEMENT: The mission of AHRMA Vintage Motocross is to preserve a particular time in the history of the sport of motocross. This time period may not be the very beginning of the sport, but marks the period of international recognition after WWII. It ended in the mid-1970s and is considered to many around the world as one of the greatest eras of the sport. We want to demonstrate why this is stated.

At the beginning of this time period, the machines raced were basic transportation-based models with slight modifications. They were raced over farmland settings with natural challenges. Higher speeds, terrain and off-camber turns provided the main challenges on these tracks that are typical of those used into the early '70s. Our era ends with the advent of specially-designed racing machines on specially prepared tracks. The main things consistent during this time period were the amount of suspension travel and the technique used to race these machines on natural tracks.

AHRMA Vintage Motocross is dedicated to preserving these machines, the sights and sounds, the racetracks and the riding techniques and strategies of this bygone era. Our rules are carefully crafted to make sure these machines will never become obsolete again.

Note: *A 10-year moratorium on adding new vintage motocross classes is in effect, beginning in 2018.*

11.1 CLASSES AND ELIGIBILITY

These classes are intended for model year 1974 and like-design machines that are essentially unchanged. Other 1975-model motorcycles are not eligible. Rider age-based Open Age, 40+, 50+, 60+ and 70+ classes also are available. The minimum age for riders is 16 years.

11.1.1 PREMIER LIGHTWEIGHT: Certain pre-modern era machines, 150-250cc. Eligible models include:

- Aermacchi
- BSA C15, must retain original left-intake-port cylinder head. B25 heads are not legal.
- CZ Trial, Type 475
- Ducati Scrambler
- ESO
- Honda CB/CL160, maximum 200cc
- Honda CB/CL7
- Husqvarna three-speed Silver Arrow and other specials based on this engine
- Jawa
- Maico with OEM iron barrel
- Matchless G2
- Parilla Wildcat
- Triumph Cub
- Triumph Tiger 70
- Villiers-powered machines (Greeves, Dot, James, Norman, Francis-Barnett, etc.)

a) Ineligible are all models of Yamaha, Suzuki, Bultaco, Ossa, Montesa, alloy-barrel Maico, and Greeves (unless Villiers powered). Refer to Sportsman and Classic classes.

b) Replacement frames, including Cheney, Rickman and replicas are not allowed. Premier Lightweight may mix-and-match any class-legal frame and engine. OEM frames may have period modifications. When using non-standard engine/frame combinations, said modifications must be approved by the Rules and Eligibility Committee.

c) Premier Lightweight machines are restricted to expansion chambers of period technology. The head pipe must be of constant diameter, and the chamber must have two cones maximum of constant angle, with no constant-diameter center section.

11.1.2 **PREMIER 350:** Certain 1960s-era four-stroke machines 300-350cc.

Eligible models include:

- All pre-unit models, built to Premier 500 specifications.
- Aermacchi 350, all
- AJS Model 8
- Benelli 350
- BSA B40
- Ducati 350, all
- ESO 350
- Honda CB/CL77
- Matchless G5
- Triumph 3TA, T90
- Unit-construction machines must retain original rear hubs and frames;
- period modifications are allowed. All engines must use original stroke
- and bore (plus allowable overbores). BSA B40 must use iron cylinder and
- left-intake-port cylinder head. Any machines with extensive
- modifications or exhibiting exemplary performance will be moved to Classic 500.

11.1.3 **PREMIER 500:** Certain pre-1965 and like-design, non-unit construction (removable gearbox) of 350-500cc and unit construction of 360-500cc. (Eligible exceptions: Matchless or AJS 600cc single using original, non-Norton oil pump crankcases with standard stroke and bore (+.080").

Examples of eligible machines include:

- BSA A7 twin and pre-unit 350/500 singles
- ESO 500
- Jawa 350cc Type 575, etc.
- Matchless G80, G50
- TriBSA, MaBSA, etc.
- Triumph T100 pre-unit; may use 650 crankshaft with maximum .030" overbore.
- Triumph 500 unit-construction twin; see below

d) To better preserve the machines of this era, standard frames are encouraged. How-ever, TriBSA specials, and period aftermarket units such as Rickman (MkIII max), Cheney, or accurate replicas, are eligible. Standard frames may have period modifications.

e) Triumph unit-construction twins are intended as entry level and must include the following: The frame must be the pre-1967 Triumph 500 "gooseneck" design (factory-produced with the gas tank as a structural member of the frame, a bolt-in backbone piece, or the 1966-style welded-in small-diameter tube from the top of the steering head stock to the tank/seat junction. Up to serial number H49832). The stock Triumph rear hub must be used. The engine must be of the type that uses a bushing on the timing side of the crank's mainshaft, although it is not necessary to utilize the distributor-type ignition. The cylinder head must be of the pre-'67 "squishband" type.

11.1.4 **PREMIER OPEN TWINS:** Certain pre-1965 and like-design non-unit construction (removable gearbox), four-stroke machines with two or more cylinders, manufactured as 600cc and larger.

The following machines are eligible:

- BSA A10 twin
- Matchless 600, 650 and 750 twin
- Norton 650, 750 and 850 twin
- Triumph 650 twin

f) To better preserve the machines of this era, standard frames are encouraged. How-ever, TriBSA specials, and period aftermarket units such as Rickman (MkIII max), Cheney, or accurate replicas, are eligible. Standard frames may have period modifications.

11.1.5 **100cc MOTOCROSS:** 88-100cc two-stroke and 88-120cc four-stroke production motorcycles manufactured as up to 1974-model-year machines, and like-design. All motorcycles in this class must have been manufactured 100cc, or smaller, displacement bikes.

Eligible machines include:

- Bridgestone
- Bultaco Lobito or Sherpa S
- Harley-Davidson/Aermacchi Baja 100
- DKW
- Hodaka 90 or 100
- Honda CT90 or CB/CL/SL/XL100
- Honda CB/CL/SL125
- Indian
- Kawasaki 90 or 100
- Moto Beta
- Penton
- Rickman-Hodaka
- Sachs
- Suzuki TC/TS90 or TS/TM100
- Van Tech frames with any eligible engine
- Yamaha YL1E, HT1, LT2 or DT/MX100
- Zundapp

a) Engine displacement can be increased to class limit, plus allowable overbore.
b) Engines may use six-speed transmissions if OEM-equipped on that particular machine. Six-speed conversions are not permitted.
c) Electronic ignitions and reed-valves are allowed.
d) Aftermarket frames are limited to those listed, pending approval of the Rules & Eligibility Committee.

e) Engine/frame combinations must be as manufactured; no mixing-and-matching of engines and chassis into "specials."
f) Hubs and forks from any 1974 or earlier production motorcycle are permitted.
g) Honda four-strokes are limited to the standard one-piece cylinder head. No major engine components from 125cc engines are allowed, including the large-valve, one-piece XL125 head.
h) **No machine or major component** manufactured as/for a 125cc motorcycle is eligible.
i) Monark frames are not permitted.

11.1.6 **CLASSIC 125:** 88-125cc two-strokes and four-strokes 88-150cc, manufactured through December 1971 and any like machines.

Eligible machines include:

- American Eagle Tyran 125 (Sachs)
- Ancilotti-, Sachs-, or Morini-powered bikes
- Bultaco, up to Sherpa S 125
- Carabela
- CZ, '71-75
- DKW
- Harley-Davidson 100 and 125
- Hodaka, all 100s and 125s (except as noted below)
- Honda CB/CL/SL up to 150cc
- Honda XL100K1
- Husqvarna, '72-74
- KTM, '71-72 Sachs engine
- Maico, '72-74 square barrel only
- Monark, '71-74
- Montesa Cappra
- Pentons with Sachs engine
- Puch, all
- Rickman Zundapp, all
- Rupp 125 with Sachs motor
- Sachs, all
- Suzuki TS100/125
- Wassell, all Sachs-powered
- Yamaha AT1
- Zundapp MC 125
- Any motorcycles powered by Sachs engines 125/5A or 6A, 125/5B or 6B.

Ineligible Classic 125 machines are:

- All Japanese except those listed above
- Bultaco Pursang 125
- Can-Am, all
- '74 Hodaka Super Rat and Super Combat
- Ossa Phantom
- Pentons with KTM engines

a) The only acceptable change from the OEM frame is to use "specials" no newer than 1972.
b) No major engine components may be changed or updated to later-model parts (i.e., cylinder head, barrel, cases, etc.). Reed valves are not allowed. Carburetors on two-strokes may be no larger than 32mm. Any OEM exhaust may be used only on the original machine; any replacement of original exhaust must be made of up to four rolled cones and a single-diameter center section and a single-diameter head pipe.
c) Four-stroke Hondas may be increased to 150cc (plus .020" overbore), but must use 1971-type crankcases, and the small-valve one-piece cylinder head.
d) 100cc two-strokes may be increased to 125cc.
e) Honda leading-axle forks are not eligible.
f) Anyone with a purpose-built machine, or one which is later than December 1971 but may be a "like" model, should submit an eligibility request form.
g) Machines which exhibit unusual performance may be required to run in Sportsman 125.

11.1.7 **CLASSIC 250:** Certain machines introduced just after the Premier Lightweight era. Also included are 350cc non-unit-construction four-strokes.

Eligible machines are:
- AJS Stormer 250
- American Eagle 238 Greenstreak
- Bultaco four-speed, including Metisse
- CZ twin pipe
- Greeves Challenger/Griffon with cast-beam or steel frame
- Honda CL175, SL175
- Husqvarna "bolt-together" four-speed (pre-'68 only)
- Kawasaki 238 Greenstreak
- Maico oval barrel
- Montesa four-speed
- Ossa four-speed
- Rickman Montesa four-speed (see below)
- Any all-alloy 250cc BSA or Triumph (B25, TR25W)
- Any 350cc non-unit-construction four-stroke such as Matchless, BSA, Ariel, and ESO
- Suzuki TM250 twin-pipe

a) Rickman or Cheney frames may be used with the above engines. Only Rickman MkIII, MkIV or Petite Metisse may be used. Original four-speed Rickman Montesas (up to frame #1824 and fitted with 53M-series engines) are allowed, but must retain their original Metal Profiles forks, Rickman hubs and exhaust pipe (or an accurate replica of the OEM pipe); replica bikes utilizing later Rickman frames originally built for five-speed engines are not allowed. Any "special" built from any Rickman Montesa chassis and any other engine runs in the Sportsman class. 1973-74 CCM or Dick Mann frames are eligible.
b) Ineligible are "bolt-together" enduro Husqvarna or any major components from this machine; single-port CZ; Japanese makes with single-cylinder, two-stroke engine, or five-speed transmission.
c) No major engine components may be changed or updated to later model parts (i.e., cylinder head, barrel, cases, etc.).
d) No machine may use a carburetor larger than 32mm, except 33mm IRZ on Ossa only. No reed valves allowed.

e) Any replacement of the original expansion chamber must be of period design, with only two cones maximum of constant angle. The center section must be of constant diameter and the head pipe must be of constant diameter until it meets the opening cone. Fitting a more modern expansion chamber will move the machine to the Sportsman class.

11.1.8 **CLASSIC 500:** Certain 500 class machines introduced just after the Premier 500 era.

Eligible machines are:
- Aermacchi/Harley-Davidson 350
- AJS Stormer 370/410
- American Eagle 360
- Bultaco 350/360 El Bandido and Montadero
- CZ 360 twin port, 360cc plus allowable overbore, must use original lower-end with crankshaft-mounted clutch.
- Ducati wide-case 350/450
- Greeves 360 or 380 twin-port in cast-beam or steel frame
- Honda CL77, CL450 and CB450
- Husqvarna 360 bolt-together, pre-1968 only
- Maico 360 oval barrel
- Montesa 360 Cappra, serial number prefix 36, 46
- Any BSA B44, 441 Victor in any BSA-designed frame
- BSA B44 with Weslake conversion
- Any Triumph unit-construction 500 twin in any BSA- or Triumph-designed frame

a) Rickman or Cheney frames may be used with the above engines. Only Rickman MkIII, MkIV or Petite Metisse may be used. Rickman Montesa and Rickman 125 Zundapp are not eligible. 1973-74 CCM or Dick Mann frames are eligible.
b) Ineligible are: BSA B50, CCM or Triumph variants; bolt-together enduro Husqvarna or any major components from this machine; single-port CZ; square-barrel Maico; single-port Greeves QUB.
c) No major engine component may be changed or updated.
d) Any AHRMA-legal carburetor may be used; no reed valves allowed.
e) Any replacement of the original expansion chamber must be of period design, with only two cones maximum of constant angle. The center section must be of constant diameter and the head pipe must be of constant diameter until it meets the opening cone. Fitting a more modern expansion chamber will move the machine to the Sportsman class.

11.1.9 EARLY SPORTSMAN STOCK (ESS) 250: Certain 250cc-class machines introduced after the Classic-class era. To preserve this historic period of American motocross, modifications are very restricted. Bikes normally eligible for Premier and Classic classes may compete, providing they are built to ESS class specifications.

Eligible models are:

- Bultaco Pursang, Model #42, 48, 68
- Cooper MX 250
- CZ "sidepipe"
- Husqvarna four-speed
- Kawasaki F7, F8, F81
- Maico "square barrel" w/full-width front hub
- Montesa Cappra (not VR)
- OSSA Stiletto
- Suzuki TS185, TS250
- Yamaha CT1, DT1

11.1.10 EARLY SPORTSMAN STOCK (ESS) 500: Certain 500cc-class machines introduced after the Classic-class era. To preserve this historic period of American motocross, modifications are very restricted. Bikes normally eligible for Premier and Classic classes may compete, providing they are built to ESS class specifications

Eligible models are:

- American Eagle 360, 405
- BSA B50/Triumph TR5MX, all variants
- CZ "sidepipe"
- Greeves QUB
- Honda CL/SL350
- Husqvarna four-speed
- Kawasaki F9
- Maico "square barrel" w/full-width front hub
- Yamaha RT1

Mechanical and cosmetic requirements for Early Sportsman Stock classes are as follows:

a) Must retain stock frame and swingarm; swingarm may be lengthened as per period modification.
b) Must retain stock wheel hubs.
c) Must retain stock forks and triple clamps.
d) No piggyback shocks.
e) No major engine components may be changed or updated beyond the model-year of any given machine.
f) Reed-valve induction is not allowed.
g) Carburetors may be updated according to Rule 11.2 c); maximum venturi size for 250 class is 34mm, 500 class is 36mm.
h) Stock placement of the exhaust pipe position must be retained. Original exhaust pipes are encouraged; if the original exhaust is replaced, a dimensionally-accurate replica of that pipe or a pipe of Classic-class specification must be used (See 11.1.7.e and 11.1.8.e). Two-strokes must have silencers.
i) BSA B50 (and all variants) must use OE crankcase, cylinder, and cylinder-head castings.

j) All machines must retain stock bore and stroke (plus allowable overbore).
k) The OE fuel tank and fender shape must be maintained. OE is encouraged; however, construction materials may vary from OE. Factory-issue paint schemes and graphics are encouraged.

11.1.11 **SPORTSMAN 125:** 88-125cc two-stroke and 88-150cc four-stroke motorcycles through the 1974 model year, and like-design machines.

Eligible like-design 1975 model machines include (see "like design" note below):
- Bultaco, see note at end of Sportsman rules
- Can-Am 125 TNT
- Honda CR125 (VIN CR125ME-200000 and CR125M-200000 series only)
- Honda MT 125 1975/1976 (VIN MT125E-200000, MT125-200000, MTE125E-300000 and MT125-300000 series only)
- Honda XL 125 1974-1975
- Kawasaki KX125
- Suzuki TM100, TM125
- Yamaha DT 125, 1975
- Yamaha YZ125, MX125

11.1.12 **SPORTSMAN 250:** Motorcycles manufactured as 126-250cc two-strokes or 151-300cc four-strokes through the 1974 model year, and like-design machines.

Eligible like-design 1975 model machines include (see "like design" note below):
- Bultaco 250 Pursang (serial #135; must use 1974-configuration swingarm). Also see note at end of Sportsman rules.
- Can-Am 175 TNT, 250 TNT (also 1976 175 TNT/OR). 250cc engines must have 57.5mm stroke
- CZ 250 Falta (1974-configuration swingarm encouraged)
- Honda MT 250 1975 (VIN MT250E-2000001-2013866, MT250-2000001-2013866)
- Honda MT 250 1976 (VIN MT250E-3000001-3004003, MT250-3000001-3004003)
- Honda XL 175 1975-1978
- Honda XL 250 1975
- Husqvarna 250WR (Eng N. MK-10500, Fr N. 2043)
- Kawasaki KX250 (also 1976)
- Ossa Desert Phantom 250 (1974-configuration swingarm encouraged)
- Suzuki TM250 (1974-configuration swingarm encouraged), also TS model
- Yamaha MX175
- Yamaha DT 175 1975 and Yamaha DT 250 1975

11.1.13 **SPORTSMAN 500:** Motorcycles manufactured as 325-625cc through the 1974 model year, and like-design machines.

Eligible like-design 1975 model machines include (see "like design" note below):
- Bultaco, see note at end of Sportsman rules
- CZ Falta (1974-configuration swingarm encouraged)
- Honda SL350 and CL360
- Husqvarna 400WR
- Kawasaki KX400 (also 1976), F5 Bighorn
- Suzuki TM400 (1974-configuration swingarm encouraged), also TS model
- Yamaha DT 360/400 1975

11.1.14 **SPORTSMAN OPEN TWINS:** Unit-construction or pre-unit, four-stroke motorcycles with two or more cylinders through the 1974 model year, and like-design machines, manufactured as 600cc and larger (see "like design" note below).

Note: Like-design Sportsman machines:
a) 1975 Maicos are **not legal** for AHRMA vintage competition, although the 1975 frame may be used as a replacement for the 19741/2 GP models. The '74-1/2 fork assembly, swingarm, hubs and engine must be retained. Any and all 1975 models must meet the seven-inch-front/four-inch-rear wheel suspension travel requirement measured at the axle.
b) 1975 Bultaco model 134-136, 143 and 144 frames may be used as replacement frames in Sportsman. Swingarm must be pre-1975, four-inch travel.
The Sportsman eligibility list is now complete with regard to non-like-design post-1974 machines. However, proposals for inclusion of like-design machines are always welcome.

11.1.15 **Open Age:** Any eligible rider on any size or type of eligible vintage machine.
11.1.16 **40+:** Riders aged 40 and older on any size or type of eligible vintage machine.
11.1.17 **50+:** Riders aged 50 and older on any size or type of eligible vintage machine.
11.1.18 **60+:** Riders aged 60 and older on any size or type of eligible vintage machine.
11.1.19 **70+:** Riders aged 70 and older on any size or type of eligible vintage machine.
Notes: A rider may not advance to the next age-related class until after that birthday. Due to difficulties in laying-out the race day program, competitors may enter no more than two rider-age classes.
11.1.20 **WOMEN:** Female riders on any size or type of eligible vintage machine.
11.1.21 At the MX coordinator's discretion, non-AHRMA support classes may be run at local and regional events only. Support races must run at the end of each round of motos to preserve the integrity of AHRMA's race day schedule and the track surface Any support classes and support-class practice sessions must run separately from the AHRMA classes. These classes will not run at National events. With the addition of the AHRMA Post Vintage MX program, coordinators are encouraged to use these as support classes (see Section 12). Only official AHRMA classes are to be run at Nationals. Any exceptions must be approved in advance by the Executive Director.

11.2 TECH INSPECTION & MODIFICATIONS

a) **SUSPENSION: All machines must have no more than seven-inches of front wheel travel and four-inches of rear wheel travel, measured at the axle, regardless of original specification.** The field check for rear wheel travel is as follows: 1) Both shocks are removed from the bike, then one bare (without spring) damper unit is reinstalled. 2) The machine is supported in such a fashion that the rear suspension is at maximum extension, and a measurement is taken from the center of the rear axle to a point marked directly above the axle on the rear fender or subframe. 3) With both wheels on the ground, the rear suspension is fully compressed by the examiner with the rider aboard to compress any rubber bumpers; a measurement is again taken from the center of the rear axle to the same marked point above. 4) The measurement obtained in step 3 subtracted from the measurement in step 2 is the wheel travel.

An alternative method of determining wheel travel may be used by tech inspectors using a pre-programmed computer. The program converts three dimensions—distance from swingarm pivot to rear axle, to lower-shock mount and top-shock mount, to show the amount of travel of the shock shaft plus 50 percent of the rubber bumper.

Due to the use of non-standard or different types of rubber bumpers, this check may be overridden by the tech inspector's discretion. Manual measurement of shock movement is the overriding factor in determining whether a shock is legal.

To help preserve the motorcycles and represent the era, stock shock mount positions are strongly encouraged. Forward-mounted or laydown shock mounts will be closely scrutinized and checked for travel, with three-fourths of the rubber bumper counted as shaft travel.

Some manufacturers listed a limited number of machines for sale with specifications that exceed the suspension limits. Those machines are not eligible unless the amount of actual wheel travel is restricted to conform with the seven-inch/four-inch rule. Regardless of the year and model of machine, it is the rider's responsibility to actually measure and ensure that his or her machine is legal. Do not rely on printed specifications. There will be no exceptions to the suspension limits. Some of the machines sold with more than four inches of rear wheel travel are Honda, Yamaha, Kawasaki, Maico GP, 1974 Husqvarna, 1974 Bultaco, 1974 Montesa, 1974 CCM and 1974 KTM.

Any shock absorber may be used, providing the technology and design was commercially available in 1974 or was supplied as OEM on any AHRMA-legal machine. Piggyback reservoirs and external rebound adjusters are allowed.

Legal shocks include:
- Armstrong
- Bilstein
- Betor
- Ceriani
- Curnutt
- Fox Shox
- Girling
- Hagon
- Marzocchi
- Mulholland
- NJB
- Noleen
- Ohlins
- Race Tech
- S&W
- Progressive Suspension
- Works Performance

Illegal shocks include:
- Any shock with a separate remote reservoir (i.e., connected by a hose) or an external compression damping adjuster.
- Any post-1974 technology, such as Fox Air shocks, etc.
- Single-shock machines are prohibited.
- Pre-1975 OEM or aftermarket forks must be used; travel is limited to seven inches. Legal leading-axle 35mm forks include: AJS Stormer; Bultaco Sherpa S, Sherpa T and Matador; Montesa; Kawasaki enduro; early Betor aftermarket; and external-spring Maico (36mm). Regardless of year manufactured, leading-axle 35mm forks which are not allowed include alloy- and magnesium-slider Marzocchi and magnesium-slider Ceriani.

b) **ENGINES:** Modifications are many, though they must be consistent with the spirit of the period and class.
   1. Reed valves may be used only on Sportsman machines.
   2. Liquid-cooled components are prohibited.
   3. Hydraulically-assisted clutches are prohibited.
   4. Cylinders may be overbored a maximum of .080" on singles, .060" on twins, .040" on triples and .020" on fours. Displacement limitations follow the three "era" breakdowns:

   Premier-class bikes may be built to class limits, plus allowable overbores. The Premier Open Twins limit is 650cc (eligible exceptions are Norton 750/850, and unlimited-displacement sidevalve machines); no 750cc or big-bore kits are allowed on OHV machines. Premier Lightweight four-strokes must utilize the original cylinder-head castings. Villiers Starmaker-powered machines are limited to the early "MkI" style, coarse-finned cylinder. Villiers 31A-37A-powered machines may use any period aftermarket alloy cylinder, the Greeves Challenger head/cylinder and/or Alpha-type crankcases.

   Classic-class machines must run at original bore and stroke, plus allowable overbores. Exceptions are: 150cc Honda four-stroke in Classic 125 and Weslake conversion for BSA B44 in Classic 500.

   Sportsman-class machines may be built to the class limit (using period components), plus overbores. Sportsman Open Twins have no displacement restrictions.

   The formula for calculating engine displacement is: bore x bore x .7854 x stroke x number of cylinders.

c) **CARBURETORS:** Flat-slide or Lectron-type and injection-type carburetors are not permitted. "Power Jet" and "Pumper" type carburetors are not permitted unless such mechanisms are disconnected or removed. Fuel injection is not permitted. Period carburetors are encouraged. Smoothbores with concentric float bowls are not permitted, except where they were fitted as original equipment or supplied as factory kits on that model motorcycle. Modern replacement smoothbore carburetors are not permitted.
   1. All motorcycles must be equipped with a functional handlebar-mounted electrical or mechanical kill switch.
   2. Footpegs must be folding type and should fold back at a 45-degree angle.
   3. Sidestands and protruding lugs must be removed or rubber-covered. At the discretion of the Tech Inspector, certain sidestands which are completely tucked away may be left in place but must be safety wired or strapped in the folded position.
   4. Disc brakes are prohibited (except Rokon and Yankee OEM). Hydraulically-assisted drum brakes are prohibited.
   5. Paddle-type tires are prohibited.
   6. All two-stroke machines must be fitted with efficient silencers. The only exception is Premier machines fitted with "blooie" pipes.
   7. Minicycles are prohibited. All machines must have a minimum OEM wheel size of 17 inches (except 125-350cc CZ and Jawa).
   8. Swingarms in the Premier and Classic classes must be steel. The only exception is the period cast-aluminum swingarm made by A&A Racing for BSA unit singles.
   9. All modifications must be consistent with the spirit of the class and period.

10. No major components may be later than 1974 (i.e., frame, fork, engine, gearbox, wheels, etc.) The burden of authenticating is on the rider. Press clippings and photos with identifiable dates may be helpful. Premier machines are restricted to Premier-type frames. Period modifications are allowed on all standard legal frames. However, no parts of later-period frames may be used for those modifications.
11. Appearance and workmanship of a reasonable standard shall be enforced.

d. **NUMBERS AND NUMBER PLATES:** All machines must display three number plates -- one mounted on the front and one on each side, mounted in a way that they will not be blocked by the rider. For race number policies, please see SECTION 3.9.

1. Numbers must be six-inches tall. If a rider's assigned competition number ends with a letter, that letter must be at least three-inches tall, and placed in the lower-right corner of the number plate. For assigned competition numbers that begin with a letter, that letter must be six-inches tall, and placed to the left of the numeric digits. It is strongly recommended -- and may be required at some events -- that riders also display three-inch numbers on each side of their helmet and eight-inch numbers on the back of their jersey.
2. All number plates in AHRMA vintage events will use a white background with black numbers and letters. To help solve past scoring problems, no other colors may be used.
3. It is the rider's responsibility to ensure number legibility. If a rider appeals his score and numbers are not properly displayed, the protest will be disallowed. There will be no exceptions to this rule.
4. Expert-class motocross champions from the previous year will be awarded a No.1 plate (with a letter suffix), which they may use in any class during the season. If they choose not to use their assigned AHRMA competition number, it will be held for them until the following season. A rider who wins more than one class championship should use only one of the No. 1/letter combinations to aid in scoring and identification.

    Number/letter combinations for each Expert class champion are:

Premier Open Twins	1B	Sportsman 500	1H
Premier 500	1A	Sportsman 250	1J
Premier 350	1S	Sportsman 125	1K
Premier Lightweight	1C	100cc	1R
Classic 500	1D	Open Age	1L
Classic 250	1E	40+	1M
Classic 125	1F	50+	1N
Early Sptmn Stock 500	1T	60+	1P
Early Sptmn Stock 250	1U	70+	1Q
Sportsman Open Twins	1G	Women	1W

5. All competitors must display their AHRMA-assigned number unless granted prior permission to run a different number at that event only.

e) In addition to the rules in Section 11, riders must comply with all applicable rules in Sections 3 (events and race procedure), 4 (entry procedure) and 6 (offenses, penalties, protests and appeals), rule 9.7.11 (fuel) and rule 9.7.17 (AHRMA decals; two required and may be placed on any readily visible part of the motorcycle).

f) Steering dampers are not allowed unless OEM or friction-type.

11.3 MOTOCROSS RIDER GRADING SYSTEM

All AHRMA motocross classes are further divided into Novice, Intermediate and Expert categories. This is an "ability" system, as opposed to an "award" system. The ability system is designed with the idea that most vintage riders do not intend to advance to the professional ranks, and that many of the riders may not improve and their ability will remain the same. Novice classes are as follows: Premier, Classic, Sportsman, Open Age, 40-60, 60+ and Women. There are no displacement classifications in any Novice class. Novice classes shall not be combined with any Intermediate or Expert class. All Novice classes shall run in Novice-only motos.

a) It is AHRMA's intent that rider ability levels are standardized within each region and across the nation.
b) Riders are graded by a committee of their peers and will be advanced only if their ability is deemed to be well above the other competitors in their class. A rider can also be moved to a lower class, in special instances, by the same method. If a rider's placement in a class is obviously wrong, that rider can be moved at any time. The executive director will make the final determination in any dispute over rider grading.
c) Each region will appoint a Regional Rider Grading Chairman and a minimum committee of one Novice, one Intermediate and one Expert. The committee will perform an annual review of ability levels but may make an immediate ability level change with a three-member quorum. The committee has overall authority and responsibility for rider ability levels in its region, whether or not a specific rider competes in its regional series.
d) Any three regional grading committee members present at a national event can make a grading decision on the spot. If the rider's home regional committee disagrees with the decision, it can be appealed to the executive director.
e) Riders who are new to AHRMA motocross must sign up as at least an Intermediate until status is confirmed by the grading committee, optimally at that rider's first event. This is done by interview or observation at the request of the new competitor. Final determination of points scored in national or regional events will not be made until status is confirmed.
f) A rider may move up a skill level at his discretion. However, no rider may move back a skill level without permission from the AHRMA grading committee.
g) So that rider skill levels are recognizable, a vertical stripe approximately 2x6 inches must be placed in the center of the rear of the helmet, with the lower end of the stripe even with the base of the helmet. Such stripes are available at tech inspection. Ability level stripes are:

    Novice .... Red
    Intermediate.............. Yellow
    Expert .... Black

h) Riders with dual ability levels must clearly display both helmet stripe colors. If a rider is observed competing without a helmet stripe, a penalty of one position may be imposed in that moto.
i) If the rider grading committee deems it appropriate, riders in the 50+ and 60+ classes may have a dual ability level. Riders in the 70+ class may apply to the rider grading committee for a lower ability rating in any class but 60+. Women may apply to the rider grading committee for any lower ability rating in any class but Women. (An Expert woman, for example, could be classified as a Sportsman Novice.) **Dual ability levels are granted only by the rider grading committee and must be listed on the rider's competition card.**

11.4 EQUIPMENT REQUIRED OF ALL MOTOCROSS RIDERS

a) It is the responsibility of the rider to select a helmet and apparel which will provide appropriate protection. AHRMA does not endorse or certify any manufacturers or products. Riders must rely on their own judgement in the selection of any helmet and apparel for durability and safety. Open-face helmets are permitted; mouth guards are recommended. See Section 3.3.14.
b) Shatterproof eye protection is required.
c) Riders' tops must have long sleeves, and full-fingered gloves must be worn.
d) Leather or plastic boots must be worn and be of sufficient height to overlap the bottom of the trouser leg at all times and in no case less than eight inches high.

11.5 SCORING AT MX EVENTS

a) The Olympic scoring method is used for each moto: 1 (one) point for first, 2 (two) points for second, 3 (three) points for third, etc. The smallest score wins.
b) Riders must complete at least one full lap to be scored.
c) A **non-starter** is anyone who does not complete one full lap, following the circuit in its entirety; a DNS receives no points. A **non-finisher** is anyone who completes one full lap but does not reach half-distance of the race; a DNF receives last-place points plus two positions, to avoid scoring problems. A **finisher** is anyone who completes at least half the number of laps completed by the class winner in a moto (e.g., three laps of a five-lap moto); points are paid in the order of finish. If there are fewer than three entrants in a class, the winner must complete at least half the prescribed race distance (track conditions allowing, as determined by the referee or race director), to receive first-place points.
d) Each race concludes with the display of the checkered flag, even if a competitor believes the number of laps is not consistent with pre-race instructions. If there has been a flagging error, the race referee may revise the results if he deems it appropriate.
e) Ties are decided by the finishing position in the last moto.
f) If two classes are run together in one race, a rider may ride one motorcycle in one class and be scored in the other class, provided the machine is eligible and entered in that other class. The rider shall start from the least favorable wave or grid position.
g) The rider, not the motorcycle, is the entry. A rider may switch to a second eligible motorcycle for the second moto in a given class.
h) If there are too many entrants for one moto, a class will be split at random and run as if there were two separate events. Series points will be awarded as if there were two separate events.
i) Results will be posted as soon as possible after the finish of a race. Once posted, there will be a 30-minute review time. If a rider believes there is an error in scoring, he or she must draft a written protest and deliver it to an AHRMA official or Referee within 30 minutes of the provisional results being posted. Unprotested results will stand. Any discrepancies will be resolved at the track. All results posted on the AHRMA website are considered final and can only be modified under direction of the Off-Road Director. This process is subject to appeal.

11.6 SERIES POINTS, AWARDS

a) Points will be awarded according to each moto finish, without regard to a rider's overall performance for the day.
b) A rider will receive points if he or she is the sole class competitor.
c) A rider must score points in at least four events to be eligible for series awards, or according to requirements as published in *AHRMA MAG* from time to time

d) National Championship Series year-end awards are based on a rider's best finishes in a maximum number of events. The maximum number of "best finishes" to count toward the championship will be specified by the Off-Road Director and announced prior to the beginning of each season. A rider must earn points in the minimum number of events specified by the Off Road Director to be eligible for year-end awards.

Position	Points	Position	Points
1	20	8	7
2	16	9	6
3	13	10	5
4	11	11	4
5	10	12	3
6	9	13	2
7	8	14	1

e) Year-end scoring ties will be broken as follows: Year-end scoring ties will go to the rider who accumulated the most points during head-to-head competition. If still tied or if they did not compete against each other, year-end scoring ties will be broken by the greatest number of moto wins, then second-place moto finishes, third place, etc. In the event of an absolute tie, the oldest rider wins.

f) In the event that only one moto is run during a Race Day, double points will be awarded.

g) National-championship events also award regional-championship points for the region in which the event takes place.

11.7 RACE PROCEDURES

a) Engine-displacement class bumping is prohibited (e.g., no 250s in the 500 class). Bumping up into later-era classes is permitted, provided the machine is of corresponding engine size (e.g., Classic 500 into Sportsman 500 in Vintage or Historic 125 into Gran Prix 125 in Post Vintage).

b) During an event, it is expressly forbidden to ride any vehicle in the direction opposite to that in which the event is being run without specific approval of a race official.

c) In the event that a rider leaves the marked racetrack, every effort should be made to reenter the track at the same place he/she exited. If this is not possible, the rider must re-enter in a safe manner, before the next track marker, without improving his/her position in relation to other competitors. If time or position is gained, the penalty will be left to the discretion of the referee.

d) A red flag means the race has been suspended. Competition must cease immediately, with all riders slowing to a safe speed and proceeding in a safe manner to the starting area, where an official will give further instructions. If a race is called complete by a red flag, scoring will revert to the last lap completed by all competitors.

e) All events where a "rubber band" or "flag" start is used, riders must have their front wheels in the start line ditch, behind the line of the rubber band, or other start line markers as specified by the starter), at the time the rubber band is released or flag is waived. Failure to do so will result in the loss of three finishing positions in the moto. A rider who jumps the start and causes a false start requiring the moto to be restarted will be penalized four finishing positions in the moto. There are no other penalties, i.e. starting backwards, hand-on-helmet, etc.

f) A yellow flag indicates a dangerous situation on the track ahead. Competitors are cautioned to ride accordingly. The intent of this rule is that riders may not use this situation to an advantage.
g) If a rider who is scheduled to start in the second wave or gate of a race leaves with the first wave or gate, there will be an automatic one-lap penalty for that rider.

■ SECTION 12 - POST VINTAGE MOTOCROSS

MISSION STATEMENT: The mission of AHRMA Post Vintage Motocross is to showcase an innovative and revolutionary period of MX racing. This relatively short time frame is recognized as the beginning of the long-suspension-travel era of motocross which lasts to this day, and also the emergence of the American domination on the world racing scene. Machines of this era were purpose-built motocross racers which introduced many technologies, from the very first long-travel suspension through to the advent of water-cooled engines and linkage-controlled rear suspensions found at the end of this exciting time in motocross.

These technological advances result in a motorcycle which has the ability to travel at incredible speeds over very rough terrain and endure punishment that would have inflicted race-ending damage to earlier machines. These capabilities, coupled with advancing riding styles and techniques, dictated changes in the racetracks. Tracks became specially prepared, permanent-style circuits, which utilized some man-made obstacles in addition to natural terrain features. The Post Vintage era ends as we start to see the inclusion of Supercross-style obstacles in the tracks, and the inclusion of disc brakes and other advanced features from the factories as original equipment.

The primary purpose of AHRMA Post Vintage Motocross is to provide an appropriate place for these machines to be preserved and ridden by those who are interested in reliving the era, in addition to educating and exposing the history to those who may not have been participants the first time around. With careful attention to racetrack preparation, and to rules crafting, AHRMA is making certain that Post Vintage Motocross bikes will be enjoyed by its members of today and tomorrow.

AHRMA's Post Vintage Motocross structure is intended to include and categorize the motocross bikes that inspired the "long-travel" revolution that transformed motocross into a sport that's very different from the earlier, short-travel era. This program groups similar motorcycles into classes that are similar to the changes that were taking place at the racetracks throughout the intended era of each class.

Please submit any requests for new rules or machine eligibility to the Post Vintage Motocross Rules & Eligibility Committee (see Section 17).

Proposals for Post Vintage Motocross Rules Changes or general machine (year/make/model) Eligibility Class changes must be made via the **Rule Change Proposal Form (See section 19.9)** during the annual period for Rules Change Proposals announced on the AHRMA.ORG web site. Approved changes become effective on an annual basis. Note: The Eligibility Request Form (see section 19.10) is not to be used for this purpose. The Eligibility Request Form is used when classification for a specific "one-off" machine or approval of its individual components is required.

NOTE: All modifications must be consistent with the intended time frame of the class.

12.1 HISTORIC - CLASSES AND ELIGIBILITY

The Historic classes are intended to represent the "first generation" of long-travel bikes that were commercially available in the 1975-'77 period. The time frame is provided only as a guideline, as some 1977 models are of the second-generation long-travel bikes that would clearly outclass the earlier models if allowed to run together. For this reason, we do not classify motorcycles strictly by the year they were produced, but by some similar characteristics that were possessed by the majority of these first-generation long-travel motorcycles, such as suspension travel.

12.1.1 **TECHNICAL SPECIFICATIONS:** The following specifications apply to all motorcycles, regardless of the year of manufacture, which fall within the scope of the Historic classes.

a) Regardless of original specification, no Historic class motorcycle may have more than nine inches of suspension travel at the front and rear wheels. Period aftermarket suspension modifications, including shock reservoirs, are allowed in the Historic classes, provided they still meet the nine-inch travel limit.
b) No liquid-cooled motorcycles.
c) 35mm leading-axle Husqvarna and Betor forks are allowed, provided travel is limited to a maximum of nine-inches. Early nine-inch travel Simons forks are allowed. Fox Factory Forks are prohibited.
d) The maximum fork stanchion diameter for Historic classes is 38mm.
e) Overhead-cam four-strokes (TT Yamahas, XL Hondas, etc.) are limited to a maximum of 500cc of displacement, plus allowable overbore.

12.1.2 **HISTORIC 125:** Certain 88-125cc machines built up to and including the 1977 model year that made up the first generation of long-travel, small-bore motorcycles.
Eligible machines include:

- 1975-'77 Bultaco Pursang 125
- 1975-'77 Can-Am TNT, Qualifier and MX 125, up to MX3 (MX4 and later, see Gran Prix classes)
- 1975-'78 CZ 125
- 1975-'78 Honda CR125, Honda MT125
- 1974-'77 Honda XL125
- 1975-'77 Husqvarna CR, WR 125
- 1975-'77 Kawasaki KX, KE, KD 125
- 1978 Kawasaki KX125 A4
- 1975-'77 Maico 125 GP
- 1975-'77 Montesa Cappra 125 VA & Enduro 125. VB, 1977-'78 models only; no later-model components, including swingarm.
- 1975-'77 Penton/KTM 125 with Sachs or KTM engine. (1978 Penton/KTM is not a like-design model. See GP classes.)
- 1975-'77 Suzuki RM, TM 125
- 1976-'78 Suzuki RM100
- 1976-'79 Yamaha YZ100
- 1975-'77 Yamaha MX, YZ, DT 125

12.1.3 **HISTORIC 250:** Certain 126-250cc machines built up to and including the 1977 model year that made up the first generation of long-travel motorcycles. Eligible machines include:

- 1975-'77 Bultaco Pursang, Frontera, Alpina 250, to include the 1977 Mk10 Pursang
- 1975-'77 Can-Am MX, TNT and Qualifier 175-250, up to MX3 (MX4 and later models, see the Grand Prix classes)
- 1975-'78 CZ 250 Falta Replica
- 1978 Harley-Davidson MX250
- 1975-'77 Honda CR, MT, MR, XL 175/250
- 1975-'76 Husqvarna CR, WR 250 and 1977 WR 250.
  1977 Husqvarna CR/OR models are allowed, with fork travel limited to nine inches. Otherwise, see GP 250.
- 1975-'77 Kawasaki KX, KLX, KD, 175/250. 1978 Kawasaki KX250A4.
- 1975-'77 Maico MC, AW 250. 1977 model AW 250 must comply with the Historic class suspension limits.
- 1975-'77 Montesa King Scorpion & Cappra VR 250 V-75, VA & Enduro 250H. VB, 1977 & 1978 models only; no later-model components, including swingarm. All later model Montesas, see GP classes.
- 1975-'77 Ossa Phantom & Desert Phantom 250, up to GPIII model. Ossas equipped with Bolger rear suspension are allowed; suspension-travel limits must be met.
- 1975-'77 Penton-KTM 175/250. 1977 models must meet the Historic-class suspension limits. (1978 Penton/KTM is not a like-design model. See GP classes.)
- 1975-'76 Puch 250 MX (twin-carb Harry Everts replica)
- 1975-'77 Suzuki RM, TM, PE 175/250
- 1975-'77 Yamaha MX, YZ, DT, IT 175/250
- 1975-78 Yamaha MX, DT, IT 175/250. 1978 YZ 250 prohibited.

12.1.4 **HISTORIC 500:** Certain 325-460cc two-stroke and up to 636cc four-stroke machines, built up to and including the 1977 model year, which make up the first generation of long-travel motorcycles.
Eligible motorcycles include:

- 1975-'77 Bultaco Frontera, Alpina, Pursang 350/360/370
- 1975-'78 CCM MX up to 636cc. No CCM four-valve heads are allowed
- Wheel travel must comply with Historic class requirements
- 1975-'78 CZ 400 Falta Replica
- 1975-'77 Honda XL350, side- or center-port engine
- 1975-'76 Husqvarna CR, WR 360. 1977 WR 360 is allowed. 1977 Husqvarna CR and OR 390 are allowed (frame numbers between ML16000 and ML21000), with fork travel limited to nine inches. Otherwise, see GP 500. 1975-'77 Husqvarna 360 and 390 Automatics are allowed
- 1975-'77 Kawasaki KX400/450
- 1974-'77 Maico MC, AW 400/440. 1977 AW 400/440 must comply with the Historic class suspension limits
- 1975-'77 Montesa Cappra 360 VA. VB, 1977-'78 models only, with original 360cc four-speed engine; no later-model components, including swingarm. All later-model Montesas, see GP classes
- 1975-'77 Penton-KTM 400. 1977 models must meet the Historic-class suspension limits. (1978 Penton/KTM is not a like-design model See GP classes)
- 1975-'77 Suzuki RM370, TM400
- 1975-'77 Yamaha YZ, MX, DT, IT 360/400, 1978 IT 400
- 1975-'80 Yamaha TT500, up to 500cc displacement, plus allowable overbore

12.1.5 **HISTORIC FOUR-STROKE:** Certain four-stroke motorcycles built up to and including the 1978 model year with up to 636cc (with restrictions). All overhead-cam four-stroke engines are limited to a 500cc maximum displacement, plus allowable overbore.
Eligible motorcycles include:

- 1975-'78 CCM MX up to 636cc. No four-valve CCM heads are allowed. Wheel travel must comply with Historic class requirements
- 1975-'78 Honda XL350 with side- or center-port head
- 1975-'80 Yamaha TT500; must meet nine-inch suspension travel limit
- Any AHRMA-legal four-stroke vintage MX machine, regardless of displacement
- Any period "special" that meets the Historic-class technical requirements and was built within the intended time frame of the class (e.g., Triumph engine in a Husqvarna frame)

12.1.6 Any Historic-class motorcycle may use an aftermarket frame. Many were available during the intended time frame of the class, including, C&J, Champion, Dick Mann, Cheney, Cycle Factory, Hallman-Aberg, and many others. Regardless of the manufacturer, all motorcycles must meet the Historic-class technical specifications for wheel travel and suspension components.

12.1.7 **POST VINTAGE 100cc:** 88-100cc two-stroke and 88-200cc four-stroke motorcycles manufactured as up to 1984 model-year machines, and like-design. All two-stroke motorcycles in this class must have been manufactured 100cc or-smaller displacement bikes. And four-strokes manufactured as 200cc or smaller displacement bikes. Maximum engine displacement for two-strokes is 100cc, plus allowable overbore. Maximum engine displacement for four-strokes is 200cc, plus allowable overbore. Electronic ignitions and reed-valves are allowed. Hubs from any Post Vintage eligible machine are permitted. Forks may not exceed 43mm in diameter. Suspension travel is not limited. Disc brakes are not allowed.

Eligible Machines to include:

- Suzuki TM, TS, and RM to 1981
- Yamaha DT, MX & YZ to 1983
- Hodakas all 100cc models
- Honda XR 100, XL 125, XL 175, and XL 185 to 1985 and like design
- Honda XR200, all years
- Kawasaki KE 100

12.2 GRAND PRIX - CLASSES AND ELIGIBILITY

The Grand Prix classes are intended to represent the motorcycles that made up the "second generation" long-travel motorcycles generally available in the 1977-81 period (or like design). During this period innovation came rapidly and motorcycles changed dramatically in a fairly short time. For this reason, the Grand Prix Classes follow a formula rather than a specific year cutoff.

12.2.1 **TECHNICAL SPECIFICATIONS:** Gran Prix-class motorcycles feature technology later than that found in Historic, but **do not** include linkage-type rear suspensions, liquid-cooling, or disc brakes. There are no suspension-travel limitations, but upside-down forks are not allowed (see the Ultima classes). Aftermarket frames and forks are permitted, and many were available during the intended time frame of the classes. If there is a question regarding the eligibility of any component, please submit a Request for Eligibility Form found near the back of this Handbook.

12.2.2 **GRAND PRIX 125:** Certain post-1977 motorcycles 88-125cc. The year of manufacture is not important, as long as the motorcycle meets the class formula.

- 1978-'83 Husqvarna 125s are allowed
- 1978-'80 Yamaha, Honda, Suzuki, Can-Am and KTM 125cc motocrossers are allowed
- 1981-model Honda, Suzuki, Yamaha, KTM and Kawasaki models are prohibited. See the Ultima class

12.2.3 **GRAND PRIX 250:** Certain 126-250cc post-1977 motorcycles. The year of manufacture is not important, as long as the motorcycle meets the class formula.

- 1978-'81 Can-Am Qualifier and MX, up to MX6, are allowed
- 1987-'89 CZ 250 is allowed
- 1978-'83 Husqvarnas are allowed
- 1978-'81 Maico 250s are allowed
- 1978-'80 Suzuki, Yamaha, Honda motocross and enduro models are allowed
- 1981 Yamaha YZ250 is allowed
- 1980 and later Kawasakis are prohibited. See Ultima class
- 1981-model Honda and Suzuki are prohibited. See Ultima class

12.2.4 GRAND PRIX 500: Certain post-1977 motorcycles, 325-500cc two-stroke and 580cc four-strokes. The year of manufacture is not important, as long as the motorcycle meets the class formula, with a few exceptions (see below).

- 1978-'81 Can-Am Qualifier and MX 370/400 up to MX6 are allowed.
- 1987-'92 CZ 400 is allowed.
- 1978-'84 Husqvarna CR, XC, OR, WR 390-500 two-strokes are allowed.
- 1978-'84 Husqvarna 390, 420 and 500 Automatics are allowed.
- 1978-'81 Maico 400-440-490 are allowed.
- 1978-'80 Mugen 360-kitted Honda CR250 is allowed.
- 1982 Suzuki DR500Z is allowed.
- 1982 and later Can-Am Sonic with Rotax engines are prohibited. See Ultima class.
- 1981-model Honda and Suzuki are prohibited. See Ultima class.
- 1983-'84 Husqvarna TE, TC, TX four-Stroke 510s are prohibited. See Ultima class.
- 1980 and later Kawasakis are prohibited. See Ultima class.

12.2.5 GRAND PRIX FOUR-STROKE: Certain 185-580cc four-stroke-powered motorcycles that came just after the Historic Four-stroke class period.

Eligible motorcycles and modifications include:

- All Honda XR185, 200, 250 and 500 models produced with dual-shock rear suspension
- Four-valve CCMs
- Yamaha TT250 and 500 with more than 9" of suspension travel, front and rear
- Suzuki DR models to include the 1982 DR500Z
- Kawasaki KLX models
- Period specials that meet the class requirements
- Can-Am Sonic and Husqvarna 510TE, TC and TX models are prohibited (See Ultima Four-stroke class.)

12.3 ULTIMA - CLASSES AND ELIGIBILITY

The Ultima classes are for machines that bring us to the brink of the modern motocross motorcycle. Generally, the distinguishing specifications for the Ultima classes **are** as follows: Motorcycles produced with liquid-cooling and linkage-type rear suspension **are** acceptable, but those having disc brakes or any type of power-valve mechanism built directly into the engine **are not**.

12.3.1 TECHNICAL SPECIFICATIONS: Upside-down forks, such as Simons and early White Power, are allowed only on Ultima-class motorcycles, as are aftermarket single-shock frames (such as C&J).

12.3.2 ULTIMA 125: Certain motorcycles 88-125cc within the guidelines of the Ultima-class specifications. Eligible machines, and exceptions, include but are not limited to:

- Honda CR125 up to 1983 is allowed.
- Suzuki RM125 up to 1984 is allowed.
- Yamaha YZ125s, up to 1982-'84 with YPVS system, are allowed. (**Note:** These are the only eligible motorcycles allowed to use a power-valve mechanism.)
- Any Post Vintage 100cc model is allowed.
- KX125 meeting Ultima guidelines up to 1984 is allowed.
- 1985-model Husqvarna 125 is prohibited.

page 106 *2024 AHRMA HANDBOOK_REV 2024.02.23*

12.3.3 **ULTIMA 250:** For certain 126-250cc motorcycles within the guidelines of the Ultima Class specifications.

Eligible machines, and exceptions, include but are not limited to:
- Up to 1983 Hondas are allowed
- Up to 1984 Suzukis are allowed
- 1982-'84 Maico and/or MStar, air-cooled, drum-brake only
- Yamaha YZ250s, up to 1982-'84 with YPVS system, are allowed (**Note:** These are the only eligible motorcycles allowed to use a power-valve mechanism.)
- KX250 meeting Ultima guidelines up to 1984 is allowed.

12.3.4 **ULTIMA 500:** For certain 325-580cc motorcycles produced within the guidelines of the Ultima Class specifications.

Eligible machines include but are not limited to:
- 1982-'83 Can-Am Sonic with Rotax four-stroke engine
- 1983-'84 Husqvarna 510 four-strokes
- 1981-'83 Honda CR450/480, 1981-82 XR500. 1983 XR500 is prohibited.
- 1980-'81 Kawasaki KX420; KX500 meeting Ultima guidelines up to 1984 is allowed.
- 1982-'84 Maico and/or MStar, air-cooled drum brake only.
- 1983-'84 Yamaha TT600 (**Note:** XT600 is prohibited). This is the only model allowed that is over 580cc (the maximum overbore is +.080").

12.3.5 **ULTIMA FOUR-STROKE:** Certain 200cc-580cc four-stroke motorcycles produced with either single-shock rear suspension or an engine of newer technology.

Eligible motorcycles and modifications include:
- 1982-'84 Can-Am Sonic with Rotax engine
- 1981-'82 Honda XR200/250/500 with Pro-Link rear suspension (1983 XR500 is prohibited). 1983 model XR350 with RFVC is allowed. XL350 models are prohibited.
- 1983-'85 Husqvarna TC, TE, TX 510 four-stroke
- 1983-'84 Yamaha TT600 (**Note:** XT600 is prohibited). This is the only model allowed that is over 580cc (the maximum overbore is +.080").

12.4 ADDITIONAL CLASSES
12.4.1 **Open Age:** Any rider on any size or type of eligible machine.
12.4.2 **40+:** Riders age 40 and older on any size or type of eligible machine.
12.4.3 **50+:** Riders age 50 and older on any size or type of eligible machine.
12.4.4 **60+:** Riders age 60 and older on any size or type of eligible machine.
12.4.5 **70+:** Riders age 70 and older on any size or type of eligible machine.

Note: A rider may not advance to the next age-related class until after that birthday. Due to difficulties in laying out the race day program, competitors may enter no more than two rider-age classes.

12.4.6 **WOMEN:** Female riders on any size or type of eligible machine.
   a) Historic Novice
   b) Grand Prix Novice
   c) Ultima Novice
   d) Post Vintage Novice Age 40+
   e) Post Vintage Novice Age 60+
   f) Post Vintage Women Novice

12.5 TECH INSPECTION AND MODIFICATIONS

   a) **SUSPENSION:** The field check for rear wheel travel, where applicable, is as follows: 1) Both shocks are removed from the bike, then one bare (without spring) damper unit is reinstalled. 2) The machine is supported in such a fashion that the rear suspension is at maximum extension, and a measurement is taken from the center of the rear axle to a point marked directly above the axle on the rear fender or subframe. 3) With both wheels on the ground, the rear suspension is fully compressed by the examiner with the rider aboard to compress any rubber bumpers; a measurement is again taken from the center of the rear axle to the same marked point above. 4) The measurement obtained in step 3 subtracted from the measurement in step 2 is the wheel travel.

   An alternative method of determining wheel travel may be used by tech inspectors using a pre-programmed computer. The program converts three dimensions—distance from swingarm pivot to rear axle, to lower shock mount and top shock mount—to show the amount of travel of the shock shaft plus 50 percent of the rubber bumper. Due to the use of non-standard or different types rubber bumpers, this check may be overridden by the tech inspector's discretion. Manual measurement of shock movement is the overriding factor in determining whether a shock is legal.

   b) Alloy swingarms in the Historic classes must be period aftermarket or OEM units. Use of later-model OEM alloy swingarms on Historic-class motorcycles is prohibited. Modification of Ultima-class single-shock alloy swingarms for use on dual-shock Gran Prix motorcycles is prohibited. Use of period aftermarket or accurate replica alloy swingarms in all Post Vintage classes is allowed.

   c) **ENGINES:** Modifications are many, though they must be consistent with the spirit of the period and class. Cylinders may be overbored a maximum of .080" on singles, .060" on twins, .040" on triples and .020" on fours.

   d) **CARBURETORS:** Period-type carburetors are strongly encouraged. Period flat-slide carbs are allowed on Historic and Gran Prix class motorcycles. Examples include Lake, Lectron, Posa and other period-type flat-slides. Active accelerator- pump-equipped carburetors are allowed only on Ultima-class motorcycles; all others must be disconnected or removed, even if OEM-equipped. Dell'Orto accelerator pump carburetors are allowed in the Historic and Gran Prix classes only if the accelerator pump mechanism is disconnected or removed. Period flat-slide Mikuni TM carburetors are allowed only on Ultima class motorcycles. Mikuni TMX and Keihin PJ and PWK flat-slide carburetors are not permitted. Modern D-shape-slide or similar equivalent aftermarket OKO, and Chinese made reproduction carburetors are not allowed in AHRMA Post Vintage off-road competition.

   e) Hydraulically-assisted clutches are prohibited.
   f) For Gran Prix and Ultima machines, any OEM or aftermarket fork may be used up to and including the Ultima era.

g) All motorcycles must be equipped with a functional handlebar-mounted kill switch.
h) Footpegs must be folding type and should fold back at a 45-degree angle.
i) Sidestands and protruding lugs must be removed or rubber-covered. At the discretion of the Tech Inspector, certain sidestands which are completely tucked away may be left in place but must be safety wired or strapped in the folded position.
j) Disc brakes are prohibited (except OEM on Rokon and Yankee). Hydraulically-assisted drum brakes are prohibited. OEM Yamaha and Honda motocross and off-road dual-leading-shoe front brake hubs are allowed only in the Grand Prix and Ultima classes.
k) Paddle-type tires are prohibited.
l) All two-stroke machines must be fitted with efficient silencers.
m) Minicycles are prohibited. All machines must have a minimum OEM wheel size of 17 inches.
n) All modifications must be consistent with the spirit of the class and period. The burden of authenticating is on the rider. Press clippings and photos with identifiable dates may be helpful.
o) Appearance and workmanship of a reasonable standard shall be enforced.
p) **NUMBERS AND NUMBER PLATES:** All machines must display three number plates -- one mounted on the front and one on each side, mounted in a way that they will not be blocked by the rider. For race number policies, please see SECTION 3.9.
   1. Numbers must be six-inches tall. If a rider's assigned competition number ends with a letter, that letter must be at least three-inches tall, and placed in the lower-right corner of the number plate. For assigned competition numbers that begin with a letter, that letter must be six-inches tall, and placed to the left of the numeric digits. It is strongly recommended—and may be required at some events—that riders also display three-inch numbers on each side of their helmet and eight-inch numbers on the back of their jersey.
   2. All number plates will use a "school bus yellow" background with black numbers and letters. Competitors on machines eligible for AHRMA's Vintage MX program may retain their black-on-white number plates and Vintage number but must inform Registration. To help solve past scoring problems, no other colors may be used.
   3. It is the rider's responsibility to ensure number legibility. If a rider appeals his/her score and numbers are not properly displayed, the protest will be disallowed. There will be no exceptions to this rule.

4. Expert-class champions from the previous year will be awarded a No. 1 plate (with a letter suffix), which they may use in any class during the season. If they choose not to use their assigned AHRMA competition number, it will be held for them until the following season. A rider who wins more than one class championship should use only one of the No. 1/letter combinations to aid in scoring and identification.

Number/letter combinations for each Expert class champion are:

Historic 500	1A	Ultima 500	1H
Historic Four-Stroke	1B	Ultima 250	1J
Historic 250	1C	Ultima 125	1K
Historic 125	1D	Ultima Four-Stroke	1S
Gran Prix 500	1E	Open Age	1L
Gran Prix 250	1F	40+	1M
Gran Prix 125	1G	50+	1N
Gran Prix Four-Stroke	1R	60+	1P
Women	1W	70+	1Q
Pre-Modern 125	1T	Pre-Modern 250	1U
Pre-Modern 500	1V	Pre-Modern 4-Stroke	1X

All competitors must display their AHRMA-assigned number unless granted prior permission to run a different number at that event only.

5. In addition to the rules in Section 11, riders must comply with all applicable rules in Sections 3 (events and race procedure), 4 (entry procedure) and 6 (offenses, penalties, protests and appeals), rule 9.7.11 (fuel) and rule 9.7.17 (AHRMA decals; two required and may be placed on any readily-visible part of the motorcycle).

6. Steering dampers are not allowed unless OEM or friction-type.

12.6 GENERAL MOTOCROSS RULES

The following rules in the Vintage Motocross section also apply to AHRMA Post Vintage MX:

- **11.3 Motocross Rider Grading System** (Note: Rule 11.3h, dual-ability level, does not apply in Post Vintage classes.)
- All AHRMA Post Vintage motocross classes are further divided into Intermediate and Expert categories. Novice classes are as follows: Historic, Grand Prix, Ultima, Pre-Modern, Open Age, 40-60, 60+ and Women. There are no displacement classifications in any Novice class. All Novice classes shall run in Novice-only motos and shall not be combined in a moto with any Intermediate or Expert class.
- **11.4 Equipment Required of All Motocross Riders**
- **11.5 Scoring at AHRMA Events**
- **11.6 Series Points Awards**
- **11.7 Race Procedures**

page 110   *2024 AHRMA HANDBOOK_REV 2024.02.23*

■ SECTION 13—OBSERVED TRIALS

MISSION STATEMENT: Observed trials is a very significant part of historic motorcycle competition. It began as a wintertime sport for European enthusiasts, who tested themselves by tracing ancient Roman roads. These riders negotiated various obstacles along the way, all of which gave test to both man and machine. As the "gentleman's sport" developed, such obstacles became more specific, and more challenging. From the 1980s until today, the obstacles presented to trials competitors have been inconceivable for most motorcycle riders.

AHRMA's observed trials goal is to provide its members a safe, historically accurate environment to showcase and experience vintage machinery. The key to this enjoyment is the observed sections. From the 1950s into the '70s, sections were mainly composed of wide-open areas of challenging terrain, with the rider's choice of line determining his/her success. Observed sections reminiscent of this era are critical in AHRMA's representation of classic observed trials. With period-accurate sections, machines will remain true to their original concept, and the techniques required to ride them will do the same, enhancing the entire vintage trials scene. The trials-riding experience will undoubtedly result in good friends, good rides, and good fun.

<u>**NOTE:**</u> <u>A 3-year moratorium on adding new observed trials classes is in effect, beginning in 2024.</u>

13.1 CLASSES

All of the following classes are further divided into the following ability levels: Expert, Intermediate and Novice. A non-points-scoring **Beginner** class is available to riders on any AHRMA-legal machine (see 13.3b). There is no minimum age for riders.

13.1.1 **PREMIER HEAVYWEIGHT:** Certain pre-1965 era and like design, non-unit construction (separate, removable gearbox), four-stroke machines, 350cc and larger. Examples: BSA B32, Ariel HT, Triumph Trophy, Royal Enfield Bullet, etc., or accurate replicas of such machines. Modifications and major components are limited to the era and must be typical of the heavyweight machines of the 1960s. The following requirements apply to Triumph unit twin works replicas: Any unit Triumph twin engine may be used; the standard pre-1966 twin frame and rear hub must be employed; only the rear frame section may be modified to period specifications; must use any year all-steel Triumph forks, standard length; must use any year all-steel Triumph oil tank; must use any Triumph steel or iron front hub; and may use any period gas tank, seat, rims, etc.

13.1.2 **PREMIER LIGHTWEIGHT:** Certain pre-1965 era and like design, unit- or non-unit construction, two- or four-stroke machines, 250cc and smaller. Also, unit-construction, four-stroke machines over 300cc. Examples: Greeves, Dot, Cotton (Villiers-powered), unit-construction BSA singles or twins, Royal Enfield Crusader, Triumph Cub, Triumph 500 unit twin or Triumph-powered Greeves. Hondas are limited to CB160, CL72 and CL77. Modifications and major components are limited to those of the era, typical of machines in the 1960s.

13.1.3 **RIGID LIGHTWEIGHT:** Any non-swing-arm machine, including those equipped with plunger or sprung-hub rear suspension, typical of those used in the pre-swing-arm era. Engine displacement up to 300cc, as manufactured, two- and four-strokes. Modifications and major components are limited to those typically used into the 1950s. Ceriani-type forks are not allowed.

13.1.4 **RIGID HEAVYWEIGHT:** Chassis and modifications as above, utilizing 301cc and larger non-unit-construction four-stroke engines.

13.1.5 **GIRDER FORK:** Any rigid-frame, girder-fork machine. Modifications and major components are limited to those of the era, typical of pre-war machines. Plunger frames and sprung hubs are not permitted.

13.1.6 **MODERN CLASSIC:** Any unit-construction machine up to and including model year 1979. Examples: Bultaco 125 and five-speed 250-350, Suzuki RL250 & TS models, Beamish Suzuki, Montesa Cota 123-348, Ossa 250-350 MAR and BLT, Yamaha TY175/250 & AT/CT/DT models, Kawasaki KT250 & enduro models, Honda TL125/250 & SL/XL models, GRM Maverick rigid frames with four-stroke engines. TMI-framed Hondas and Frazier frames are eligible. Modifications and major components are limited to those of the era, typical of machines of the mid-'70s. SWM, Fantic or Beta motorcycles are not allowed.

13.1.7 **CLASSIC:** Any kit-framed two-stroke machine 175cc or less. Examples: Wassell, Penton, Gaunt, Minarelli-powered Cotton, Puch-powered Greeves, Dalesman and Hodaka specials. Also any Spanish four-speed up to 250cc in original OEM frame. Examples: Ossa four-speed, Montesa four-speed, Bultaco four-speed, also GRM Maverick rigid frames with Classic-legal engines and GRM four-speed. Eligible four-strokes include those legal for Premier Lightweight and Honda S90 and SL90.

13.1.8 **MODERN TWIN SHOCK:** Post 1979 factory-designed twin shock motorcycles with drum brakes and air-cooled engines.

Eligible machines include:
- Beamish Suzuki
- Beta TR240
- Bultaco 6 speed
- Cagiva 350
- Fantic 80, 125, 200, 240, 300
- Garelli
- Honda TLR200, TLR250, Reflex, Seeley and Metatechno
- Italjet Montesa 242, 348, 349
- JCM
- OSSA Gripper, BLT
- Merlin
- Yamaha Majesty 175, 200, 250

13.1.9 **BEGINNER:** A non-championship class for beginning trials riders on any motorcycle eligible for AHRMA trials.

13.1.10 **VINTAGE YOUTH CLASSES:** AHRMA Vintage Youth Classes are open to any rider through 14 years old. Skill levels are: Youth A riding the "2" line, Youth B riding the "3" line, and Youth C riding the "4" line. There is no minimum age requirement, just an ability to ride the loop and attempt the sections.
Eligible machines include any air-cooled, twin shock, drum brake motorcycle as manufactured of 125cc or less. Examples include 1974-1975 Yamaha TY80s, some European Mini Trials bikes, and "homebuilt" specials using period correct components and techniques.

g) **YOUTH A:** Rides the "2" line
h) **YOUTH B:** Rides the "3" line
i) **YOUTH C:** Rides the "4" line

13.1.11 **AIR COOLED MONO** (ACM) with drum brakes only. Trials machines manufactured just after the twin shock era, but before significant performance advances were introduced to trials bike technology.
Typically, mid-to-late 1980s models.

Eligible machines include:

- Yamaha TY250/350 monos
- Honda RTL250
- Beta TR32-34
- GasGas Halley 325
- JCM 32
- Montesa 304/330
- Fantic 301
- Merlin DG350 mono
- Mecatechno Dragonfly
- Armstrong 240-350
- Can-Am 240-350
- Alfer TX300
- Aprilia TX125-311, etc.

Some of these machines came standard with disc brakes (particularly on front), and period correct retrofits are permitted.

Eligible drum brake machines include:

- 1984-1987 Yamaha TY250/350 monos
- 1985-1986 Honda RTL250
- Beta TR32
- JCM – all drum brake models
- 1986 Fantic 301
- Armstrong 240-350 – drum brake models only
- Can-Am 240-350 – drum brake models only

13.1.12 At the discretion of the trials promoter, non-AHRMA support classes may be run at regional and national events.

NOTE: It is the rider's responsibility to consult with the Trials Rules & Eligibility Committee to determine class eligibility. This is especially important when building a special which is not traditionally used as a trials machine.

13.2 TECHNICAL INSPECTION AND MODIFICATIONS

13.2.1 **TIRES AND WHEELS:** Trials tires are required in all classes. Motocross knobby-type tires may be used in the Beginner class at the discretion of the promoter. Any pre-1975 hubs and any type of rim from the proper era for that machine are acceptable. Only the Modern Classic class may use pre-1980 components.

13.2.2 **SUSPENSION:** No single-shock or cantilever-type-suspension machines may compete, except Vincent. Suspension travel is limited to four-inches in the rear and seven-inches in the front. Rear dampers may be replaced with any units using technology available prior to December 31, 1974. Ossa Bolger Long Travel (BLT) machines may compete in Modern Classic, with rear wheel travel limited to four-inches.

13.2.3 **SOUND:** Silencers are required; no machine may compete with an open exhaust system.

13.2.4 **No major components may be later than 1974** (specifically, engine, frame, gearbox, fork, and hubs). Only Modern Classic may use components later than 1974 (but limited to pre-1980). Hydraulically-assisted brakes and clutches are prohibited.

13.2.5 **All motorcycles must comply with all applicable AHRMA competition and safety rules**, including rule 3.2.6 (AHRMA decals), 3.3.8 (operating brakes) and 11.2d (handlebar-mounted kill switch). Fuel shall be gasoline only; maximum 115 octane [using formula (R+M)/2].

13.2.6 **ALL MODIFICATIONS MUST BE CONSISTENT WITH THE SPIRIT OF THE CLASS.** Period modifications have been extensively documented and machines with obvious non-period or excessive modifications will be disqualified or required to compete in the next-higher-level class. Two-strokes in Classic classes must have piston-port induction; reed valves will be permitted if it was a factory modification by a recognized service agent in the same production series for such motorcycle. 125cc and smaller would also be exempt are not legal. Only round-slide carburetors may be used (see 11.2.c)

13.2.7 When entering a "special" constructed from various pre-1974 components of different classes and eras, the machine must be entered in the latest class that either the chassis or the engine dictates. **Example:** Triumph Cub engine in a five-speed Bultaco frame rides in the Modern Classic class. Otter-type chassis are not allowed in Premier and must run in Classic or Modern Classic.

13.2.8 **NUMBER PLATES:**
a) All machines must have a front number plate with a white background at least 5x5-inches with a black number or letters at least three inches tall, indicating the line that will be ridden.
b) In an instance where two riders competing on different lines are sharing one machine, it is each rider's responsibility to notify the Observer which line is being attempted.

13.2.9 The rider, not the motorcycle, is the entry. A rider may switch to another motorcycle at any time during the event, provided the second machine is eligible for the class in which the rider is entered.

13.3 CLASS AND ABILITY LEVELS

The sections of an AHRMA trial course are divided into various "lines" of difficulty as follows:

a) The number-four line is extremely simple and, except for Girder Fork and Rigid Novice competitors, is intended only for entry-level riders. If only three lines are used, number-four riders will ride the number-three line.
b) The riders in the Beginner class using the number-four line may compete on any AHRMA-legal machine and will be scored together in one class.
c) A rider's ability level is shown on his/her AHRMA membership card. A change in a rider's ability level must be done with the approval of the AHRMA National office and the change will be indicated on the rider's AHRMA membership card.
d) Riders may be asked to advance in ability level by the AHRMA Trials Rules & Eligibility Committee or an AHRMA-recognized grading committee. A rider may advance in ability levels at his/her own discretion (see (f) below), but must receive permission from the grading committee to move down in ability level if the committee's evaluation concludes that the rider would be better suited at that lower level.
e) A rider may only enter one class per day.

f) A rider will ride for an entire calendar year at the ability level as shown on his/her AHRMA membership card, with the following exception: A rider may temporarily ride an ability level higher than indicated on the membership card if:
   1. The rider declares the intention to move up at registration
   2. The rider rides no more than the total number of events that equal the number of rounds needed to qualify for national championship points, minus one.

   Example: If four rounds are needed to qualify for national points, then the rider may ride three rounds without permanently advancing his/her ability level. If the rider does permanently move up in ability level, the rounds ridden before formally moving up will then count toward National championship points.

g) Members of the AHRMA Trials Rules & Eligibility Committee shall make up the trials grading committee.

h) Typically, a Trialmaster will lay-out four separate "lines" within each section, marked 1, 2, 3 or 4, to correspond with the number on each rider's number plate. Some Trialmasters may elect to designate a separate PI line within the sections. When utilizing the four-line format, PI riders will ride either the 2 or the 3 line, at the discretion of the Trialmaster. In this instance, the Section Begins card is to be marked "PI=2" or "PI=3." Likewise, riders with EX on their number plates will find "EX=1" or "EX=2" on the Section Begins card.

i) A number 4-line shall always be made available for Beginners at both National and Regional trials events.

TRIALS LINES BY CLASS & ABILITY LEVEL
(Numbers indicate which line to ride)

CLASS	MASTERS	EXPERT	INTERMEDIATE	NOVICE
MODERN TWIN SHOCK	1	EX	2	3
MODERN CLASSIC	1	EX	2	3
CLASSIC		2	PI	3
PREMIER LIGHTWEIGHT		2	PI	3
PREMIER HEAVYWEIGHT		2	PI	3
RIGID		PI	3	3
GIRDER FORK		3	3	4
BEGINNER	4			

Premier Intermediate, Classic Intermediate and Rigid Expert riders are to display "PI" on their front number plate

Modern Classic and Modern Twin Shock Expert riders are to display "EX" on their front number plate

13.4 EVENT PROCEDURES

13.4.1 The object of observed trials is to ride specified "sections" with "Start" and "End" gates and side boundaries. The right-side outermost boundary is to be marked with a red ribbon, and the left-side with blue ribbon. Any markings within a section may be marked with a color other than red or blue. Scoring will be based on the "points-lost" (marks) system. The numerical score will increase from a starting score of zero. Final placement will be inverse to the numerical score; i.e. the lowest score wins. The sections are laid out in a loop configuration, where the competitor rides each of the sections one at a time before his/her subsequent attempts.

a) Section Scoring shall begin when the machine's front wheel axle passes the "Start" markers and stops when the front axle passes the "End" markers. The rider is required to ride the sections toward the side of the split gates on which the arrows are displayed. Section points are allocated as follows:

Error	Penalty Points (mark)
None (clean section)	0
One dab	1
Two dabs	2
Three or more dabs	3
Failure in a section	5
Section not attempted	10

A rider is penalized in each section only for the one error that results in the most penalty points. In any given section, penalties are not cumulative, except for the first three "dabs." (Example: If a rider dabs twice before riding out of bounds, the score for the section is 5 points, not 7).

b) Sections are to be separately numbered and should be ridden in numerical sequence. No section may be ridden more than once per lap without consent of the Course Marshal. Riders shall start Loop One at the point designated at the rider's meeting by the Course Marshal. Second and subsequent loops will start at Section One. The loop must be ridden in one direction only.

c) If a rider completes at least one full loop before retiring, the rider will be scored as having finished the event and will be assessed 10 points for each subsequent section required to complete the event.

d) Unsportsmanlike conduct or offensive behavior can result in a penalty of 10 points at the sole discretion of any Observer or authorized event official.

e) A lost loop card will result in a score of 10 points per section for that loop.

f) Practice in any marked section before or during the event will result in disqualification of the rider from the event. Riders may stop and inspect sections on foot prior to riding for a score, providing their machine is parked off the course.

g) While walking the section, a rider that alters a section by moving rocks, making a path, changing the condition of the section, etc. shall be given a score of 5 by the Observer for that section.

h) When a rider leaves his/her machine to inspect the section, the machine does not hold the rider's place in line. When the rider returns to the motorcycle, he/she goes to the back of the line. Failure to do so may result in a five-point penalty.

i) The rider must obtain permission from the Observer to enter the section for a score. Failure to obtain permission may result in a score of 5 points if the Observer is unable to monitor the competitor's ride though the entire section.

j) Time limits may be imposed in any one of a number of ways. At the riders' meeting, the promoter or Course Marshal shall announce the type of time limitations being implemented, and any details thereof.
k) A punch-type scorecard is normally utilized, and will be carried by the competitor in a way that does not obscure the number plate. At events where separate scorecards are used for each loop, the rider will turn in his/her scorecard to the scorekeeper when the loop is complete, and obtain a new scorecard for the next loop.
l) It is the sole responsibility of the rider to make sure his/her scorecards are properly marked at each section, are completed with the rider's name and class information, and are turned in to the scorekeeper on time.
m) All competitors, whether completing the entire event or not, must turn in their scorecards to the scoring area before the end of the event. A competitor who does not do so will receive a "DNF" (did not finish) status for the events and will not receive series points.
n) The scorekeeper will post each competitor's individual loop points, time penalty (if applicable) and final score by class and ability level. The rider with the lowest number of points will be declared the winner in his/her classification.
o) In the case of a tie score, the winner will be the competitor with the most cleans. If the tie is still unbroken, the oldest rider will be the winner.

13.4.2 PROTESTS
a) It is the rider's responsibility to acknowledge his/her score on each section immediately upon completion of the attempt. Disagreement with the Observer must be noted and settled, if possible, without inconveniencing or delaying other riders, while the situation is fresh in everyone's mind. Section scoring protests will not be heard if the Observer was not made aware of the conflict immediately after the section attempt. If the rider elects to protest, he shall file a formal written protest with the Course Marshal not later than 30 minutes after the attempt in question.
b) No person may protest another rider's score in a section. Only the rider can protest a penalty. Any rider may protest any matter relating to the event. All protests must be in writing and filed with the Course Marshal not later than 30 minutes after the scoring results have been posted. The Course Marshal shall render all decisions on protests as soon as possible.
c) Even though awards may be announced on the day of the event, the results shall not be come official until all decisions on protests have been finalized and the results have been checked for incorrect calculations.

13.5 DEFINITIONS FOR TRIALS RULES
a) **GENERAL DEFINITIONS**
Axle In - Axle Out: All scoring is to take place as the front wheel axle passes an imaginary straight line between the "Start" markers and all scoring is to cease as the front axle passes an imaginary straight line between the "End" markers. If a split marker is used at either gate, the imaginary line runs between the "Start" or "End" marker and the split marker.
Balk: While riding a section for a score, a rider is severely distracted or his line is blocked by spectators, other riders, an animal, blowing debris, etc., the rider may claim a "balk" and request a re-ride. At the discretion of the Observer, a re-ride of the section may be permitted, with the score of the re-ride the one to be counted.

Course Marshal: The Course Marshal is the person with final authority for all aspects of the event and has the ability to perform any of the workers' duties on the day.

DNF (Did Not Finish): A competitor who retires before attempting all sections on the first loop is DNF and will not receive series points.

Observer: Any event official who is authorized to score a competitor's ride. Observers report directly to the Course Marshal.

Rider's Meeting: Meeting for all competitors, prior to start time, at which the promoter or Course Marshal gives the final instructions for the day's event. This meeting is intended to be an open format to allow competitors to ask for clarification of any rules or procedures.

"Rider!": Term used by an Observer to notify a competitor that he/she has permission to enter the section **and** to simultaneously notify all persons walking the section to immediately vacate. The competitor riding for a score always has the right-of-way within a section. Failure to vacate can be deemed unsportsmanlike conduct.

b) **SCORING DEFINITIONS**

Clean: No points (zero). The rider completes the section without committing an error.

Dab: Any intentional contact ("dab") between a rider's foot, or any other part of the body, and a supporting surface or object either inside or outside the boundary is scored one point.

Examples:

1. Rider removes a foot from the footpeg and touches the ground once to maintain balance or extends the foot out to push off of a vertical object such as a tree = 1 point.
2. Rider's feet are on the footpegs and hands are on the handlebars when any part of his/her body inadvertently brushes against or is hit by a vertical object = 0 points.
3. Rider's foot is accidentally knocked from the footpeg after unintentional contact with a rock or other object = 0 points.
4. Rider removes hand from the handlebar and reaches to touch or "push off" an object = 1 point.
5. Rider's foot rotates or pivots on the ground without picking up or dragging the foot = 1 point.
6. Rider's foot touches the ground or an object on the outside of the section-marking ribbon, while the machine remains inside the section = 1 point.
7. Touching both feet to the ground at the same time while astride the machine = 2 points (one dab for each foot).
8. Rider drags or slides one or both feet while astride the machine and maintains forward motion = 3 points.
9. Footing: three or more dabs, or paddling with both feet = 3 points.
10. A machine with a dead engine that is paddled out of the section without loss of forward motion (rider may not dismount) = 3 points
11. A machine with a dead engine is ridden out of the "End" gate without loss of forward motion and the rider does not dab = 0 points.
12. An engine dies and is restarted without loss of forward motion and the rider does not dab = 0 points.

Failure: The following instances during a section attempt will result in a score of five points:
1. A complete loss of forward motion whether intentional or not, with or without the rider dabbing.
2. Rider dismount: both feet to the ground on the same side or behind the machine.
3. Rider receives outside assistance (not to be confused with interference that results in a balk).
4. The motorcycle crosses its own track with both wheels (unless the section is so designed and is duly noted by the Observer or Course Marshal).
5. Either tire breaks, removes, or knocks over a section marker or a ribbon defining the rider's line (i.e., "1" markers for the 1-line rider, "2" markers for the 2-line rider, etc.) in a manner that requires the marker to be reset. A rider may knock over any section marker that does not define his/her line without penalty.
6. Missing a marker: rider completely misses or goes on the wrong side of a marker, including split gates within a section. If your line number is NOT on a split gate you may go to either side.
7. Ribbon out-of-bounds: a machine may ride on a ribbon, but not beyond it. There must be ground visible between the inner edge of the tire and wrong side of the ribbon to be considered a 5. This also applies to the ribbon used in a split gate.

13.6 SERIES POINTS, AWARDS

The National Championship Trials Series runs from January 1 to December 31 of each year. The official schedule of events that award series points will be published in *AHRMA MAG*. A competitor will earn National Championship points for each series event based on the rider's finish position as follows:

Position	Points	Position	Points
1	20	8	7
2	16	9	6
3	13	10	5
4	11	11	4
5	10	12	3
6	9	13	2
7	8	14	1

a) Riders receive National Championship points only if they enter the event and ride in the ability class indicated on their AHRMA membership card.
b) A rider will receive points if he or she is the sole competitor in a class.
c) Even though the Beginner class is included in a National Championship trial, the competitors in this class will receive awards from that day but will not earn National Championship Series points.
d) <u>National Championship Series year-end awards are based on a rider's best finishes in a maximum number of events. The maximum number of "best finishes" to count toward the championship will be specified by the Off Road Director and announced prior to the beginning of each season. A rider must earn points in the minimum number of events specified by the Off Road Director to be eligible for year-end awards. In the event of a year-end scoring tie, the advantage will go to the rider who accumulated the most points at the National Championship Final. If after the Final there is still a tie, the older rider on the date of the Final will win.</u>

e) National-championship events may also award regional-series points. A competitor may not be charged any additional entry fee to earn regional points.
f) At any AHRMA national trial, all sections must be managed by an observer. A rider will receive his/her score from only the observer. If it is not possible for the promoter or coordinator to supply enough observers to cover each section, the number of sections must be reduced. The number of loops may be increased to make up the discrepancy in the number of sections.
g) Support class will be offered at AHRMA nationals trials.

■ SECTION 14 - DIRT TRACK

MISSION STATEMENT: Dirt track racing has been the mainstay of American motorcycling since the earliest days and blossomed into a unique American sport with the advent of Class C racing by the AMA in the 1930s. The proliferation of dirt ovals throughout America led to further development of this 100% American sport up through the 1970s, resulting in several distinctly different forms of racing motorcycles—each developed to suit the rules of the time period and optimized for dirt oval racing.

The American Historic Racing Motorcycle Association has attempted to preserve the sights and sounds of this uniquely-American sport and display it to the public by providing a set of governing rules intended to capture each distinct period of dirt track racing (Class C, brakeless, vintage, and Seventies-era) and pit the motorcycles of that period against each other in fair competition and types of motorcycles which are historically under-represented in modern dirt track racing. Races are held on a variety of dirt tracks, ranging from short tracks, half-miles, miles, and Tourist Trophy circuits, with National points awarded to encourage participation and recognize achievement. The rules are written to provide safe and suitable competition classes for as many period motorcycles as possible while maintaining level competition between different types and preserving the historical basis for each class. A concerted effort is made to maintain a stable rules structure so that members may participate with their machines for an extended period of time without having to upgrade or modify their motorcycles to adapt to changing rules. The Committee strongly recommends no front brakes on <u>Dirt</u> Track Machines.

Our objectives are:
a) To provide a set of consistent competition rules to govern the dirt track competition classes with the acknowledged intent of preserving the historically significant periods of American dirt track racing cited above.
b) To sanction a series of appropriate public racing venues for members to compete and spectators to enjoy this American sport, with special attention paid to race track safety and suitability for historic machines, especially the brakeless classes, as well as to ensure a reasonable geographic spread of events.
c) To encourage competition and recognize accomplishments by administering a national championship series for each AHRMA dirt track class.
d) To actively promote AHRMA dirt track racing and events so as to reach a broad spectator base and expose the public to historical dirt track racing.
e) To actively promote safe competition, monitor rider skills and behavior and continually address rider and member concerns.
f) To provide a forum for communication via *AHRMA MAG*, the AHRMA web site and any other appropriate means to convey dirt track information and event news.

14.1 RIDER ELIGIBILITY/EQUIPMENT:

a) Competitors must demonstrate that they can ride up to Junior level, or be vouched for in writing by an AHRMA-accredited dirt track rider.
b) Riders who have raced as a professional Expert (or have accumulated enough points to qualify) in the preceding 12 months may not compete in AHRMA dirt track events, to protect AHRMA amateur riders. Pro-Sport/Pro-Am riders and Division 2 and Division 3 speedway riders are eligible to compete.
c) Any rider entered in an AHRMA Novice class event may not compete in any other AHRMA classes that day.
d) Rider age:
Displacement/Age Progression:
Vintage Classes:
- 0-500cc's 4-stroke- 16yrs old or older (with Minor Release and Waiver of Liability and Indemnity Agreement* under 18yrs)
- 501cc's and up 4-stroke- 18yrs old and older
- 0-400cc's 2-stroke- 16yrs old or older (with Minor Release and Waiver of Liability and Indemnity Agreement* under 18yrs)
- 401cc's and up 2-stroke- 18yrs old and older

Modern Classes:
- 0-250cc's 2- and 4-stroke- 16yrs old and up (with Minor Release and Waiver of Liability and Indemnity Agreement* under 18yrs)
- 251cc's and up 2- and 4-stroke- 18yrs old and up

18 years plus:
- Dinosaur
- Light Brakeless
- Heavy Brakeless
- Sportsman 750
- Vintage Heavy
- Hooligan

16 years minimum:
- Sportsman 125
- Sportsman 250
- Sportsman 600
- Seventies Singles
- Spanish Cup
- Vintage Light
- Novice
- 250 Pro/Am
- 450 Pro/Am
- Mad Dog

*Note: see section 19.13 for Minor Release and Waiver of Liability and Indemnity Agreement information

e) Riders must wear full leathers on track a half-mile in length or longer. Leathers are strongly recommended for all types of dirt track races. The use of back protectors is strongly recommended. Boots covering at least the top of the ankle and gloves are required of all competitors. Helmets must be full-facial type and certified by the manufacturer by having a sticker affixed to the helmet stating the helmet meets or exceeds the Snell M2010 standard or other applicable standards listed in rule 3.3.14.

14.2 DIRT TRACK and TT CLASSES

14.2.1 **DINOSAUR:** 1951 and earlier, 500cc OHV or 750cc sidevalve. Like-design models also are permitted. All major components must be OEM parts that existed prior to 1951, or accurate, detailed replicas of the same parts using the same type materials and technologies. The burden of authenticating is upon the rider.

Press clippings and photos with identifiable date may be helpful. There are no restrictions on internal modifications, except the stroke may not be changed from the original specifications and the bore may not exceed the .080" overbore limit.

14.2.2 **LIGHT BRAKELESS:** Open to all machines 1968 and older up to and including 300cc. The motorcycle engine, transmission and frame must be from the same manufacturer and model. An aftermarket rigid racing frame may be substituted, e.g., Sonicweld or Swanson.

14.2.3 **HEAVY BRAKELESS:** Open to all machines 1968 and older 301cc and larger. The motorcycle engine, transmission and frame must be from the same manufacturer and model, an aftermarket rigid racing frame may be substituted, e.g., Sonicweld or Swanson.

14.2.4 **SPORTSMAN 125:** Motorcycles using 125cc two-stroke or four-stroke production engines in either production or aftermarket racing frames of the period (up to 1974 and like design). Engines must have been manufactured for 125cc or smaller displacement machines; engines originally manufactured as larger than 125cc may not be downsized for this class.

Eligible machines include but are not limited to:
- Bridgestone Bultaco Lobito or Sherpa S
- DKW Hodaka 90 or 100
- Harley-Davidson/Aermacchi Baja 100
- Honda CT90 or CB/CL/SL/XL100
- Indian
- Kawasaki 90 or 100
- Moto Beta
- Penton
- Rickman-Hodaka
- Sachs
- Suzuki TC/TS90 or TS/TM100
- Yamaha YL1E, HT1, LT2 or DT/MX100
- Zundapp

a) Aftermarket frames are limited to those using technology and design from the period (up to 1974).
b) Hubs and forks may be period racing type, or production items from the period.

14.2.5 **SPORTSMAN 250:** 1974 and earlier machines up to 250cc, including like-design models.

Eligible machines include:

- Bultaco, all
- Can-Am 175; all 250cc machines must run in Seventies Two-Stroke
- CZ single-port
- Greeves Griffon 250
- Harley-Davidson two-strokes; MX250-based machines must run in Seventies Two-Stroke
- Honda CR250M, XL250
- Husqvarna, pre-reed-valve, plus '74 Mag 250CR
- Kawasaki A1R, Greenstreak 238, pre-reed-valve KX250 (engine number K2E900001-K2E911400 only)
- Maico square-barrel and radial, up to GP
- Montesa, all five-speed
- Ossa four-speed w/DMR frame, all five-speed
- Suzuki T250, TM250, TS250 all
- Yamaha DT singles (engine # prefix DT1, 438 or 450), MX250 (#364), YZ250 (#431 or 483)
- Yamaha air-cooled twins up through RD250 or TD3B

Note: Yamaha singles with engine number prefixes 509, 1W3, 2K7 or later are prohibited.

14.2.6 **SPORTSMAN 360:** 1974 and earlier machines manufactured as 251-600cc, including like-design models.

Eligible machines include:

- Bultaco, all 350, 360, 370 five-speed
- CZ single-port 360, 380
- Greeves Griffon 380
- Honda CB350, CB450, 500T
- Kawasaki Bighorn 350, F12M, KX450, 1975-'76 KX400
- Maico square-barrel and radial, up to GP
- Suzuki T350, TM400, TS400, T500
- Yamaha RT singles (Engine # prefix RT1), DT360 (#446), MX360 (#365), YZ360 (#432 or 484), SC500 (#363)
- Yamaha air-cooled twins TR2, TR3, R5, RD350, TX500
- Honda XL350.

a) Yamaha TT/XT/SR500s are prohibited.
b) Yamaha singles after serial #484 are prohibited.

14.2.7 **SPORTSMAN 750:** 1974 and earlier machines manufactured as 601-750cc, including like-design models.

Eligible machines include:

- BSA A65, A70
- Harley-Davidson Sportster-based bikes, XR750 (iron-barrel only)
- Norton 750
- Nourish/Weslake twins
- Triumph 650, 750 twins, triples
- Yamaha XS650

a) Aftermarket swingarm frames are allowed, including Champion, Cheney, Redline, Rickman and Trackmaster.
b) 1972-up alloy-cylinder H-D XR750s are prohibited.
c) Norton 850s are prohibited.
d) 38mm maximum fork tube diameter.

14.2.8 **SEVENTIES SINGLES:** Late 1970s-era four-stroke single-cylinder motorcycles up to 600cc such as were raced in period dirt track events.

Eligible machines include:

- 1982-83 Honda FT500 Ascot
- 1976-78 Honda XL350 (center port head)
- 1979-81 Honda XL500 (all engine numbers with prefix PD01E-), maximum 38mm carburetor 1979-80 Honda XR500 (engine # PE01E-5000001 up to -5200001), maximum 38mm carburetor 1978-79 Suzuki DR370 and SP370
- Yamaha TT500 (engine prefix 583, 1T1 or 240), XT500 and SR500
- Sportsman 600 vintage four-stroke singles not exceeding 600cc may bump up into this class. Radial-four-valve-head Honda XR500s are prohibited. Reed valve Honda XR500s are prohibited.

a) All frames must be dual-shock, including period-style aftermarket
b) Shocks with remote reservoirs are not permitted; piggyback-type shocks are allowed
c) 43mm maximum diameter fork stanchions
d) Up to 5 (2.75 inches) rims are allowed
e) Modern-style, "wide" tires (27.5×7.5×19) are allowed on the rear
f) Adjustable-type fork triple clamps are not allowed
g) A 600cc limit (plus allowable overbore of .080") will be strictly enforced for all Seventies Singles
h) Maximum carburetor size is Any flat-slide carburetors are permitted; Lake, Lectron, Posa and Gardner only
i) Unless otherwise noted, all general vintage class rules

14.2.9 **SPANISH CUP:** All air-cooled Spanish motorcycles (Bultaco, Montesa, Ossa) to 360cc.

14.2.10 **50+:** Riders age 50 or older on any AHRMA class-eligible machine.

14.2.11 **VINTAGE LIGHT:** Open to all machines 1990 and older up to and including 400cc. Custom tubular racing frames allowed.

14.2.12 **VINTAGE HEAVY:** Open to all machines 1990 and older 401cc and larger. Custom tubular racing frames allowed.

14.2.13 **NOVICE:** A non-championship class for entry-level riders on any Sportsman-eligible machine; displacement breakdowns for 0-250cc, 251-600cc and 601-750cc may be run, but will be combined into one class in the instance of a low rider turnout.

14.2.14 **SUPPORT CLASSES:** May be run as support classes at the promoter's discretion.
   Modern Support Classes:
   - 250 Pro/Am
   - 450 Pro/Am
   - Hooligan (multi-cylinder, 700cc and larger production machines)
   - Mad Dog (four-stroke, air-cooled up to 150cc)

14.2.15 **EXHIBITION CLASSES:** AHRMA dirt track exhibition classes include:
   a) Board Track and like-design dirt track machines
   b) Two-valve speedway machines (on soft tracks where conditions allow)

14.2.16 A rider is allowed to receive a waiver, at no charge, exempting the rider's machine from all DT equipment eligibility rules except for: engine displacement, model year of engine, and safety items. Upon receiving the waiver, the rider will remain eligible to win or podium (including trophies) in his/her class, but only receive 80% of the normal championship points for his/her finish. Waivers are available upon request at trackside registration.

14.3 RACE PROCEDURES
   a) Riders may "bump up" from one period class to another, providing the machine meets all the rules of the newer-period class (e.g., a Brakeless oval-track machine may run in Sportsman after attaching brakes). Machines may not move up to a larger displacement class.
   b) Shifting gears is allowed during any event in any class.
   c) Brakeless and brake-equipped machines must never occupy the track at the same time, either in practice or during competition.
   d) A rider must make every effort to use the same motorcycle in a heat race as he/she does in the main event (if transferred). If a replacement bike is necessary, the rider must start the main from the penalty line.

14.4 DIRT TRACK TECHNICAL INSPECTION & MODIFICATIONS
   a) **TIRES:** Knobby tires are not permitted. The use of 19-inch wheels and new tires is encouraged, for the safest and most predictable setup. The maximum tire size (both front and rear) for vintage classes, up through Sportsman 750, is 27.0x7.0x19. Seventies Singles classes may use "wide" 27.5x7.5x19 rear tires. If you have questions, please contact the Dirt Track Rules & Eligibility Committee.
   b) **WHEELS:** Rim width must not exceed WM3 (2.15") for all vintage-era classes, from Dinosaur through Sportsman 750.
   c) **BRAKES:** Brakes are not permitted in Dinosaur or Brakeless classes. As an alternative to brake removal, an effective mechanical lockout may be used to disable rear brakes for these classes. Any disc-brake caliper with up to two op-posed pistons is acceptable for Sportsman. Operating front brakes are not permitted in dirt track racing. Hydraulically-operated drum brakes are prohibited.
   d) **CHASSIS:** Must be of the same period as the class in which the machine is entered. Dinosaur machines' chassis and engine must be made by the same manufacturer (i.e., OEM chassis or replacement type offered by the engine manufacturer). Frame modifications for Dinosaur class must be of period style. Weld-on rear axle holders are permitted but bolt-on adjustable-height rear axle supports (i.e., Sonicweld type) are not.

e) Swingarm frames are allowed in Classic classes only if they are production components for that make and year motorcycle and equipped with stock-configuration swingarms. Any aftermarket racing frame must be of rigid type (hardtail or strutted) to compete in Classic classes. Post-1967 Champion, Redline, Trackmaster, Ossa DMR, Bultaco Astro and similar-type dirt track frames are not allowed in Classic classes, even if fitted with struts. Aftermarket frames cannot be used in the Classic Open TT class.

f) Sportsman-class machines may use a production chassis from 1974 or earlier, or an aftermarket chassis of the type and configuration used in North American dirt track competition prior to 1975. Typical eligible models include Champion, Trackmaster and Redline. Others must be submitted to the Dirt Track Rules & Eligibility Committee for an eligibility decision. Requests must be accompanied by documentation and photographs establishing the configuration and appropriate timeline. Accurate replicas of eligible dirt track aftermarket chassis are acceptable as long as they conform to the original design and other class rules.
See roadrace rule 9.7.3f for a diagram of a braced swingarm eligible for Sportsman and Seventies Singles machines only.

g) No machine in any category may have more than 7" of front wheel travel and 4" of rear wheel travel, measured at the axle, regardless of original specification.

h) All of the following must be covered with rubber and conform with AHRMA competition rules: footpegs, stand mounting lugs, brake rods and anything else that might present a hazard.

i) Footpegs must be of the folding type able to pivot upwards and aft at 45-degrees.

j) **FORKS:** Machines must use OEM or pre-1975 aftermarket forks, with maximum 35mm diameter tubes. Ceriani, Red Wing, Betor or other non-period telescopic forks are not allowed on Dinosaur class machines. No adjustable fork triple clamps are allowed in any class except for OEM adjustable steering stems on Can-Am and certain period C&J frames. Non-adjustable, billet triple clamps are allowed.

k) **SHOCKS:** No single-shock chassis are permitted. Dual-shock machines may use any shock absorber, providing the technology and design was commercially available in 1974 or was supplied as OEM on any AHRMA-legal dirt track machine.

l) **ENGINE:** No major engine components may be changed or updated to later model parts (e.g., cylinder, head, cases, etc.). Hydraulically-operated clutches are prohibited.

m) Machines in all classes may be built to the class limit, plus overbores (in TT racing only, Dinosaur and Brakeless Open must use the stock displacement, plus overbores). Overbore limits for all classes are as follows: +.080" for singles; +.060" twins; +.040" triples; +.020" fours. Pre-unit Triumph 500 twins may use 650cc crankshaft but must not exceed +.030" overbore. Any AHRMA official may ask for a random engine teardown at any event, without posting the protest fee. Any rider refusing to teardown or found to be using an oversize engine in any AHRMA competitive event is subject to an immediate 13-month suspension of his/her racing license.

n) Two-strokes are limited to no more than two cylinders; multi-cylinder four-strokes are permitted. Use of compression releases is allowed on any two-stroke machine. All two-strokes must be equipped with an effective silencer. Throttles must be self-closing. All motorcycles must be equipped with a functional handlebar-mounted kill switch. If the motorcycle is equipped with a magneto where an operational kill switch cannot be fitted, then the carburetor settings must be such that a running engine shuts off when the throttle is fully closed.
o) **CARBURETORS:** No flat-slide or injection-type carburetors are allowed. "Power jet" and "Pumper" type (accelerator pump-equipped) carburetors are not permitted unless such mechanisms are disconnected or removed. Fuel injection is not permitted. Smoothbores with concentric float bowls are not permitted. Period carburetors are encouraged.
p) Brakeless 250 two-strokes are restricted to 32mm for singles, 28mm for twins, except Ossa, which may run the OEM 33mm IRZ carburetor.
q) All Dinosaur bikes must use OEM or period-type carburetors with specific exceptions as identified in 10.4.1A.d of the Class C road racing rules.
r) All drain plugs must be lockwired.
s) All modifications must be consistent with the spirit of the class; period modifications only.
t) Appearance and workmanship of a reasonable standard shall be enforced.
u) For race number policies, please see SECTION 3.9. All machines must carry three 10x12-inch (minimum) rectangular number plates—one on the front, and one clearly visible on each side of the motorcycle. Novice entrants shall have yellow plates, all others must be white. All numbers must be black, at least eight-inches tall, with a minimum one-inch brush stroke. Any letters must be at least three-inches tall. It is the rider's responsibility to be scored; legible numbers on the rider's back and helmet are highly encouraged. All competitors must display their AHRMA-assigned number unless granted prior permission to run a different number at that event only.
v) In addition to the rules in Section 14, riders must comply with all applicable rules in Sections 3 (events and race procedure), 4 (entry procedure) and 6 (offenses, penalties, protests and appeals), rule 9.7.11 (fuel) and rule 9.7.17 (AHRMA decals; two required and may be placed on any readily visible part of the motorcycle).

14.5 TT TECHNICAL INSPECTION & MODIFICATIONS
a) Dirt track rules 14.4.a, b, and d through o apply.
b) **BRAKES:** All TT machines must have a functional rear brake; front brakes are optional but highly recommended. Brakeless and Dinosaur bikes must use OEM drum brakes. Dinosaur bikes must use OEM drum brakes or single-leading-shoe/single-trailing-shoe type with a maximum brake diameter of 8.75 inches and a maximum shoe width of 1.75 inches. Hydraulically-operated drum brakes are prohibited.
c) **SUSPENSION:** Maximum suspension travel for machines in all classes, including Seventies Singles, is seven-inches in the front and four-inches rear, measured at the axle.

14.6 SERIES POINTS, AWARDS
a) A rider will receive points if he or she is the sole class competitor.
b) National year-end awards will be based on a rider's best finishes in half the events conducted, plus one.
c) If there is less than a full field for the final, a rider who failed to start his heat race may run in the final but will start from the penalty line.

d) Riders who start a main event will be scored in the order they cross the finish line at the pre-determined number of laps. Any rider not completing the entire distance will be scored according to the number of laps completed. There are no "DNFs."
e) Results will be posted as soon as possible after the finish of a race. Once posted, there will be a 30-minute review time. If a rider believes there is an error in scoring, he or she must draft a written protest and deliver it to an AHRMA official or Referee within 30 minutes of the provisional results being posted. Unprotested results will stand. Any discrepancies will be resolved at the track. All results posted on the AHRMA website are considered final and can only be modified under direction of the Dirt Track Director. This process is subject to appeal.

The following series points are awarded:

Position	Points	Position	Points	Position	Points
1	20	6	9	11	4
2	16	7	8	12	3
3	13	8	7	13	2
4	11	9	6	14	1
5	10	10	5	15-on	0

f) Points will be paid only to entrants who start the main event. In the case that fewer than 14 riders compete in a main event, points through 14th position will be paid. This will be determined by the finishing order in a "B" main, or in qualifying semis or heats, whichever is appropriate. A rider must complete at least one lap to earn points.
g) Year-end scoring ties will be broken by the greatest number of first place finishes, then second place finishes, third place, etc. In the event of an absolute tie, the oldest rider wins.
h) TT National races award Dirt Track series points for their respective classes.

■ SECTION 15 - CROSS COUNTRY

MISSION STATEMENT: Cross country riding is how motorcycling began because roads were very few and far between when motorcycles were born. As the motorcycles and roads improved, the riders still challenged themselves with off road competitions on ancient Roman roads in Europe and "cow and wagon" trails in the U.S.A. Eventually, the competition organized into ISDT type reliability runs in Europe and Enduros and "Hare and Hounds" in the U.S.A. Further organization and land closure issues brought the closed course Hare Scrambles to prominence.

It is AHRMA's mission to recreate these different types of Cross Country events and to provide its members with a safe, historically-accurate racing environment to showcase and experience Vintage and Post Vintage machines for all skill levels of riders.

While cross country rules specifically cover events of short duration at the moment, it is envisioned that all types of cross country events can be incorporated into the championship schedule. They must be announced in a timely manner so that the integrity of the schedule is maintained. From time to time it is possible that hare scrambles, GPs, hare and hound, desert events, enduros, ISDT-type events will be part of the schedule. Specific rules for types of competition not covered by the accompanying rules will be created by the Cross Country Rules & Eligibility Committee as required.

15.1 CLASSES

15.1.1 VINTAGE: In most aspects, machine eligibility and other requirements mirror those of AHRMA vintage motocross (Section 11), with the exception being engine displacement, as defined below. The minimum age for riders is 16 years. Each of the following classes is further divided into Novice, Intermediate and Expert skill-levels.

a) **100cc:** 88-100cc two-stroke and 88-120cc four-stroke production motorcycles manufactured as up to 1974-model-year machines, and like-design. All motorcycles in this class must have been manufactured 100cc-or-smaller-displacement bikes.

b) **SPORTSMAN 200:** Machines manufactured as 88-200cc; includes Sportsman 125 motocross machines, plus pre-1975 Bultaco 175/200, Husqvarna 175, Penton/KTM 175, Puch 175, 1975-1977 Honda MR175 Elsinore. Regardless of original displacement, engines may be built to the class limit (plus allowable overbore).

c) **SPORTSMAN OPEN:** Machines manufactured as 201cc and larger. Regardless of original displacement, engines may be built to the class limit (plus allowable overbore).

d) **CLASSIC:** Includes all machines eligible for Classic classes in vintage MX (not further divided into engine-displacement classes; Classic 125 machines may compete in Sportsman 200). Sportsman Open Twins MX machines are eligible for this class (see rule 11.1.14). Regardless of original displacement, engines may be built to the class limit (plus allowable overbore).

e) **PREMIER:** Includes all machines eligible for Premier classes in vintage MX (not further divided into engine-displacement classes). **Note:** The BSA B40 is eligible for this class. Regardless of original displacement, engines may be built to the class limit (plus allowable overbore).

f) **50+:** Riders age 50 and older on any size or type of eligible vintage machine.
g) **60+:** Riders age 60 and older on any size or type of eligible vintage machine.
h) **70+:** Riders age 70 and older on any size or type of eligible vintage machine.
i) **WOMEN:** Female riders on any size or type of eligible vintage machine.

15.1.2 POST VINTAGE: In most aspects, machine eligibility and other requirements mirror those of AHRMA post vintage motocross (Section 12), with the exception being engine displacement; regardless of original displacement, engines may be built to the class limit (plus allowable overbore) The minimum age for riders is 16 years. Each of the following classes is further divided into Novice, Intermediate and Expert skill-levels

a) **HISTORIC 200:** Historic-class machines manufactured as 88-200cc.
b) **HISTORIC OPEN:** Historic-class machines manufactured as 201cc and larger.
c) **POST VINTAGE 200:** Gran Prix and Ultima-class machines manufactured as 88-200cc.
d) **POST VINTAGE OPEN:** Gran Prix and Ultima-class machines manufactured as 201cc and larger.
e) **50+:** Riders age 50 and older on any size or type of eligible post vintage machine.
f) **60+:** Riders age 60 and older on any size or type of eligible post vintage machine.
g) **70+:** Riders age 70 and older on any size or type of eligible post vintage machine.
h) **WOMEN:** Female riders on any size or type of eligible post vintage machine.
i) **PRE-MODERN** (Expert, Intermediate, Novice Class only)

15.2 EQUIPMENT REQUIRED OF ALL CROSS COUNTRY RIDERS

a) It is the responsibility of the rider to select a helmet and apparel which will provide appropriate protection. AHRMA does not endorse or certify any manufacturer's or products. Riders must rely on their own judgement in the selection of any helmet and apparel for durability and safety. Open-face helmets are permitted; mouth guards are recommended. See Section 3.3.14.
b) Shatterproof eye protection is required.
c) Riders' tops must have long sleeves, and full-fingered gloves must be worn.
d) Leather or plastic boots must be worn and be of sufficient height to overlap the bottom of the trouser leg at all times and in no case less than eight inches high.

15.3 RACE PROCEDURES

15.3.1 It is recommended that a cross country track not be less than three miles in length. For safety reasons, the course should be laid out and pre-run by someone riding a four-wheeler. One parade lap for all competitors is strongly encouraged.

15.3.2 A race should run no less than one hour before the first finisher is flagged off, unless track conditions require an earlier finish.

15.3.3 Classes may start in waves or may be consolidated to form suitable waves. There will be a time gap between waves of not less than 30 seconds. If a rider leaves the starting grid in a wave *prior* to the one he/she is assigned to, there will be an automatic one-lap penalty. There is no penalty for leaving in a later wave. Dead-engine starts are encouraged. There will be no overall winner, only class winners.

15.3.4 If more than one event is run on the same course on the same day, classes may be mixed or added but must be advertised prior to the event.

15.3.5 A competitor must pass between all gates created by marking and within 15 feet of any trail marker.

15.3.6 A rider must complete at least one full lap to be scored as a finisher in hare scrambles/cross country type events or the first regular checkpoint in enduros, hare and hound and ISDT-type events.

15.3.7 Every rider must come to a complete stop each lap at the scoring point until signaled to proceed.

15.3.8 A rider may not enter more than one class in a one-hour race.

15.3.9 A rider's motocross skill level designation is used as the basis for his/her cross country skill designation. However, the rider grading committee may assign a rider a separate skill level designation for cross country.

15.3.10 A rider who cuts the course will be docked a minimum of one lap. If the infraction is more serious, rule 6.2 may also apply.

15.3.11 Cross country races may be split into two sessions at the discretion of the race director, with the vintage motorcycles first, followed by the post vintage motorcycles with a sufficient break to allow those entering both events to have a short rest.

15.3.12 Enduro, hare and hound, and ISDT-type events can run vintage and post vintage at the same time, but every effort should be taken to separate them on the course (e.g., post vintage early numbers, vintage later numbers, etc.).

15.4 SERIES POINTS, AWARDS

a) National Championship Series year-end awards are based on a rider's best finishes in a maximum number of events. The maximum number of "best finishes" to count toward the championship will be specified by the Off Road Director and announced prior to the beginning of each season. A rider must earn points in the minimum number of events specified by the Off Road Director to be eligible for year-end awards. In the event of a year-end scoring tie, the year-end scoring ties will be broken as follows: Year-end scoring ties will go to the rider who accumulated the most points during head-to-head competition. If still tied or if they did not compete against each other, year-end scoring ties will be broken by the greatest number of first place race finishes, then second-place race finishes, third place, etc. In the event of an absolute tie, the oldest rider wins.

b) Results will be posted as soon as possible after the finish of a race. Once posted, there will be a 30-minute review time. If a rider believes there is an error in scoring, he or she must draft a written protest and deliver it to an AHRMA official or Referee within 30 minutes of the provisional results being posted. Unprotested results will stand. Any discrepancies will be resolved at the track. All results posted on the AHRMA website are considered final and can only be modified under direction of the Off-Road Director. This process is subject to appeal.

c) The following points are awarded:

Position	Points	Position	Points
1	20	8	7
2	16	9	6
3	13	10	5
4	11	11	4
5	10	12	3
6	9	13	2
7	8	14	1

d) Separate points may be awarded if two separate events are held on two consecutive days, but not for a single overall event that runs for two days.

15.5 NUMBERS AND NUMBER PLATES:
For race number policies, please see SECTION 3.9.

■ SECTION 16 - NEXT GEN MOTOCROSS

Mission Statement: The Mission of AHRMA Next Gen Motocross is to showcase the technological advancements that continued in rapid succession after the Post Vintage Period. Most of these advancements can be found in modern Motocross bikes produced to this day.

16.1 GENERAL RULES:
General Motocross rules apply to the Next Gen Series of classes, with the exception of machine specific details which will be noted within the class structure.

16.2 NUMBERS AND NUMBER PLATES:

16.2.1 RACE NUMBER POLICIES: For race number policies, please see SECTION 3.9.

16.2.2 NUMBER PLATES: All Next Gen Class eligible machines shall use a white background with black numerals.

16.2.3 Expert-class champions from the previous year will be assigned a No. 1 plate (with a letter suffix), which they may use in any class during the season. If they choose not to use their assigned AHRMA competition number, it will be held for them until the following season. A rider who wins more than one class championship should use only one of the No. 1/ letter combinations to aid in scoring and identification. Number/letter combinations for each Expert class champion are:

    Pre-Modern 125................. 1T (Moved from Sec 12.5.p.4)
    Pre-Modern 250................. 1U (Moved from Sec 12.5.p.4)
    Pre-Modern 500.................1V (Moved from Sec12.5.p.4)
    Pre-Modern 4-Stroke ....1X (Moved from Sec12.5.p.4)
    Next Gen-1 125..................1A
    Next Gen-1 250..................1B
    Next Gen-1 500..................1C
    40+....................................1M
    50+.....................................1N
    60+.....................................1P
    Women............................. 1W

All competitors must display their AHRMA-assigned number unless granted prior permission to run a different number at that event only.

16.3 TECHNICAL INSPECTION: All Next Gen eligible machines and riders are subject to the pre-race, technical inspection. All equipment must adhere to the rules for the class entered. All riders must meet safety and eligibility standards for AHRMA Motocross.

16.4 COURSES: Tracks will follow the same design principles as those created for Post Vintage Motocross. All "SuperCross" or "Extreme" steep faced, sharply-lipped jumps are to be avoided. Tracks shall be traditional outdoor style MX. Safety will be considered when designing track obstacles with the Race Director being the final authority in making track changes.

16.5 PRE-MODERN CLASSES

16.5.1 **PRE-MODERN:** Pre-Modern machines are on the cusp of incorporating all features of modern technology, including linkage rear-suspension, engine power valves, and disc brakes. Class eligible machines shall consist of circa 1982 to 1988 two- and four-stroke motorcycles which were factory-produced with hydraulic front disc brake and *rear* drum brake. Bikes equipped with a factory-produced rear hydraulic disc brake are ***not*** allowed.

16.5.2 **PRE-MODERN 125:** Certain two-stroke motorcycles 100-125cc that were produced within the guidelines of the Pre-Modern class specifications.

Eligible machines include, but are not limited to:

- 1984-'87 Cagiva WMX125
- 1984-'86 Honda CR125R
- 1985-'88 Husqvarna 125CR
- 1986-'88 Husqvarna 125WR, 125XC
- 1982-'85 Kawasaki KX125
- 1983-'85 KTM 125GS, 125MX
- 1985-'86 Suzuki RM125
- 1985-'87 Yamaha YZ125
- 1990-'93 Yamaha RT180 (air cooled)

16.5.3 **PRE-MODERN 250:** Certain two-stroke motorcycles 126-250cc that were produced within the guidelines of the Pre-Modern class specifications.

Eligible machines include, but are not limited to:
- 1984-'87 Cagiva WMX250
- 1986- 87 Can Am 200/250
- 1984-'86 Honda CR250R
- 1985-'88 Husqvarna 250CR
- 1986-'88 Husqvarna 250WR, 250XC
- 1982-'85 Kawasaki KX250
- 1986-'88 Kawasaki KDX200, KDX250
- 1983-'85 KTM 250GS, 250MX
- 1985 M-Star 250
- 1985-'86 Suzuki RM250
- 1986 Yamaha IT200
- 1985-'87 Yamaha YZ250

16.5.4 **PRE-MODERN 500:** Certain two-stroke motorcycles 280-500cc that were produced within the guidelines of the Pre-Modern class specifications.

Eligible machines include, but are not limited to:
- 1984-'87 Cagiva WMX500
- 1986 -87 Can Am 406/500
- 1984-'86 Honda CR500R
- 1985-'86 Husqvarna 500CR
- 1986 Husqvarna 500WR, 500XC
- 1986-'88 Husqvarna 430AE
- 1987-'88 Husqvarna 430CR, 430WR, 430XC
- 1983-'85 Kawasaki KX500
- 1983 KTM 420GS, 420XC, 495MC, 495XC
- 1985 KTM 500MX
- 1985 M-Star 500
- 1985 Suzuki RM500
- 1985-'90 Yamaha YZ490

16.5.5 **PRE-MODERN FOUR-STROKE:** Certain four-stroke motorcycles 250-600cc that were produced within the guidelines of the Pre-Modern class specifications.

Eligible machines include, but are not limited to:

- 1984 ATK 560
- 1984 Honda XL350R, XL600R
- 1984-'89 Honda XR250R
- 1984-'85 Honda XR350R
- 1983-'84 Honda XR500R
- 1983-'89 Honda XR600R
- 1987-'88 Husqvarna 510TC, 510TE, 510TX
- 1982 KTM 500K4, 500XC
- 1983-'88 KTM Any four-stroke, rear drum
- 1986-'87 Yamaha TT250
- 1985-'86 Yamaha TT600
- 1985-'00 Yamaha XT350
- 1984-'89 Yamaha XT600
- Four-stroke, dual-disc, up to 1997 and like-design models. Examples are:
    - 1985-'01 ATK DS/XC/MX 350-605
    - 1990-'98 Husaberg FE/FC 350-650
    - 1989-'99 Husqvarna TC/TE/TX/WXC/WXE 350-610
    - 1994-'03 Vertematti/VOR EN/MX 495-503
- Japanese off-road and trail bikes: Honda XL/XR, Kawasaki KLX, Suzuki DR, Yamaha TTR/XT
- Yamaha YZ400F, and its variants, are not allowed
- Modern, liquid-cooled Japanese four-stroke motocross bikes (CR-F, KX-F, RMZ, YZ-F) are not allowed

16.6 NEXT GEN CLASSES

16.6.1 **NEXT GEN 1:** Next Gen machines incorporate nearly all of features of current motorcycle technology, including front and rear hydraulic disc brakes, upside-down front forks, and twin-spar frames. Class eligible machines shall consist of circa 1986 to 1998 two- and four- stroke motorcycles which were factory-produced with steel main frames. Aluminum sub-frame and swingarm are allowed. Motorcycles equipped with an aluminum main frame are **not** allowed.

16.6.2 **NEXT GEN 1- 125:** Certain two-stroke motorcycles 100-125cc that were produced within the guidelines of the Next Gen 1 class specifications.

Eligible machines include, but are not limited to:

- 1987-'97 Honda CR125R
- 1989-'99 Husqvarna 125 all
- 1989-'02 Gas Gas 125
- 1986-'98 Kawasaki KX125
- 1986-'00 KTM 125
- 1987-00' Suzuki RM125
- 1986-'98 TM Racing 125
- 1988-'01 Yamaha YZ125

16.6.3 **NEXT GEN 1 250:** Certain two-stroke motorcycles 126-250cc that were produced within the guidelines of the Next Gen 1 class specifications.

Eligible machines include, but are not limited to:
- 1988-'93 ATK 250
- 1987-'96 Honda CR250R
- 1989-'99 Husqvarna 250
- 1989-'02 GasGas 250
- 1986-'98 Kawasaki KX250
- 1986-'06 Kawasaki KDX200, KDX220, KDX250
- 1988-'02 KTM 250
- 1987-2000 Suzuki RM250, RMX250
- 1994-'98 TM Racing 250
- 1988-'98 Yamaha YZ250, WR250

16.6.4 **NEXT GEN 1 500:** Certain two-stroke motorcycles 256-500cc that were produced within the guidelines of the Next Gen 1 class specifications.

Eligible machines include, but are not limited to:
- 1988-'95 ATK 406
- 1987-'03 Honda CR500R
- 1989-'91 Husqvarna 300xx
- 1986-'04 Kawasaki KX500
- 1986-05" KTM 300, 360, 380 (up to MXC/EXC)

16.7 TWO-STROKE CLASSES

16.7.1 **MILLENNIUM TWO-STROKE (Promoter Optional Class, see 16.8.4):** Millennium Two-Stroke: machines incorporate nearly all features of current motorcycle technology. Class eligible machines shall consist of circa 1997 to 2008 two-stroke motorcycles which were factory-produced. These machines represent the era when two-stroke motocross bikes were nearing the end of their development cycles and were being phased out of the Japanese manufacturer's model lines in favor of modern four-stroke motocross bikes. OEM engine and main frame combination/configuration must remain as produced by the original manufacturer for a given model. Motorcycles built using engines and frames from different models/displacements, even if from the same manufacturer, are not allowed.

16.7.2 **MILLENNIUM TWO-STROKE 125:** Certain two-stroke motorcycles 100-125cc that were produced within the guidelines of the Millennium class specifications.

Eligible machines include, but are not limited to:
- 1997-'07 Honda CR125R
- 2000-'13 Husqvarna CR125 (Pre-Austrian)
- 1999-'06 Kawasaki KX125
- 2001-10' KTM 125 SX (PDS Shock, No Linkage)
- 2001-'07 Suzuki RM125
- 1999-'07 TM Racing 125 MX (Steel Perimeter Frame)
- 2002-'05 Yamaha YZ125 (Pre-KYB SSS Front Fork, No Ti Shock Spring)

16.7.3 **MILLENNIUM TWO-STROKE 250:** Certain two-stroke motorcycles 126-250cc that were produced within the guidelines of the Millennium class specifications.

Eligible machines include, but are not limited to:
- 1997-'07 Honda CR250R
- 1999-'09 Husqvarna CR250 (Pre-Austrian)
- 1999-'07 Kawasaki KX250
- 2003-'10 KTM 250 SX (PDS Shock, No Linkage)
- 2001-'08 Suzuki RM2501999-'07 TM Racing 250 MX (Steel Perimeter Frame)
- 1999-'06 Yamaha YZ250 (Pre-KYB SSS Front Fork, No Ti Shock Spring)

16.7.4 **CURRENT TWO-STROKE**: Current two-stroke: Included machines are those produced to the current era. Modern two-strokes, including those currently in production by contemporary manufacturers and future models not yet in production, which maintain the modern structure. All modifications currently known are permitted, with the exception, of those which create an unsafe operating condition.

16.7.5 **CURRENT TWO-STROKE 125 AM:** two-stroke motorcycles 100-125cc that were produced within the guidelines of the current two-stroke class specifications.

Eligible machines include, but are not limited to:
- Husqvarna TC125
- KTM 125 SX
- TM Racing 125 M
- Yamaha YZ125

16.7.6 **CURRENT TWO-STROKE 250 AM:** two-stroke motorcycles 126-250cc that were produced within the guidelines of the current two-stroke class specifications.

Eligible machines include, but are not limited to:
- Husqvarna TC250
- KTM 250 SX
- TM Racing 250 MX
- Yamaha YZ250

16.7.7 **TWO-STROKE UNLIMITED (Promoter Optional Class, see 16.8.4):** This class shall not have OEM production machine restrictions, unlimited modifications are allowed, two-stroke engines ONLY. No displacement limits.

16.8 ADDITIONAL CLASSES

16.8.1 **AGE CLASSES**
 a) 40+ Expert & Intermediate. Any bike of this generation is eligible for this class
 b) 50+ Expert & Intermediate. Any Bike of this Generation is eligible for this class
 c) 60+ Expert & Intermediate. Any Bike of this Generation is eligible for this class (Note: There is no novice classification in the Age Groups)

16.8.2 **WOMEN:** Female riders on any size or type of eligible machine.

16.8.3 All AHRMA Next Gen motocross classes are further divided into Intermediate and Expert categories. Novice classes shall not be combined with any Intermediate or Expert class. All Novice classes shall run in Novice-only motos. Dual ability level does not apply in Next Gen classes.

Next Gen Novice Classes
- Next Gen Novice
- Next Gen Women's Novice

16.8.4 **PROMOTER OPTIONAL CLASSES:** Promoter Optional Classes shall be run at the race promoter's discretion when and where prudent scheduling allows and shall be subject to AHRMA's written prior approval when taking place at a National event. Next Gen Promoter Optional Classes include those in sections 16.7.1 to 16.7.7. of this Handbook. Promoter Optional Class machines in the previously listed Millennium and Current 2-Stroke sections are not eligible for section 16.8.1 Next Gen Age classes, section 16.8.2 Next Gen Woman's classes, and section 16.8.3 Next Gen Novice classes. No national series points shall be awarded in Promoter Optional classes.

16.9 GENERAL MOTOCROSS RULES

The following rules in the Vintage Motocross section also apply to AHRMA Next Gen MX:
- **11.3 Motocross Rider Grading System** (Note: Rule 11.3h, dual-ability level, does not apply in Next Gen classes.)
- **11.4 Equipment Required of All Motocross Riders**
- **11.5 Scoring at AHRMA Events**
- **11.6 Series Points Awards**
- **11.7 Race Procedures**

■ SECTION 17 - AHRMA, THE ORGANIZATION

17.1 **THE ORIGINS OF AHRMA:** The seeds of today's American Historic Racing Motorcycle Association were sown in the late 1970s and early 1980s as different groups and individuals began to organize vintage racing on a regional basis. Roadracing was the first type of competition to appear, spearheaded in the Northeast by Robert Iannucci. In the Southeast, Bob and Marrie Barker and Will Harding launched the Historic Motorcycle Racing Association (HMRA). Other groups also began emerging around the nation, adding motocross, trials, flat-track and concours events to the competition options available for vintage riders. In the West, Fred Mork, Dick Mann, and Mike Green were nurturing the California Vintage Racing Group (CVRG).

By 1986, it was clear that a national organization would be necessary to administer this burgeoning sport. AHRMA was originally formed as a privately-held business corporation. Other groups were brought together under one banner and one set of rules. In 1989 AHRMA was reorganized into the current member-owned, not-for-profit association. Along the way, many other individuals and organizations have lent a helping hand. The late Tom McGill, the late Mike Smith, Beno Rodi, Jeff Elghanyan, Gary Winn, the American Motorcyclist Association, Daytona International Speedway, the Championship Cup Series, BMW of North America, and the American Motorcycle Institute are just a few who have contributed greatly toward AHRMA's success.

17.2 AHRMA ORGANIZATION: AHRMA is governed by a 12-member Board of Trustees, six from east of the Mississippi River and six from west of the Mississippi, elected from and by the membership. Trustees serve three-year terms and may be reelected any number of times. The accompanying organizational chart gives an overall view of AHRMA's structure, as described in greater detail below.

17.3 GETTING MORE INVOLVED: Opportunities for involvement cover a wide range, from assisting at events to serving on the Board of Trustees. To volunteer your help putting on an AHRMA event, contact the National office or one of the race coordinators listed in Section 17. To discuss other ways you might become involved, contact the Executive Director.

Four Trustees are elected each year, two from the West and two from the East. The process begins when a call for nominations is published in *AHRMA MAG*. Any full member in good standing is eligible to run. Members vote by means of a ballot provided either electronically or by mail. Trustees take office at the Board meeting held during the first quarter of the year. Trustees meet three times per year—in person—at revolving locations. These meetings are generally open to AHRMA members, and members are encouraged to attend. Other meetings are held as necessary in person, by telephone or video conference call. The Board chooses three officers–Chairman, Treasurer and Secretary, who make up the Executive Committee. This committee meets frequently, usually by conference call, to consider various matters of importance.

The Board also appoints committees, such as the eight Rules & Eligibility panels, the Awards Committee, and the Risk Management Committee. Rules & Eligibility Committees consider rules issues and make recommendations to the Board of Trustees for changes to the annual Handbook. These committees also consider questions of eligibility for specific machines and offer interpretations and clarifications of rules. Suggestions for rules changes may be made using the form provided near the back of the Handbook. The Awards Committee oversees the various special awards given to the prior year's outstanding competitors at the annual awards banquets early each year. The Risk Management Committee objectively reviews AHRMA rules, procedures, and policies to ensure the organization exercises proper standards of care, providing a reasonable balance of safety and fun for entrants and the public.

The Executive Director oversees the day-to-day operations of AHRMA, directs other staff members, and serves as the staff representative to Board committees. The Executive Director is responsible for appointing the various Directors and Coordinators, who head the volunteer staffing at each of AHRMA's events.

17.4 COMPETITION OPPORTUNITIES: AHRMA provides National-championship series in road racing, cross country, motocross, observed trials and dirt track. These series are coordinated by the National office in Tennessee. At the same time, regional and local groups often organize other series and individual events. Information on all AHRMA competition, including a calendar of events, appears each month in the association's newsletter, *AHRMA MAG*, and on AHRMA's website, **www.ahrma.org**.

17.5 AHRMA MEMBERSHIP: Eligibility: AHRMA, at its sole discretion, may accept as an AHRMA member any individual or business entity interested in vintage motorcycle racing, so long as the individual or entity has properly filed a membership application and thereby agrees to abide by AHRMA rules, has paid the fee prescribed for membership, and meets the required qualifications. The decision to admit an applicant shall be made by the Executive Director.

AHRMA is dedicated to the highest degree of safety, sportsmanship, and integrity in the sport of motorcycle racing. Participation or involvement by a member (including in the case of a business entity, involvement by any stockholder, director, officer, employee, partner, or agent thereof) in conduct deemed inappropriate by AHRMA, at its sole discretion, shall result in such penalties as may be imposed by AHRMA, including but not limited to, suspension, revocation of AHRMA membership, and/or banishment. AHRMA reserves the right to reject any application or revoke any membership for cause, so long as such rejection is not based on race, creed, color, sex, or national origin.

The decision to reject or revoke membership, or impose banishment or other penalties, shall be made by the Board of Trustees. Suspension may be imposed only by the AHRMA Executive Director, who shall immediately notify the member so suspended, in writing, of the suspension. The suspended member shall thereafter be entitled to a reasonable opportunity to be heard, in person or through a representative, by the Board of Trustees or a committee appointed by it. The Board of Trustees may thereafter rescind or terminate the suspension, or continue the suspension for a definite term, or expel the member, and its decision
shall be final.

17.6 BENEVOLENT FUND: The Benevolent Fund was created in 1992 as a means of helping AHRMA members in need (anyone who wants to make a request or suggestion for assistance should contact the AHRMA office). AHRMA offers a variety of raffles and other fundraisers benefiting the Benevolent Fund. Members also are encouraged to contribute directly.

Assistance of up to $1000 for any incident is available from the fund. To be considered, the person must be a member in good standing for at least one year, and the injury must have occurred at an AHRMA-permitted event. The person's injuries must have been reported to a race official by the end of the day when it occurred. Application forms are available from the AHRMA National office. The form may be completed by someone other than the injured member. Final decisions on assistance are made by the Executive Committee, after a recommendation from the Benevolent Fund Advisory Committee. All applications for assistance are kept confidential. The available funds in the Benevolent Fund shall be capped at a maximum of $100,000 at any time. Funds in excess of the cap shall be moved to the Safety Fund.

17.7 AGREEMENT NOT TO SUE AND TO INDEMNIFY: In order to promote the sport of motorcycle racing, to achieve prompt and final competition results, and in consideration of receiving the numerous benefits to them, all members, including competitors and officials, expressly agree that determinations by AHRMA officials (and rulings of the Board of Trustees when made) as to the applicability and interpretation of AHRMA rules are non-litigable, and they covenant that they will not initiate or maintain litigation of any kind against AHRMA or anyone acting on behalf of AHRMA, to reverse or modify such determination or to recover damages or to seek any other kind of relief allegedly incurred or required as a result of such determination. If a member, competitor, or official initiates or maintains litigation in violation of this covenant, that member, competitor or official, agrees to pay AHRMA for all damages, costs, travel expenses and attorney fees incurred by AHRMA, its officers, directors and/or agents in such litigation.

17.8 COMMUNICATIONS: AHRMA's publication, AHRMA MAG and the AHRMA website, www.ahrma.org, are the official conduits of information from AHRMA to its members and from member to member. You are encouraged to contribute articles, columns, letters, race reports and photographs. Our extensive website is maintained at www.ahrma.org, featuring event schedules, results, points standings, member information, this Handbook, featured machines, classified ads, suppliers and more.

Advertising opportunities are available in *AHRMA MAG*, the Handbook, and other special publications. See Section 19 for the address and phone number of AHRMA's Communications office to inquire about marketing and advertising.

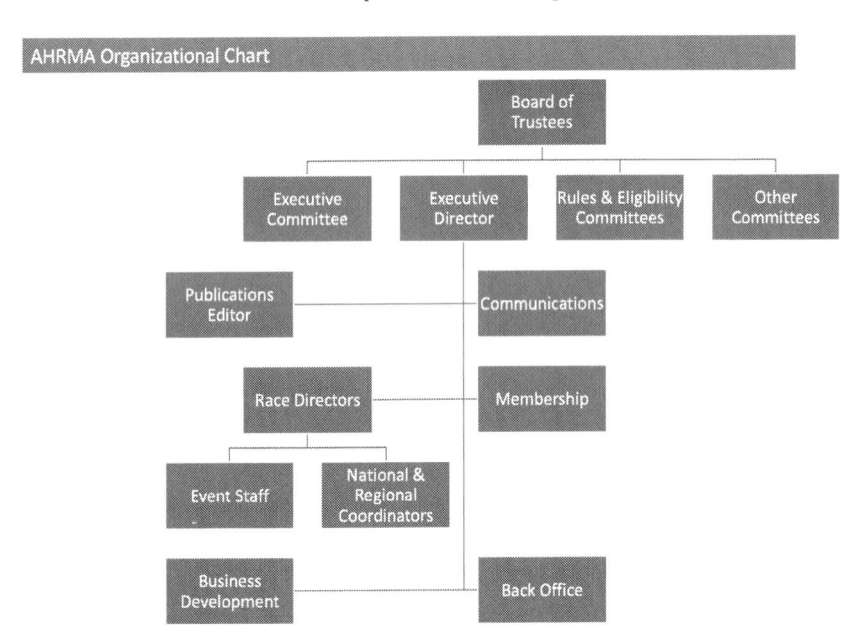

AHRMA Organizational Chart

- Board of Trustees
  - Executive Committee
  - Executive Director
  - Rules & Eligibility Committees
  - Other Committees
- Publications Editor
- Communications
- Race Directors
  - Event Staff
  - National & Regional Coordinators
- Membership
- Business Development
- Back Office

17.9 SPECIAL AWARDS

Numerous special awards are presented by AHRMA each year. Among them are:

a) **Barber Vintage Motorsports Museum Trophy:** awarded to the Sportsman 750 road racing champion by George Barber.
b) **Barker Constructor/Rider Award:** sponsored by Bob Barker for outstanding machinery and performance by its owner.
c) **Bill Nilsson Trophy:** honoring the first 500cc World Motocross Champion (1957), is presented to the Premier 500 Expert motocross champion.
d) **Brad Lackey Trophy:** honoring the first American World Motocross Champion (1982, 500cc), it is presented for an outstanding performance in the Sportsman 500 Expert motocross class.
e) **Brian Martin Trophy:** awarded to the Premier Lightweight Expert trials champion.
f) **British Bike Woman's Award:** given by *British Bike* magazine for outstanding contributions by a female AHRMA member.
g) **CB160 High Point Award:** Moto LeMans (FKA CB160) High Point winner.
h) **Daniel Beher Brakeless High Point Award:** awarded to highest points total for any one of the three qualifying brakeless dirt track classes.
i) **Dave Bickers Trophy:** for the Premier Expert Lightweight Champion (first recipient in 2019).
j) **Debbie Evans Trophy:** awarded to the Modern Classic Master trials champion.
k) **Dick Mann Sportsman of the Year:** AHRMA's highest award, presented to a member for outstanding contributions to the vintage movement.
l) **Don Schmutzler Award:** presented by the family of the late Don Schmutzler for outstanding contributions to the sport of vintage observed trials.
m) **Dwaine Williams Memorial Trophy:** presented to the 200 Grand Prix roadrace champion.
n) **Enders Cup:** for outstanding Sidecar racing support.
o) **Gary Moore Spirit Award:** awarded to the Dirt Track racer who displays sportsmanship, competition, dedication, and passion for the sport of dirt track. (nominated by Dirt Track racers and selected by Dirt Track Committee from nominations)
p) **Hailwood Cup:** a trophy won by the late Mike Hailwood racing in the U.S. (and donated by his wife, Pauline Hailwood), presented to the 500 Premier roadrace champion.
q) **Hensley Handshift Trophy:** awarded to the Class C Handshift road racing champion. This award was donated by Jeff Glasserow in memory of Indian restorer Dean Hensley.
r) **Irene Smith Trophy:** presented for an outstanding performance by a female competitor in an off-road discipline.
s) **Ivan Harkness Trophy - Sportsman 500 Road Race Champion:** will be whoever wins the season championship for the Sportsman 500 Road Race class.
t) **Jeff Smith Trophy:** for the Expert-level motocross rider with the highest points total on a four-stroke in any Classic or Premier class.
u) **Jim McClinton Award:** for outstanding performance on a four-stroke in a motocross rider Age or Sportsman class.
v) **Jimmy Nation Trophy:** for off-road mechanic of the year.
w) **Jim Pomeroy Trophy:** honoring the first American to win a World Motocross Gran Prix on the first attempt (1973, Spain). It is presented for an outstanding performance in the Sportsman 250 Expert motocross class.
x) **John & Ginny Demoisey Memorial Award:** presented to the outstanding road racing couple, by Ginny Demoisey in memory of Johnny Demoisey.

y) **Lady Roadracer of the Year:** presented for outstanding performance by a female roadrace competitor.
z) **Mick Andrews Trophy:** awarded to the Modern Classic Expert trials champion
aa) **Mike Lightfoot Trophy:** presented by the Santa Clara Riders Unlimited in honor of the late AHRMA Trustee for outstanding contributions to the vintage motocross program.
ab) **Mike Smith Trophy:** presented by Ed and Jean Smith in memory of the late AHRMA Trustee to a committed AHRMA official or volunteer.
ac) **Nobby Clark Trophy:** for road racing tuner of the year.
ad) **Paco Bultó Trophy:** for current year's 250GP Champion, (first recipient 2018).
ae) **Rookie of the Year:** (sponsored by D.R.S. Limited, David & Stephanie Wells), presented for exemplary participation and performance to a competitor new to AHRMA road racing.
af) **Stan Dibben Award - Side car Co-Pilot:** celebrates (subjectively) the sidecar passenger who best represents the sidecar discipline.
ag) **Syd Tunstall Trophy:** sponsored by Malcolme Tunstall and awarded to the Sportsman 350 road racing champion.
ah) **Tommy McDermott Trophy:** honoring the first American to earn a Gold Medal in the International Six Days Trial (1949, Wales). It is presented for an outstanding performance in AHRMA's National Cross Country series.
ai) **Tony Hendon Trophy:** for outstanding performance in post vintage cross country.
aj) **Triumph International Owners Club Award:** to the rider with the highest points total earned while riding a Triumph motorcycle in any individual road racing class.
ak) **Vintage Iron Premier Award:** for the rider who accumulates the most points in any Premier motocross class.
al) **Young AHRMA Racer of the Year:** recognition of excellence in a young AHRMA racer 35 years of age or younger. Cycles through disciplines each year, Road Race, Off-Road, Dirt Track.

■ SECTION 18 – AHRMA MEMBER CODE OF CONDUCT

As a condition of membership, all Members agree to abide by the AHRMA Member Code of Conduct as set forth in the then-current AHRMA Handbook in effect. AHRMA's Member Code of Conduct sets forth the obligations and required behavior of all AHRMA Members and the associated processes.

In addition to the requirements set forth herein, AHRMA expects that all of its Members will at all times: be considerate of other Members, their guests and families; exhibit respect and appreciation for all AHRMA workers and volunteers; comply with track and event rules and regulations.

18.1 MEMBER CODE OF CONDUCT – OFFENSES

Behavior which may result in disciplinary action is that behavior, whether physical, verbal, or written, which in the sole reasonable discretion of the Board of Trustees, fails to comform with the Member Code of Conduct, causes or may cause AHRMA harm or adversely prejudices AHRMA, or adversely affects any AHRMA Member or any person or entity associated with AHRMA.

Prohibited behavior, whether by physical action or published in any form of communication, whether verbal, written via phone, in person, email, social media, or other digital platform includes, but is not limited to:

a) Derogatory Statements: Making derogatory statements about or with respect to another Member and/or that Member's family or business, any AHRMA Associate and/or that Associate's family or business, any sponsor, any track personnel, any workers or volunteers, or any AHRMA Trustee, contractor, or vendor regarding or concerning:

- Religion
- Political beliefs
- Heritage
- Family members
- Gender, Gender Expression, Sexual orientation
- Physical appearance or characteristics
- Financial status or work status
- Ability to compete or be competitive (outside of friendly trackside banter)
- Integrity or honesty
- Moral, professional, or ethical conduct or reputation

b) Any use of profanity directed at another member, associate, sponsor, vendor, track personnel, volunteer, Trustee, contractor or worker, and/or family or business of same.
c) Defamatory Statements: Making any defamatory statement concerning or regarding any member, associate, sponsor, vendor, track personnel, volunteer, Trustee, contractor, or worker.
d) Any action which in any way defrauds, denigrates, defames, or deprives any organization, person, contractor, promoter, other Members or Associates, or any persons related to or involved with AHRMA.
e) Failure to follow any applicable AHRMA rules or AHRMA policies.
f) Willful failure to follow track rules or regulations that causes or may cause safety risk.
g) Any communication, publication or disclosure of AHRMA confidential, proprietary, privileged, or protected AHRMA legal matters in any way or format, including but not limited to oral, written, electronic or via digital and/or social media.

h) Any communication, publication or disclosure of AHRMA confidential, proprietary, privileged or protected financial information in any way, including but not limited to oral, written, electronic, or via digital and/or social media.
i) Any threats or actions of physical violence, assault, or battery off or on the track.
j) Aiding, abetting, or causing another to engage in any prohibited conduct as set forth in a) – i) above.

18.2 MEMBER CODE OF CONDUCT - SUBMISSION OF A COMPLAINT

a) AHRMA recognizes that motorcycle competition involves commitment, enthusiasm, and passion. In the event an ostensible violation of the Member Code of Conduct occurs, Members shall seek to resolve such matters amicably and in the spirit of Member cooperation. If necessary or appropriate, the assistance of another Member, Race Official, or Trustee may be sought.

b) AHRMA does not encourage submitting a complaint regarding alleged violations of the Member Code of Conduct. A formal complaint is a last resort and is not favored. If Member-resolution is not possible, any Member Code of Conduct Complaint shall:

- be submitted in a timely fashion
- set forth in detail the person(s) alleged to be in breach, the nature of the alleged breach pursuant to Section 18.1, above, the date, time, location/event of the alleged breach, and all material facts, circumstances, and witnesses concerning the alleged breach
- include a sworn statement by the person bringing the complaint of all actions and efforts made to amicably resolve the issue pursuant to Section 18.2 (a).

c) Complaints may be submitted to the Race Director, a Trustee, or the Executive Director. All complaints shall be in writing, within 7 days of last efforts to resolve the issue, but in no event later than 14 days after the alleged breach, transmitted in person, or via first class mail with proof of delivery, or via email with delivery confirmation.

d) Any Member who submits a complaint will be notified of the resolution action taken by AHRMA. AHRMA's handling and disposition of complaints and alleged breaches of AHRMA's Member Code of Conduct are confidential matters, except as otherwise set forth herein.

18.3 MEMBER CODE OF CONDUCT – ENFORCEMENT AND PENALTIES

Breaches of Code of Conduct are serious matters, and any enforcement or penalty is instituted after due consideration and investigation.

Notwithstanding any legal ramifications which may arise from adverse behavior, specific AHRMA penalties range from verbal warning to probation, suspension and banishment. Penalty Level (1- 4) will be adjudged by either repeated failure to comply with the Member Code of Conduct, or severity of such conduct as determined by Board of Trustees at their sole reasonable discretion.

Penalties:

a) **Level 1** – Informal verbal or written warning by an AHRMA Official with documentation sent to the Executive Director who will then forward to the Board of Trustees and record in the membership database.
b) **Level 2** – Written reprimand, by the Executive Director, with documentation sent to the Board of Trustees and written reprimand recorded in membership database.
c) **Level 3** – Fine and/or probation, by the Executive Director after majority vote by the Board of Trustees, fine and/or probation documented in membership database. Probation may range from a national or regional event to an entire season. Members on probation are not "in good standing" and are not eligible for national or regional championships in the season of record.
d) **Level 4** – Dismissal and forfeiture of dues paid. Executed by the Executive Director and after a majority vote by the Board of Trustees. Member is banned and may neither attend nor participate in any AHRMA event.
e) In AHRMA's sole discretion, AHRMA may elect to publish the result of any enforcement or penalty. Otherwise, all enforcement and any penalty is confidential between AHRMA and the involved Member(s).

18.4 MEMBER CODE OF CONDUCT – APPEALS

a) A Member can appeal any action taken against the Member. Any appeal shall be in writing, via first class mail with delivery receipt letter, or via email with delivery receipt, within 30 days of notification of the decision being appealed, and sent to the Executive Director.
b) Appeals shall be accompanied by an appeal fee of $50 (Level 1), $75 (Level 2), $150 (Level 3), $250 (Level 4). Depending upon the result of the appeal, all or some of the appeal fee may be refunded, as determined by AHRMA in its sole reasonable discretion.
c) Appeals will be heard by an Appeal Committee, established by the Board of Trustees, comprising three members, as appointed from time to time by the Board of Trustees. The Board of Trustees may appoint such Appeal Committee on a case-by-case basis or establish a standing committee. The number of committees, the length of committee service, and the persons serving on the committee(s) shall be at the sole discretion of the Board of Trustees.
d) An appeal will include a hearing, either in person, by phone, or by video conference, as the committee determines. The committee will consider all information presented, both oral and written, within 30 days of the hearing. No attorneys are permitted to represent any party. The decision of the committee is final. For Level 3 and 4 appeals, a decision found against the Member will be published in AHRMA MAG and will identify the parties, the dispute, the decision, and as appropriate, the penalty.

■ SECTION 19 - FOR MORE INFORMATION…

This section of the Handbook is intended to help put you in contact with the people who can answer your questions about vintage racing in general, and AHRMA racing in particular. Because questions about rules and eligibility are best solved prior to a race, and because machine approval is authorized only by AHRMA officials, riders and tuners are encouraged to contact the individuals listed below well in advance of an event. Note: As Trustees, officers, and committee members can change during the year, AHRMA members will be provided with an addendum to this section, if necessary, published in *AHRMA MAG*.

Contact information for each of the following committees can be found at www.ahrma.org/contact/committees/

19.1 RULES & ELIGIBILITY COMMITTEES

There is a specific timeframe for submitting Rule Change Proposals. This normally occurs during the first quarter of the year. The call for each year's Rule Change Proposals will be announced on the AHRMA website, via email and on the AHRMA Facebook page. Proposals MUST be submitted on the official **Proposal for Rule Change** form found on ahrma.org, at the link that will be included in the announcement of the opening of the Rule Change Proposal process. For rule clarifications and questions of machine eligibility, please take advantage of the extensive information available here in the AHRMA Handbook. If you are unable to find an answer to your question here, contact members of the following committees. Before contacting a Rules & Eligibility Committee member, please consult the Handbook. Rules & Eligibility Committee Member contact information may be found at **www.ahrma.org/contact/committees/**

- ☐ Vintage Roadrace Rules & Eligibility Committee
- ☐ Sound of Singles/Battle of Twins/Sound of Thunder Rules & Eligibility Committee
- ☐ Vintage Superbike Rules & Eligibility Committee
- ☐ Next Gen Superbike Rules & Eligibility Committee
- ☐ Sidecar Roadrace Rules & Eligibility
- ☐ Dirt Track Rules & Eligibility
- ☐ Vintage Motocross Rules & Eligibility
- ☐ Post Vintage Motocross Rules & Eligibility
- ☐ Trials Rules & Eligibility
- ☐ Cross Country Rules & Eligibility
- ☐ Next Gen MX

19.2 AWARDS COMMITTEE - Selects recipients of special annual awards and coordinates presentation of those awards.

19.3 RISK MANAGEMENT COMMITTEE - Addresses issues relating to safety and reducing risks to members and to the association.

19.4 BENEVOLENT FUND ADVISORY COMMITTEE - Advises on investment decisions and contribution requests for the Benevolent Fund.

19.5 EDITORIAL REVIEW COMMITTEE - Addresses correspondence that is negative or controversial in nature.

19.6 AHRMA RACING OFFICIALS

19.6.1 **NATIONAL ROADRACE OFFICIALS**
For questions about National events and procedures, contact:
  a) **Roadrace Director:** roadrace.director@ahrma.org
  b) **RR Technical Administrator:** Jim Innes, ji8772@yahoo.com
  c) **RR Referee:** Barbara Smith - roadrace.referee@ahrma.org

19.6.2 **NATIONAL DIRT TRACK OFFICIALS**
For questions about National events and procedures, contact:
Dirt Track Director: Richard Brodock, dirt.track@ahrma.org

19.6.3 **NATIONAL OFF-ROAD OFFICIALS**
For questions about National events and procedures, contact:
  a) **Off-Road Director**: Terry McPhillips, offroad.director@ahrma.org
  b) **Motocross Tech Chief (East):** James Smith, ahrma4d@aol.com
  c) **Motocross Tech Chief (West)**: Chris Todd, 462yzracer@gmail.com
  d) **Cross Country Coordinator:** TBD
  e) **Trials Coordinator** - Debbie Poole, pooleschl1@hotmail.com

19.6.4 **REGIONAL COORDINATORS**
For questions regarding regional events, contact regional coordinators or Off-Road Director at offroad.director@ahrma.org. Regional coordinator contact information may be found at **www.ahrma.org/contact/regional-groups/**

19.7 OFF-ROAD REGIONS
- **Great Lakes** (IN, KY, MI, OH, IL, WI)
- **Northeast** (CT, MA, ME, NH, NJ*, NY, PA*, RI, VT,)
- **Mid-Atlantic** (WV, MD, DE, DC, VA, NC, PA*, NJ*)
- **Northwest** (N.CA, ID, N. NV, OR, WA, W. MT)
- **Rocky Mountain** (CO, E. MT, UT, WY, NM)
- **Heartland** (KS, NE, MO, IA)
- **North Central** (SD, ND, MN [Inactive])
- **South Central** (AR, LA, OK, TX)
- **Southeast** (AL, FL, GA, MS, SC, TN)
- **Southwest** (AZ, S. CA, S. NV)

*PA and NJ are both Northeast and Mid-Atlantic, depending on race discipline

19.8 AHRMA NATIONAL OFFICES
PHONE: (888) 41AHRMA or (888) 412-4762

19.8.1 NATIONAL OFFICE
For questions about AHRMA events, sponsorship or general administrative matters, contact:

Daniel May, Executive Director
8913 Town and Country Circle #1093
Knoxville, TN 37923
executive.director@ahrma.org

19.8.2 AHRMA COMMUNICATIONS
For questions about AHRMA's website, website advertising, AHRMA's social media or other AHRMA digital products or AHRMA communications,
please contact:

Cindy McLean
communications@ahrma.org

19.8.3 MEMBERSHIP
For questions about membership and renewals, please contact:

Lorraine Crussell
membership@ahrma.org

19.8.4 ADVERTISING
For questions about *AHRMA MAG* or AHRMA Handbook advertising,
please contact:

Stephanie Vetterly, Advertising Manager
advertising@ahrma.org

19.8.5 AHRMA MAG AND PRINT MEDIA
For questions about *AHRMA MAG*, and AHRMA print and marketing products,
please contact:

Stephanie Vetterly, *AHRMA MAG* Publications Editor
ahrmamag@ahrma.org

19.8.6 AHRMA NATIONAL WEBSITE - www.ahrma.org

19.9 RULE CHANGE PROPOSAL FORM
All proposed rule changes will be forwarded to the appropriate Rules & Eligibility Committee. The committees will submit recommendations for rules changes for consideration at the summer meeting of the Board of Trustees. Any rules tentatively acted on by the Board will then be published for member comment on the AHRMA website and in the *AHRMA MAG*. Final rules decisions for next year's AHRMA Handbook will be made at the August Board meeting. Safety-related rules may be put into effect by the Board at any time. Additional information, detailed instructions and digital form can be found at:
www.ahrma.org/how-to-create-rule-change-proposal

19.10 ELIGIBILITY REQUEST FORM

A copy of this form can be found at:
www.ahrma.org/eligibility-request-form/

The Eligibility Request Form is to be used for determining the eligibility of:

- A motorcycle not specified on the class list (example: a one-off, a motorcycle from another class, a motorcycle that might meet the definition of the class but unmentioned on the class list).
- A modification to an eligible motorcycle when the mod is unmentioned in the existing rules.
- A motorcycle modification is questionable, requiring interpretation of an existing rule.

Three photos must be uploaded through the form - one of each side, and one clearly showing the engine and submitted through the form found at **www.ahrma.org/eligibility-request-form**. The form must be submitted 21 days before the event in which you want to compete (please allow longer if possible). You will be notified by email whether your eligibility has been granted or denied. The decision of the Rules and Eligibility Committee will be valid until the conclusion of the next full rules change cycle. Lasting resolution and inclusion of the determination in the Handbook must be made by the member (not AHRMA staff) by submitting a Rules Change Proposal during the specified rules change proposal period.

19.11 AHRMA MEMBERSHIP APPLICATION

You can join AHRMA at the same website used for creating your rider profile, finding upcoming event information, and signing up to compete in all events:

ahrma.motorsportreg.com/

19.12 REFUND/CREDIT REQUEST FORM

This form can be found at:
www.ahrma.org/refund-credit-request-form/

19.13 MINOR RELEASE AND WAIVER OF LIABILITY AND INDEMNITY AGREEMENT

This form can be found at:
www.ahrma.org/member-resources/forms-and-information/

- NOTES -

- NOTES -

- NOTES -

RACE TECH VINTAGE SUSPENSION

racetech.com | 951.279.6655

Race Tech Proudly Sponsors AHRMA
Ask for AHRMA Member Discount

G-3S Custom Series Shocks
- Custom Built to Order
- Made to Any Length
- Choice of Features
- Color Options

Made in U.S.A.

MODERN TECHNOLOGY

ENGINE SERVICES NOW AVAILABLE

Brake Arcing
Greatly Improves Drum Brake Stopping Power!

FOR VINTAGE MACHINES

Race Tech Hi-Performance Springs

Fork Gold Valve Emulators®
Gold Valve Cartridge Emulators offer Adjustable Damping!

TNK Fork Tubes
Made in Italy. Call or go to the website for your application.

- Fork & Shock Springs available in a variety of Spring Rates.

Made in the USA
Columbia, SC
11 March 2024